About the Author

Michael Windross was born in Carlisle in 1942. He was a chorister at St Paul's Cathedral from 1952 to 1956, and then moved on to Lancing College and St John's College Cambridge, where he read history as well as being a choral scholar. He emigrated to Belgium in 1964 and taught for forty years at the Higher Institute for Translators and Interpreters in Antwerp. He was awarded his PhD by Louvain University in 1988. He has published in the fields of historical linguistics and the history of ideas. *Catching up with the Past* is his first venture into non-academic writing. He and Elly, his wife, divide their time between Antwerp, Sussex, and Abruzzo in Italy.

Michael Windross

Catching up with the Past

Olympia Publishers

London

www.olympiapublishers.com
OLYMPIA PAPERBACK EDITION

ISBN: 978-1-80074-285-7

Every effort has been made to fulfil requirements with regard to reproducing
copyright material. The author and publisher will be glad to rectify any omissions
at the earliest opportunity.

First Published in 2023

Olympia Publishers
Tallis House
2 Tallis Street
London
EC4Y 0AB

Printed in Great Britain

For Elly, Stephen, and Oliver

Acknowledgements

For the most part the illustrations are either reproductions of family photographs, or photographs taken by me of personal items and objects collected over the years.

Photographic credits:

Detail from OS Explorer Map 315 (Crown Copyright) reproduced by permission of Ordnance Survey.

Frontispiece to the *Book of Common Prayer (1662)* reproduced by permission of the Trustees of the British Museum.

Title-page and fossils from Verstegan's *Restitution (1605)* reproduced by permission of Plantin-Moretus Museum, Antwerp. UNESCO heritage site.

Diagrammatic map of the Solway Firth area, by courtesy of Ordnance Survey.

Two letters — Fanny Windross to the Defence Department, Melbourne, and W.J. Weatherill to Sir George Reid in London, 1915, by courtesy of The National Archives of Australia.

HMS Queen (1909) reproduced by permission of the National Maritime Museum, Greenwich.

I am grateful to Christopher Watts, fellow-chorister, for sending me the photograph of the SPCCS cricket XI, 1956. The colour in my photograph of Eileen Price's painting of 'the art class on a building site' had faded badly and Anthony Price kindly provided me with a better image of the original painting for which I am most grateful. I would also like to thank Peter Eyckerman for the enhanced image of the couple in the Ambrotype (c.1860) and for pointing out to me that it was not a 'Daguerreotype' — as I had thought — but a slightly later variant.

***

With regard to the documentation: for the military records, my thanks are due to the National Archives, Kew, and to the National Archives of Australia. I have also benefitted from the online database of the National Library of Australia — 'Trove' — for early newspaper articles.

I am very grateful to Cumbria County Council Certificate Services and Portsmouth City Council Civic Offices for their kind assistance. I should also like to express my thanks to the Dumfries & Galloway Council Archives and Local Studies and in particular for the personal assistance of Erica Johnson and Helen McArthur, who provided me with an abundance of records. Stephen White, Librarian at Carlisle Library, also provided material from local newspapers, which I much appreciated.

I am most grateful to the Port of London Authority for allowing me to quote from the booklet *The Royal River*.

A special word of thanks to Alan Cole and Gail Sirmais who not only made us welcome — a touching moment for me personally — but also gave me full access to the records relating to the Little family, and the house in Aglionby Street — a crucial stepping-stone between Scotland and Cumberland in the narrative.

While the supporting cast is not large, my warmest thanks to all who so readily allowed me to refer to them by name in the book.

While I take sole responsibility for the text as it stands, the presence and advice of others has certainly made for improvements. Conversation with Larry Gibilaro about the progress of our respective books has become a regular part of our long walks together in Abruzzo, and it has helped me structure my thoughts. I am also greatly indebted to my friend Albert Gomperts – we go back a long way – for his critical reading of the entire text, for his corrections (he modestly calls them 'quibbles') and a host of valuable suggestions – thanks Albert!

I feel privileged having Olympia as my publishers. They promised to make it an enjoyable and rewarding experience, and that describes perfectly how it has been. I should particularly like to thank James Houghton, commissioning editor, and Kristina Smith, production coordinator, who has steered my work through with such patience and punctuality from manuscript to book, and the editors and graphics department for their expertise and flexibility.

Lastly, I want to thank Elly for her help and support throughout — not just 'moral' but also 'material'. It was her example that got me started on Part Two, and while I am responsible for the finished product — and its shortcomings — chasing up the family past was very much a joint effort. Without her I would not have managed.

Preface

I started writing this book when I was nearing my seventy-sixth birthday — an age when one certainly has more to say about the past than the future. It may well have been this that prompted me to start writing and it probably explains my readiness to take a cyclical view of time rather than a linear one. The book contains two parts — 'Time's Cycle' and 'The Family Circle' — which are meant to complement each other.

Part One is largely autobiographical and based on memories, though it was never my intention to write my 'memoirs' in the way that word is generally understood — an anecdotal account of events and the people one has known and met. The focus is, rather, on the world I grew up in and how my experience of that world helped form (or sometimes threaten) my own sense of identity, and because of this introspective approach my account is thinly populated and almost devoid of dialogue. The first chapter on my early childhood in Cumberland serves as a prologue, where some of the recurrent themes in the book first make an appearance. From there the narrative follows a chronological line which is frequently crossed by historical digressions and flashbacks to a past outside my own experience, thus creating an interaction or 'dialogue' between the past and an unfolding present.

Calling Part Two 'The Family Circle' (rather than, say, 'The Family History') lets me off the hook somewhat, for it allows me to delve into the family past without having to tie up the loose ends. Most of the spadework had been done before lockdown and travel restrictions were imposed in response to the Covid-19 pandemic, but since then I have had to leave a number of residual problems unresolved. The family past is seen as a number of separate threads which come together to form a web. I have chosen to work in a series of time loops, allowing the different threads to catch up and converge before moving on. Here too the narrative is interwoven with historical detours from different geographical angles.

The ordering of the two parts perhaps calls for some explanation. While the content of Part Two *precedes* that of Part One, that is not how I experienced things. My actual experience of the events in Part One was of course in the past, whereas my memory of them — a recalled experience

— is something that happens now in an ever-shifting present. The events in Part Two I never experienced at all in the physical sense and I only became aware of them recently — a mental confrontation superimposed on the other. The ordering I have chosen allows me to close the circle at my initial starting point, giving the illusion of a recurrent cycle.

The historical commentary throughout certainly reflects my own interests, but it also rests on knowledge I have acquired from the teaching and writings of others. This is not an academic study and a long list of references would have been out of place. I do, however, refer to specific books and articles in the endnotes when I borrow more detailed information. I have to confess that I have shied away from narrative works I encountered in bookshops when I thought they were so close to my subject that they might inhibit my own writing. I apologise for this omission and I now look forward to reading them.

I should add that I set out to write the book for myself and my close family, but I hope the broad sweep in time and place will give what is essentially a personal account a wider appeal.

Schoten, Antwerp, 12 November 2021

TABLE OF CONTENTS

Part One: Time's Cycle **15**

    Chapter One: Cumberland 17

    Chapter Two: St Paul's Cathedral 45

    Chapter Three: Lancing College 69

    Chapter Four: Cambridge 79

    Chapter Five: Antwerp 89

    Chapter Six: Back and Beyond 105

    Chapter Seven: Raised Beaches and an Early Start 137

Part Two: The Family Circle **161**

    Chapter Eight: The Solway Firth 163

    Chapter Nine: The Great War 191

    Chapter Ten: The Inter-Bellum 213

    Chapter Eleven: Brian Windross's war — Full Circle 225

Endnotes **261**

PART ONE

TIME'S CYCLE

The horse is taught his manage, and the wind
Of heaven wheels round and treads in his own steps;
Year follows year, the tide returns again …

[William Wordsworth, *The Prelude*]

Chapter: One

CUMBERLAND

I was born in Carlisle on 12 November 1942. My father's side of the
family had strong ties with Carlisle and he was born there too. As
for the date, in a speech at the Mansion House, Winston Churchill
had said:

"This is not the end, it is not even the beginning of the end, but it is
perhaps the end of the beginning."

That was two days before I was born. He was of course referring to
the recent victory at El Alamein and how it might influence the course
of the war. Still, you could say that my birth roughly coincided with this
critical turning-point. It would take another two and a half years of
fighting — in which my father played a part — to achieve that end.

Unlike my parents who both had two given names: Doris Irene Spong
and Brian Weatherill Windross, I had only one, Michael, which recalls
no other family member, and since there was no christening, I had no
godparents — it was all up to me.

We pick things up about our early childhood from parents and
others, but the only direct access we have to the earliest period of
our lives is through memory. Memory plays an integral part in
our sense of identity. Born in the war, what do I remember of it?
Not much. I was not even three when it ended and Carlisle did not
suffer any major catastrophes to leave a lasting impression. Belfast
was bombed, so was Glasgow; but Carlisle — an important railway
junction between Clydeside and Tyneside, and directly linked to the
industrial heartlands of England — escaped scot-free. Perhaps this is
not the happiest choice of words for the closest bomb to Carlisle was

the one that was dropped just across the border on Gretna Green, which killed twelve people.

I do have mental images of objects from that period. My Mickey Mouse gas mask for instance, and the blue and white tins of powdered milk introduced by the Ministry of Food during the war. I vaguely recall the bonfire celebrations on VE-day in our neighbourhood, and I think Auntie Olive (my mother's sister) was with us too. The one memory that stands out is my father returning home from the war in the regimental kilt of the Seaforth Highlanders. That would have been in late summer 1945, when I was two years and ten months old.

Back in civvy street, my father got a job as a clerk at Telford and Scott's, an estate agents and auctioneers in Carlisle. We lived in Currock Road, a long road leading south away from the city centre. I was aware that we had only part of the house, which belonged to the Grahams. They had a cat and three sons who were a few years older than me. The eldest was called Peter, which I thought was a very good name. One day I strayed off with them. We went down to the Caldew — a tributary of the River Eden — to an industrial area. I now know that these were old cotton mills dating from the Industrial Revolution when Shaddon Mill was the largest in England, surpassing anything at Manchester. It also boasted Dixon's Chimney, built in 1836 and at three hundred and five feet high, one of the tallest in Europe. Here the river was canalised and there was a weir. The boys were looking for stickleback, which they put into a jam jar. My mother gave them a good telling off when we got back.

There must have been a sigh of relief when the war was over, but I suppose for those who had not been fighting or bombed, daily life went on much as before. I for one, noticed no difference! Rationing continued for a number of years, not only on food but also on clothes, furniture, and luxury items. Old habits die hard, and corned beef hash, a typical wartime meal, was still served up at lunchtime. I loved it. Tucking in with my fork and 'pusher', to the background of *Workers' Playtime* on the radio, a programme introduced in 1941 to boost morale, which might account for the patriotic military-sounding signature tune. The 'wireless' (as we still called it) had a special place in my childhood; not least because it introduced me to so many different styles of music.

In spite of rationing, the shops in the city centre held a great attraction for me. It was not so much the goods on display, as all the technical novelties. Binns, the large department store, introduced me to lifts and escalators, and to all those pneumatic tubes providing an instant transfer of money and receipts around the store which popped and hissed when operated. At Oram's the grocers there was a complex system of overhead wires along which cash carriers travelled like miniature cable cars.

The shoe shops had those wooden constructions where you looked through an oval-shaped viewing shaft downwards at your feet (which showed up a like a green X-ray) to check the fit of the shoes. It looked like a cross between something in an amusement arcade and an inverted submarine periscope. Perhaps there were smaller ones for children, for we could hardly have been picked up to take a look at our own feet! I realise that many of these gadgets survived into the '50s, (lifts and escalators are of course still with us) but I first got to know them as a toddler. No wonder I had a habit of wandering off by myself when we went shopping.

The earliest memories of a wider family circle are my regular Sunday afternoon visits to Gran (my father's mother) in Chatsworth Square. This was some distance from where we lived and my father took me there by bus. I must have been three or four years old by then. As the name suggests, it was rather posh, with trees and shrubs in the middle surrounded by iron railings. She had a top-floor flat, and I always felt I was entering a slightly different world from the one at home. An old-fashioned world. This feeling persisted throughout boyhood and adolescence, whenever and wherever I visited Gran. We would have tea, often with bread and honey (from the honeycomb) and later go for a walk. She had a soft refined voice and although from Carlisle, she spoke with a southern accent with a trace of Scottish: *hwer, hwen* for 'where' and 'when'. It was from her that I first heard of Aglionby Street, where Auntie Jane and Auntie Aggie had lived; of Hastings and St Leonards, where she herself had lived between the wars. The first pieces in the family jigsaw puzzle. Our after-tea walks were usually in the parkland along the banks of the river Eden.

When I was three, I had my tonsils taken out. I have some memory of being put to sleep in the operating theatre and for some reason it was always associated with a repeated musical phrase played in octaves on the piano. Later, as a teenager, I discovered that this was in fact the musical theme from the wartime film *A Matter of Life and Death* in which there is a sequence in an operating theatre, and Mother confirmed that I had seen the film with her and Olive around that time. Leaving hospital after the operation, the doctor had advised me to eat an ice cream. At home I had a haemorrhage — which caused a bit of a panic. Perhaps this explains why I had such an aversion to ice cream as a child.

Funny, I don't remember anything about the arrival of my brothers, Colin and David, who were born on 10 June 1946. It seems I later complained to Mother:

"Why did you have to have the twins? It was much better before!"

I hope this is apocryphal. Shortly before the twins' first birthday, the three of us had our photo taken in a studio in Carlisle. It was Gran's idea and I recall her licking her fingers, trying to give my hair some semblance of a parting, and me kicking up a fuss because I was not allowed to hold my little tin horse for the photograph. On 10 June 1947 — their birthday — we moved to Hayton, a village seven miles east of Carlisle. I presume Telford and Scott had a hand in it, because we were driven there by car and that was something we did not own. I remember two older girls asking if they could take the twins for a walk in the pram. To me they seemed like young women, but they could only have been eleven or twelve years old. One of the girls was Margaret Bouch, the elder sister of Christine who was my age and later sat next to me at school.

My goodbye to Carlisle proved to be short-lived. In the middle of August, just before I was due to start school, I went down with infantile paralysis. There was an epidemic and the health service was on alert. Even so, time was lost in getting me to hospital because there had been a terrible mining accident at Whitehaven on the Cumbrian coast (15 August) in which one hundred and four miners died and all available ambulances had been rushed to the scene. With some delay I was taken to Carlisle infirmary. I remember being carried down the narrow stairs of the cottage to the ambulance wrapped in a blanket, being given a lumbar puncture on arrival, being put on a ward with older patients who shouted out to the nurses their needs (which surprised me for grown-ups) and then I was transferred to a children's ward. I can recall the nurses and especially one being cross with me because I'd 'dirtied my sheets' and the rather bossy matron with her uniform and wimple-like headgear. I must have been on an isolation ward because my parents never visited me, but Mother did send me a picture book about a family of barrage balloons and some drawings she had done of our two cats, which I liked. I don't think I was in any great pain and there were no lasting effects. After several weeks I was allowed to go home and Mother came to collect me.

***

The Solway Plain stretches away from the Solway Firth beyond Carlisle. Hayton was at its eastern edge where the foothills of the Pennine fells begin. There was a quick way to get from Carlisle to Hayton via the main road (the A69) direction Brampton, but the bus, a red 'United' single-decker, took the slower, cross-country route along Warwick Road past Brunton Park — the Carlisle United football ground — past the territorial army barracks to Warwick Bridge where it crossed the Eden, then past Toppin Castle — a nineteenth century mock fortified farm — from where you could already see the church tower, left down a narrow country lane to the signpost, right, and there it was, Hayton.

We got off at the walnut field in the centre of the village. The gnarled walnut tree with its hollowed-out trunk was said to be four hundred years old. The children would hide in it and the long straggling branch that came close to the ground provided a natural swing. The field was really our village green, surrounded by a low stone wall and it sloped gently away as it distanced itself from the road.

The bus trundled on for another fifty yards and then turned off left in the direction of Brampton. We went in the opposite direction, turning right down the 'vennel' — a cobbled lane that descended just a bit more steeply than the field, and if you were small like me the walls seemed to get gradually higher and the sound of footsteps became more and more hollow, like in a tunnel.

The vennel led to Beck Bottom, where we lived. It was hardly a road, more a gravel track, but soon after we arrived it was tarmacked and they used an old-fashioned steam roller to level it. Beck Bottom lay in a dip with an ivy-clad wall at the end which we used as our den and beyond there was an orchard where we would go scrumping. The 'beck' sounds romantic, but much of it was in a culvert and where it did run in the open it was overgrown with nettles and docks; they often grew together which was fortunate for we would spit on the dock leaves and use them as an antidote for the stinging nettles. In early spring the beck was full of frog-spawn.

Turning left, our house was the first to appear — the White Cottage — stone-built and covered in layers of flaky white-wash. There was a small garden on two sides and a stone wall all round. Everywhere in the village there were walls, and here, approaching the Pennines, even the divisions between fields were often dry-stone walls. Hadrian was simply following local custom! A stone pathway led to the door at the side of the cottage. The front windows faced south, looking towards the upper village, though this view was rather obscured by our holly hedge. There were no windows at the back, just a concrete backyard cut into the sharp incline behind. Adjoining the cottage were two outhouses. The larger one might have been a barn at one time, for it had a wide, double door, and here we stored the tea chests which had been used in the removal. The other still had the old 'copper' for doing the wash, but our laundry was picked up and delivered by the Lakeland Laundry Company.

Next to us, slightly higher and set back was a big Victorian house in sandstone. Here lived the Bird family and as their son Ian was my age, I spent a fair bit of time there. In the hall stood a grandfather clock which had an ornate face with the sun and moon, and a slow resonant tick that made me think of the popular Burl Ives song 'My Grandfather's Clock' — which 'stopped, short, never to go again, when the Old Man died'! From the Bird's house a narrow path ran along the edge of a wood overlooking our backyard. The crowns of the trees were full of crow's nests and there was a constant cawing as they circled high in the sky above. Every so often this peaceful scene would be shattered by the loud report of a double-barrel shotgun indicating that a cull had started. Tranquillity and violence were never far apart in rural life. It was said that in earlier centuries during the border raids, the women and children took refuge in this wood.

The high path led to an older Georgian house with an elegant façade and a lawn in front of it. Here lived old Mrs Bird — Ian Bird's grandmother — and with her hooked nose and pointed chin, she really did look like an old bird. I would sometimes have tea there with Ian. For us children 'tea' was simply what we had after school. It might occasionally include baked beans or spaghetti on toast, but more often it was just bread with one or other spread or simply bread and jam. This was our last meal of the day and there was nothing dainty about it. We sat at a large farmhouse table and when we were too noisy, she would shut us up with an old-fashioned "whisht, whisht!" — a raised finger pressed to her lips. I cannot recall the room, except there was a Welsh dresser and placed on it a huge ostrich egg and a whale's tooth — an odd pairing.

Outside, was a short flight of stone steps leading down to the cellar. The cobwebbed windows allowed some sunlight to pass through and there was an old motorbike propped up against the wall. The place had that distinctive smell of apples and pears stored away for the winter. On the other side of the wall was a space to which the only access was via a small trapdoor in the floor of the kitchen above. You had to climb down two planks fixed vertically against the wall with slots cut out for the feet. Little more than a shaft, it was referred to as the 'priest hole'. Whether it was made for this purpose — hiding a 'recusant' Catholic priest from his Protestant hunters in Reformation times — I don't know. The architecture was not right, but perhaps an earlier building had undergone alterations. I cannot dismiss the 'priest hole' as simply an old wives' tale.

Opposite the White Cottage lived the Hetheringtons. There were Hetheringtons in our family, but these were not relations. They had a son, Derrick, the same age as the twins and I think Mother got on quite well with Mrs Hetherington. Just beyond her house was an open stretch of land, half orchard, half paddock, known as the 'garth' — an old Nordic word and a reminder that back in the tenth century Cumberland had been settled by Norwegian Vikings. The Anglo-Saxon equivalent was 'geard' which has given us modern English 'yard'. Father once told me that a Nordic dialect survived in remote parts of Cumberland till as late as the sixteenth century.

Next to the garth, at the corner of Beck Bottom, was the blacksmith's. For me, the prototype of a forge: dark, with small, yellowed window-panes, an open air-vent in the roof, beaten earth floor, a glowing fire and bellows, anvil, hammers, tongs, iron filings, twisted metal shavings like springs. Here I would sometimes watch the process of shoeing a horse: the leather bellows bringing the coals to life, the red-hot metal being hammered into shape on the anvil then plunged into cold water before it was taken outside to the waiting horse, all tethered up. The smith, wearing a leather apron, lifting the fetlock of the horse's leg, and holding it firmly between his own legs, placing the shoe against the hoof, then taking the square nail he had between his teeth and hammering it home. The metal was still hot enough to create a lot of hissing and a foul stench of burning keratin, and sometimes the horse — huge shire horses — would kick out causing burns and injury and a lot of swearing.

Turning right at the blacksmith's you arrived at 'Briar Lonnin'. A 'lonnin' was the local word for a country lane, although this one had been tarmacked for cars. It took you past a couple of recent additions to the village. First, the Women's Institute, which was used for dances, Christmas parties, nativity plays and other local functions. It was here that I got to know 'Oranges and Lemons', 'Hokey-Kokey', 'We all keep Merry and Bright', 'Blind Man's Buff', 'Musical Chairs' and all that popular stuff handed down from previous generations. Then two houses in chalet style referred to as the 'Swiss Cottages', and just beyond, marking the end of the village, the first post-war council houses were being built. Word had it that the workers were German prisoners-of-war. They did wear those square-shaped peaked caps with ear mufflers — quite unlike the ones British workmen wore — so they might well have been.

Let us carry on further down the lonnin. After half a mile we come to the main road from Carlisle to Brampton; a normal two-lane road, with markings down the middle, and reflecting cat's eyes. These fascinated us children and we would jump up and down on the rubber encasements to feel the 'give' — not a very wise thing to do on a busy road. Crossing over, we passed the keeper's lodge which always looked empty and continued down a drive lined with tall beech trees until we got to a lake, partly hidden by the rhododendron bushes. Behind this was a rise and a large building known as 'Edmond Castle' which had a Pele Tower, a stronghold against the marauding Scots during the border raids. After the war, it had been turned into an approved school for juvenile delinquents, which was always in the back of my mind as we filled our jute sacks with kindling wood in the winter. We would watch them at a distance on Sunday mornings filing to the village church, where they sat apart in a side gallery which had been added by Thomas Henry Graham, whose family had owned the estate since the seventeenth century.[1]

Returning to the blacksmith's, the road leads up to the main village street again. From our house, it was much quicker to take the vennel, and this is how I went to school each day. The building was from 1871 and the date was clearly visible above the entrance door. While it retained its old title 'Hayton Church of England School', it was a state mixed primary school for boys and girls between the age of five and fourteen, which was soon reduced to eleven when the Labour Government's Education Act came into effect. I dreaded going to school at first. Missing the start of the year through sickness proved a handicap. Since the class contained children of different ages, teacher had to split us up into groups and I was sometimes left alone staring at an ink blot or some scratching out, aware that the bell for playtime was only a temporary reprieve and that I would soon be 'found out'. To make matters worse, she would rap our knuckles with the edge of a wooden ruler for bad work.

Our classroom was at the back of the school next to the playground and the tall windows looked across to the church. Sometimes when there was a funeral, teacher's gaze would be drawn towards the family and mourners, then suddenly remembering herself, she would spin round on her heel and instruct us not to stare (which she pronounced 'stir'). From the church there was a short driveway leading to the vicarage, maybe the grandest house in the village, reflecting the changed status of the eighteenth-century parish priest — now a 'man of leisure'. The façade of the vicarage with typical Georgian windows, overlooked a large lawn which provided the setting for the annual garden fete. From here there was a wide view westward across the Solway Plain, Carlisle in the middle distance with Dixon's Chimney, and way beyond the pale blue outline of the mountains of the Lake District.

Hayton was built chiefly along the one real street. The only pub fronted onto the road, next to the incline going up to the school and there were a number of farmhouses, distinguished from the other houses by their wide entrance gates which gave access to the rectangular farmyard behind, usually with an old barn where the grain was stored. And beyond that just fields. The one shop in the village was a newsagent, where you could also get bread, tinned food and household products, but not much else. Milk was delivered from the Bouch's farm, and eggs and vegetables were also available locally, but for general groceries a man from Oram's in Carlisle would call and take the weekly order and it was delivered by van. The post office was at the far end of the village, past the turn-off to Brampton, and thereafter the road became little more than a track as far as Town Head, the farthest limit of the village, almost a village apart. I had classmates who lived here too, like Alan Wear who had only recently returned from the Far East, where he and his family had been held in a Japanese internment camp during the latter part of the war.

It was a farming community. Not that everyone worked in agriculture; there were probably those who worked in local industry, offices, banks, and so on in Brampton or Carlisle, like my father. But farming determined the character of the village. You were more likely to see a horse or a tractor than a motor car, and at certain times of the year the street had trails of manure from the muck spreaders on their way to and from the fields. I can recall only one or two families having a car. A good friend of my father's, Tom Skelton, was one (although he lived in a nearby village) — he had a black Singer. The father of one of my friends in How Mill even had a Triumph Roadster — a convertible with a dickey-seat behind, which was pretty exceptional. So was the big red American cabriolet, with headlamps two feet deep (I don't remember the make) which suddenly made an appearance in Hayton.

"It belongs to George Formby" one of the boys said, but I didn't really believe him.

George Formby was a popular entertainer of the '30s and '40s, on both screen and stage, from Lancashire. He had a status similar to Gracie Fields and Vera Lynn, especially up north, and he died relatively young in 1961. I checked recently on google, and to my surprise Formby was indeed a collector of classic cars.

There were social differences within the farming community. The biggest landowner did not even live in the village — a certain Dick Lamb. Some of the farms still had horses for working in the fields; another used the rather slow and noisy Fordson tractor, dark green and smelling of oil; and one or two had the new sleek grey Fergusons, which went twice the speed. For us, these were status symbols. Far better to get a ride on a Fergie than a Fordson!

***

In a rural setting like this we were very aware of the changing seasons. In springtime the pussy-willow and catkin appeared in the hedgerows, and in early summer on the rougher ground of the lower fells the gorse and broom burst into flower in a vivid yellow. Here in the north the summers were perhaps less hot, but the days were longer, and I remember us children — all ages, boys and girls — playing our version of hide and seek over a huge terrain until well past nine in the evening. And when the person hiding could not be found, we would all shout in unison:

"Give a tally-ho, a whistle or a holler. If ye don't give one, we'll all give over!" in our broadest Cumbrian accents.

With this mix of ages and easy contact between boys and girls there was some sexual precociousness in our playing; you could say that we were being prepared in a natural way for a world that I was to be denied throughout puberty and adolescence.

In the summer holidays we would spend days in the fields where the harvesting was in full swing, sometimes chasing rabbits with a heavy stick when the cornfield had been cut back to a narrow triangle and the poor creatures bolted. I did not join in — it was too close to the lyrics of the popular song *Run rabbit, run* for my liking. I have a faint memory of horse-drawn reapers, but most farms had a mechanised reaper which threw the corn-sheaves out as it moved along, and these had to be gathered together in stooks of twelve, more or less upright, where they kept dry. I cannot recall there being combine-harvesters — the well-known Massey Ferguson dates from the early '50s. The sheaves of corn were stacked on a cart to be taken to a designated place, usually the piece of rough ground near the blacksmith's, where the threshing machine would arrive — a huge wooden vehicle, like a medieval siege-engine, with metal wheels on the side to which were attached heavy leather belts driven by a stationary steam traction engine.

Throughout the summer 'hound trails' were held. Races where the hounds (twenty or more) followed a trail laid out beforehand by dragging a heavy swab soaked in aniseed across the countryside behind a tractor. It was an event for the adults and a betting sport, with bookies and tic-tac men just like at the horse races, but we enjoyed it too. The dogs headed off in an easterly direction towards the fells, then they wheeled round in a wide circle, all followed through binoculars, before returning across the plain. Six or seven miles in all. As they got nearer to home, so their barking became audible, gradually increasing in volume as the whistling of the owners reached a shrill climax. Sometimes they arrived injured — that was in the nature of things — but on the whole they were well looked after.

As autumn approached, the walnut tree began to shed its nuts. There were plenty to go round, but we were impatient. We could not wait till they were properly dry, so that our hands were stained a reddish-ochre colour from peeling open the skin, in spite of the threat of a caning at school. This was closely followed by the horse-chestnuts, so shiny and beautiful like polished mahogany. I would have liked to keep them this way, but their destiny was otherwise. Like thousands of children, we played a game generally known as 'conkers' (though we usually called it 'cheggies'). I don't know whether the game is as widespread as it used to be. The conker was threaded on a piece of string, knotted at one end to hold it securely — even better were the leather laces we used to fasten our boots — then turns were taken, the idea being to smash the opponent's conker. All very simple. But there were those who developed a special technique, using for instance a shortened string wound round the fingers, and others selected 'cheesers' — the chestnuts with a flattened side when there were two in the same husk. There were some who used conkers hardened by age, which you could simulate by baking them, leading to accusations of using a 'bakey'. And there were those hardy survivors who had long lost their skin and shrunk till they resembled a piece of old Parmesan cheese, so small they were difficult to hit at all!

At half-term in early November agricultural necessities took over. 'Spud-bashing'. Not in the usual sense of peeling potatoes but *picking* potatoes. Those who were old enough were taken to the fields by cart at first light where they would follow behind the tractor which unearthed the potatoes leaving them on the soil. Our job was to pick them up and sort them, from eight till four when the light began to fade. I only did it once, around my eighth birthday. The pay for the week was five shillings, which was a lot of money for us and it came in useful because Guy Fawkes Night was approaching. Looking in the supermarkets and shop windows in the high streets up and down the country nowadays, it is apparent that Halloween has pushed Guy Fawkes into the background. Posters advertising Bonfire Night, are very much in the minority, and seem to be organised by the local council or a committee. In post-war England it was otherwise and in Hayton it was the boys of the village who were responsible for building the bonfire in the walnut field in the weeks before. By the time it was finished it was ten or twelve feet high and to make sure it did not get wet a tarpaulin was spread over it. There was no 'official' fireworks display; we simply bought our own fireworks, loose, or in boxes, from the village store or from Brampton and Carlisle. I remember *Brock's Fireworks* and, I believe, *Standard Fireworks* — funny how popular things came in pairs, like the *Dandy* and the *Beano* — and the excitement of simply looking at the different shapes and colours of the fireworks: jumping jacks, Catherine wheels, bangers, roman candles, and so on. Even letting off the fireworks was up to us, with perhaps the guiding hand of parents. The whole village would gather in the walnut field, many carrying turnip lanterns hollowed out with a primitive face and candle inside which produced a smell I liked. It all sounds like a recipe for disaster, but I can't recall there ever being an accident.

Next up was my birthday, followed by the build-up to Christmas. At school we would make our own decorations using crepe paper, tinfoil, red cellophane, and there was holly in abundance and those small cardboard nativity scenes or old-fashioned townscapes where you could pull open a window or shutter or door, revealing some new treasure. I liked these, but now decades later I see that many of the big garden centres stock them. Of the four Christmases we spent in Hayton, I know that two were white, and I'm not sure about the other two. There was hardly any street-lighting to impede our view of the star-lit sky when we went out carol singing.

It had a commercial side too. We paid Father Christmas a visit at Binns in Carlisle, but far from being the jovial red-cheeked Santa, he was a mysterious, heavily hooded Nordic figure who dwelt in a grotto. It was a time for festivity in a period of rationing, and we benefitted from having the local farms. At home we usually had a goose for the Christmas dinner. By present-day standards it was, I suppose, all rather modest.

***

How did we live as a family in this rural community? Perhaps a look inside the White Cottage will give some idea.

The original flagstone floor in the living room had been taken out prior to our moving and the flags were stacked against the side of the cottage next to the pathway where they stayed for a couple of years. In its place came a smooth concrete floor which was painted dark red, like a garage. In the course of time Mother made traditional rag rugs, usually round, which added to the cosiness. There was an open hearth, with a high mantelpiece. Formerly, the fire had served for both heating and cooking, and there was still a crane for hanging pots and griddles above the fire, which we called a 'rekken'. Since the cottage had been partly modernised — gas, electricity, and running (cold) water — not much cooking was done in the traditional way, but sometimes Mother would make drop-scones (which rhymed with 'gone' not 'bone').

These passing references to speech, to local words and pronunciations, are of course made in hindsight, but my awareness of these language variations dates from *then*, not now. Both my parents spoke with a southern English accent (though using local words for local things) and this is what I heard on the radio (except in comedy programmes) and what I spoke at home. With my friends in the village, it was different and my speech would have been peppered with the local dialect; for instance, "I'm going home" was "Am gan yam" — with the original Anglo-Saxon vowel sounds, and "shut the gate" would be "shut 'geat" with a round-lipped 'u' as in 'put' and a diphthong-vowel as in 'gear' — again very much as it would have been pronounced in Anglo-Saxon!

Like everyone else we burned coal on an open fire, delivered by the coal merchant in jute sacks; not the treated coke or nuggets, but the untreated kind straight from the coal face — big chunks, small ones and inevitably coal dust. Sometimes the coal would hiss, exude tar, and produce colourful green plumes. Spectacular but probably not very healthy.

The furniture in our living room was not the country furniture I saw in the farms and cottages of my playmates. The table, the dining chairs, and the sideboard were all 'Utility Furniture', a government-backed scheme to keep down costs and provide a decent standard. It was produced on a massive scale, but I cannot recall seeing it in other homes in Hayton. 'Utility' extended to soft-furnishings and other household goods, all of which bore the distinctive trademark. Father had his own armchair with velvet upholstery in a pattern that today would be called 'art deco'. There were a couple of plain, sturdy bookcases for he was a keen reader. When I learned to read, I began to take notice of the titles: The Bible (though my father was an atheist — it was the Odhams edition 'to be read as literature'), the Collected Works of Shakespeare, Blake's poems, and many titles you would find in the average home. But there were others with less familiar titles: *Axel's Castle, The Waste Land, Ulysses, For whom the Bell Tolls*... and large art books to which I was introduced at an early age. There were also the little King Penguins. I especially enjoyed looking at the illustrations in the slim volume *Children's Art*. Placed on the bookcases were various ornaments and curiosities: a brass camel's stirrup, a Prussian military Stein, an antique Burmese Buddha in the form of an incense burner, and more. The pictures on the walls were framed reproductions of Picasso, Matisse, Dali, and Dürer (the warrior on horseback), and there was a Zulu knobkerrie too which certainly made an impact on me, for once it fell from the wall right on my bonce! Without damage to either of us.

Next to my father's chair was the radio with lots of foreign stations and knobs; one had little coloured dots on it for the different wavelengths — medium, long and shortwave. It was an important item in our home and a link with the world beyond. In the daytime it would be tuned to the Light Programme for more popular programmes like *Music while you work, Housewife's Choice* and *Workers Playtime* — all with their signature tunes and playing the popular light music of the day, which has stuck in my mind (and I think that goes for many of my generation) and seems to capture the feel of the times.[2]

In the early evening it was time for *Dick Barton, Special Agent*, a programme that ran from 1946–51, with a peak audience of fifteen million!

The theme music was a fast tarantella, with complex cross beats and unusual harmonies. Then a quick switch of stations to the Home Service for *Radio Newsreel* at seven, with its patriotic introductory march music ('Imperial Echoes'). The 38th parallel was often mentioned and I was aware there was another war going on. At the end of the news there were police notices, for witnesses of fatal car accidents to call Whitehall 1212 and messages to family members on holiday to call a particular hospital "where their father is dangerously ill" — the tone made me shudder. Saturday evening *Radio Newsreel*, however, was followed by 'another reading of the football results' — probably for people to check their football coupons. I soon knew all the team names by heart, and some of the places have remained simply football teams for me: Bolton Wanderers, Accrington Stanley, Oldham Athletic, etc. Later in the evening, it was the turn of the 'Third Programme' for the more highbrow stuff to which my parents listened: T.S. Eliot reciting the *Waste Land* and a radio adaptation of *Murder in the Cathedral*. My father always listened to *The Critics* and to philosophy talks, which were often published in the weekly *Listener* to which he had a subscription, and I still find cuttings from *The Listener* in books of his. The radio was also an introduction to major sporting events: Raymond Glendenning's commentaries on football matches and John Snagge on the Boat Race — I can hear his voice giving the timing of the stroke, "one-out, two-out, three-out" and Oxford sinking in 1951.

It stood on top of a gramophone cabinet and you had to turn the knob to the white dot to connect the two, with the radio acting as speaker — an improvised radiogram. In the cabinet below was my father's collection of jazz 78s: Louis Armstrong's Hot 5 and Hot 7 recordings, King Oliver, Fletcher Henderson, Jelly Roll Morton, Ma Rainey, Bessie Smith, Red Allen, Bix Beiderbecke, Duke Ellington… and so on. Father would sit next to it in his armchair, smoking a pipe and tapping his right foot (with the brown brogue suedes) in time to the rhythm, and I would imitate him, and before I knew it, it had become an automatic reflex. Sometimes in the evenings after closing time, my parents returned home from the pub with a few friends — usually including Tom Skelton who shared my father's passion for jazz — and there would be a listening session and Mother would prepare coffee and snacks. Over the years this became a routine occurrence in our home on Friday nights.

I have said nothing about our *wider* family since we moved to Hayton. The White Cottage was small. There was no bathroom, washing was done at the kitchen sink, and there was only an outside lavatory. Upstairs were two bedrooms; my parents had the bigger one and me and the twins shared the small one. Mother's sister certainly spent time with us, and there are numerous photographs of her with the twins and me. Allen, my father's younger brother, also visited us. He had served in the Far East in the war and he gave us a Japanese military sword — a guntō — which hung in its scabbard above the stairs as an ornament. Both were in their early 30s, young enough to rough it for a few nights, but it would have been impossible to put up Granma and Grandad, Mother's parents. At the end of the war, they had moved up from the south-coast to Birmingham (where Granma was originally from) and, instead, we went down to visit them by train — that must have been early in 1948, for I remember seeing the streamlined Coronation Scot at Carlisle Station, and the streamlining was removed that year. I also have recollections of the journey: getting sprayed through the half-open window when the engine was taking on water, and Mother singing the old music-hall song 'Oh Mr Porter, whatever shall I do? I wanted to go to Birmingham and they've taken me on to Crewe!'. They lived in Chantrey Crescent on the Pheasey Estate, a large post-war housing development beyond Perry Barr in the north-west outskirts of Birmingham, towards Walsall and West Bromwich.

Shortly after we had moved to Hayton, Gran left Chatsworth Square and went to live at Skinburness, some twenty miles away on the coast of the Solway Firth. It was soon to become a focal point in my life.

Meanwhile Father was awarded a place at Trinity College, Cambridge. He received a grant from the Cumberland County Council and I assume also a family maintenance allowance. Anyhow he went up to Trinity in autumn 1949 to read Philosophy and Psychology — a 'mature student' of thirty-two, which was nothing out of the ordinary in the post-war years. I didn't notice his absence too much as his holidays from Cambridge were long. He often took a vacation job and I remember him working for Dick Lamb during the harvest in 1950 — until he got the sack, which embarrassed me greatly.

In the summer holidays, especially at weekends, there were the family outings. A regular one was to Warwick Bridge (to which we took the bus) on the banks of the river Eden. I can picture my parents swimming, Mother sidestroke and Father doing the crawl — he was a good swimmer — and I think I also went in the water, because it was here that I first made acquaintance with the khaki, army-issued, inflatable life jacket, that followed us around for the next ten years. It was extremely cumbersome, and fortunately never had to be put to the test. In contrast, the picnic blanket in a coarse tartan served us admirably and was in regular use over the next twenty-five years.

Another Sunday afternoon outing was to Talkin Tarn, a lake a couple of miles east of Hayton ('tarn' is another survival from Old Norse). We would set out with rucksack, picnic basket and in sunny weather my father would have on his khaki shorts. This one we had to walk, taking the twins' pushchair in case they got tired. First the road out of the village in the direction of Town Head, then the longer bit skirting Gelt Woods. I knew these woods, because I had been here with older children when we would follow the course of the river Gelt through the woods; a succession of cascades, potholes and dark mysterious pools which glittered as the sunlight pierced the beech-tree canopy. There was a long outcrop of red sandstone which in places became cliff-like, and they showed me 'Abraham's Cave' and the 'Written Rock' which bore Roman inscriptions. Here was the quarry used when constructing the Roman Wall.

Talkin Tarn — glacial in origin and maybe a mile and a half in circumference — was more placid. It had a gently sloping shore just a few yards wide at the water's edge, where rowing boats were lined up for hire and a traditional boathouse where you could admire the sleek racing-boats. Here we had our picnic and spent the afternoon playing at the water's edge and sometimes, as a treat, we would go out in a rowing boat. In late summer, we stopped to pick brambles on the return journey. These outings were the first of a long line through childhood and into adolescence. Usually very pleasant, but as I got older, I had a tendency to put my foot in it, which would spoil things.

***

At school I had by now left the infant class, and moved with Christine Bouch, Alan Wear, & Co. to the classroom at the front of the school, under the eye of the headmaster, Mr. Allinson. The desks were arranged horizontally, leaving quite a large space across the front with an old-fashioned stove in the middle, around which the bottles of school milk would be stood in a circle when it was freezing outside. In the winter, the birds sometimes pecked through the tops of bottles left out on the doorstep and drank the cream — this was before milk was homogenised — and we used to joke that it was because they preferred the cream, but the real reason, that their beaks were not long enough to get to the milk, caused even more hilarity.

This space was used for the 'music and movement' class given on the BBC at the beginning of the day. We followed a fair number of school's programmes, including music programmes. In this way I (and probably thousands of others) got to know Prokofiev's *Peter and the Wolf* and the names and sounds of the various orchestral instruments. It was also around this time that I joined the church choir, made up of older girls from the village and one or two adults — and it was then that I was finally baptised. We didn't wear choir robes and our main duty was to lead the congregational singing of the psalms, hymns, and responses — only rarely did we sing on our own. Sunday mattins was the main service; evensong attracted a very small congregation and hardly anyone from the choir save for one lady who only sang at evensong. She needed a magnifying glass to read the texts and had a frightful wobble in her voice and standing next to her singing the hymn 'Lead kindly light amid the encircling gloom' was certainly a gloomy affair!

I usually got soldiers and Dinkey Toys for my birthday. But on my eighth birthday Allen sent me something quite different; *The Happy Prince* based on Oscar Wilde's story. This was an illustrated book with a spoken commentary on an accompanying 10inch, 78rpm record, where you were regularly instructed to 'turn the page'. Beautifully produced, the illustrations did not depict an English setting, but rather some unspecified medieval town in continental Europe. I believe this helped determine my mental image of a provincial German town. And then there is the music that accompanies the spoken text throughout, by the English composer

Leslie Bridgewater. I now realise that it prepared me for music I was to encounter later, like the Debussy and Ravel string quartets. (Bridgewater himself wrote a string quartet — I must try and hear it). As for the story, I found it unbearably sad, the death of the little swallow and the broken heart of the prince. The 'happily ever after' ending provided no comfort and did not convince me.

A month later at Christmas, my parents gave me *Treasure Island* by Robert Louis Stevenson. This was the Dent edition, illustrated by S. Van Abbé, with both line drawings and colour prints. Here again the two together — story and illustrations — helped me picture how the world looked in the eighteenth century; what people wore, and the social differences (officers, country gentlemen, locals, pirates). I took the book with me when I next went to Skinburness by myself at Easter and Gran helped me with it, sometimes reading to me.

***

Skinburness was a sprawling village on the coast of the Solway Firth, a mile or so north-east of Silloth, a small Victorian seaside town. From here we had views across the Firth towards Criffel on the Scottish side. Gran lived in what is known as the 'Long House' which faced straight onto the shore. There was a stone quay the whole length of the house and the lower windows had shutters which could be closed for protection when the sea was rough. Built as one single house, at some stage partitioning walls had been introduced, dividing it into separate dwellings, while preserving the outer structure. On the upper floor this created an earie effect, for a long corridor still ran the length of the building with the planks continuing under the wall divisions, so the sound of footsteps and creaking boards could be heard without a visible agent. There were lots of stories about the Long House. Smugglers' tales. In the eighteenth century it had been a smokery and fishing boats would be pulled up on the beach in front where the catch was unloaded and treated within. For a while it had been an inn — The Greyhound — run by a Mrs Carrick, whose husband operated a regular ferry service to and fro across the Solway Firth, and at the end of the nineteenth century it had functioned as a private hotel.[3]

The entrances to the houses were all on the rear side, where presumably carriages had once pulled up. Gran's, had an entrance hall with a tiled Victorian floor, and at the far end hung a large picture which Father had bought at Telford and Scott's — far too large for the cottage — an oil painting by an American artist Edward Norton, 1890, showing Piccadilly with horse-drawn buses, London policemen, and in the foreground a fashionable couple with their small daughter crossing the street. The hall gave access to the kitchen (at the rear) where we ate, and to two front rooms which faced the shore: one was the sitting room, which had some of the furniture from Chatsworth Square; the other was hardly ever used and was rather cold, but there was a table and a large mahogany sideboard with a 400-day clock on it, which fascinated me, and inside a collection of silver-plated salvers, serving-spoons, toast racks, teapot and coffee pot — a veritable 'pirate' treasure. These two rooms were on either side of a staircase that led up to the corridor which I have already mentioned. Leading off from this were the bathroom, the boxroom, and three reasonably sized bedrooms.

Gran's house was in the middle. The only other part of the Long House I ever went into was at the Silloth end, which had an additional side-window looking along the shore towards Silloth. There was a great big stuffed bear in the living room, holding a wooden tray with a brass post horn on it, and a silver witch ball hanging in the window where it caught the light. Here lived the Heals, who were cousins of Gran.

It was said that Sir Walter Sott had spent time at the Long House when he was writing *Redgauntlet* and that it had served as a model for Crackenthorpe's Inn in the novel:

> The little cavalcade was now approaching the house of father Crackenthorpe, situated, as the reader knows, by the side of the Solway, and not far distant from a rude pier, near which lay several fishing boats, which frequently acted in a different capacity. The house of the worthy publican was also adapted to the various occupations which he carried on — the original mansion being a house of two stories, roofed with flags of sandstone....

There was indeed a door under the stairs giving access to a short flight of stone steps which led to a smugglers' tunnel. It was always locked.

> Redgauntlet next led the way into a very small room; adjoining which, but divided by a partition, was one of apparently larger dimensions; for they

heard the trampling of the heavy boots of the period, as if several persons were walking to and fro, and conversing in low whispers.

It certainly reads as though the author was familiar with the house.

One evening when the whole family was together there, I came downstairs again to the sitting room complaining that there was someone in my bedroom. My father could be very strict and he might well have ordered me back upstairs. Not this time. Instead, he went back up with me and talked to me quietly until I'd fallen asleep again.

***

Skinburness was, I said, a sprawling place, with gorse bushes, half made-up roads and bungalows; but no centre, no apparent planning. Behind it was an RAF base, a wartime airfield, where planes were now lined up waiting to be scrapped: Spitfires and Hurricanes, Wellingtons and Halifaxes. Every so often a plane would thunder over, so low you could see the yellow and brown camouflage markings. Sometimes after tea I walked with Gran in the direction of the aerodrome and she would tell me all about London Airport — she was of course referring to the pre-war airport at Croydon.

I got to know some of the local lads and began to play with them and go exploring. A place we often went to was Grune Point, at the far end of a narrow neck of land beyond the Long House. On one side was the Solway, and on the other, stretching for miles, creeks and marshes, which were highly dangerous unless you really knew the tides and currents. Frightened by the stories of drownings, we kept to the sandy paths through gorse bushes and dunes to a narrow-gauge railway line leading to a hangar where there were the remains of a glider. Continuing we finally reached our goal: a wartime pillbox which looked out across the Solway. We were always a bit hesitant about entering; it stank inside, and we never knew quite what to expect, but once I found a live bullet there which I kept quiet about.[4]

Sometimes my parents would get up early and go mushrooming on the marshes before breakfast. I didn't like mushrooms but I did enjoy looking for them and one day I found an Edward I silver penny. Though there was a piece missing, the front-on head of the King was very clear and I recognised him from the coloured Players cigarette cards 'Kings and

Queens of England' of which I had the complete set. During Edward's campaign against the Scots in 1300, twenty-seven ships from the Cinque Ports were ordered to assemble here and all supplies to the English garrisons in Dumfries were shipped from Skinburness. In 1301 Edward granted a Royal Charter to the Abbot of Holme Cultram, close by, to hold a weekly market at Skinburness and a fair in early June. Returning from his last campaign against the Scots in 1306-7, the King fell sick with dysentery, and for much of the winter he was looked after at Lanercost Priory, north of Brampton, while his entire army was encamped on the Solway waiting to be paid off. He died at Burgh Marsh. The coin is from around 1290.

***

On school trips we went to places such as Morecambe, Blackpool, and even to Liverpool, where we went through the Mersey Tunnel and travelled on the overhead railway the full length of the busy docks. With Mother, we again went down to Granma and Grandad's at Birmingham in late August 1951. That was the first time I watched television. More to the point, I watched Denis Compton knocking runs off the South African attack in the fifth test match. Compton was one of the sporting idols of the time and he was everywhere to be seen on the poster advertising Brylcreem - my introduction to television and test cricket in one fell swoop! My interest in football had already taken off when Carlisle United, from the third division north, faced Arsenal away at Highbury in the third round of the FA Cup. Hundreds of Carlisle supporters had gone down to London to cheer on their side on 6 January 1951, including Fred Nicholson, landlord of the village pub. The result was a draw. One of the biggest upsets in the history of the Cup — as they say. The replay was at the small Brunton Park stadium, Carlisle, four days later and there was a mad rush to get tickets. It was a weekday, and lessons were cancelled so the whole school could listen to the live commentary on the radio. We lost 4-1. The manager of Carlisle at the time was a relatively unknown Scot called Bill Shankly.

By the time I was eight I was allowed to do quite a lot outside the house without parental supervision — probably more than children of that age today. I would go with chums to the pictures in neighbouring

Brampton, for instance to see *Oliver Twist*, starring Alec Guinness and Robert Newton. On Saturday mornings I went with the twins and Mother to Carlisle and while she did the shopping and so forth, we headed to the ABC minors at the 'Lonsdale' — the children's matinée at all the ABC cinemas up and down the country. This was an absolute cacophony, a gradual crescendo of caterwauling, screeching kids which made the soundtrack inaudible. It was a good thing that the weekly instalments of *Sir Galahad* (my main interest) came early in the programme before the kids had got into full voice!

The annual school trip in 1951 was to Whitley Bay, a seaside resort north of Newcastle, with a huge fun fair. The headmaster announced that the coach journey would follow Hadrian's Wall, "built to keep out the Picts and Scots". I wondered whether he knew about the quarry in Gelt Woods but refrained from asking because that was *our* terrain. A few days later in a convoy of three coaches, we stopped at Birdoswald just beyond Brampton and at Housesteads closer to Hexham. These have since become prime tourist attractions — particularly the latter — but then there were only the barest facilities for visitors, and it had a much bleaker aspect.[5]

One of the things we listened to on the BBC schools programmes, rather surprisingly, was a series on the geological history of our planet. There was a large wall poster that went with the programme showing the main divisions: Precambrian, Cambrian, Ordovician, Silurian, Devonian, Carboniferous, etc. I knew this by heart at the age of eight and so it has stuck. Shortly after, I found my first fossil, a simple shell in a block of broken limestone (possibly part of a stone mantelpiece) at the end of Beck Bottom, close to the ivy-covered wall. Over the next few weeks, I found a couple more and I started going to Tullie House Museum in Carlisle where the fossil collections were kept in those old-fashioned display cases with browning labels. Mother persuaded me to take my 'specimens' with me to get them dated. Thanks to Hayton Primary School and the BBC, I was introduced to 'Deep Time' at a very early age. I am grateful to both and I still have some of my fossils.

The Festival of Britain took place in 1951. It marked the centenary of the 'Great Exhibition' but it was more a celebration of Britain's recovery from the war, a sort of 'national statement'. There was a lot of publicity in schools, where posters were put up and children took part in competitions, writing short texts and making drawings in connection with the Festival. At half-term in June, I went down to London with Mother on an overnight coach. I didn't sleep very well and looking out of the window in the early morning, I was struck by the different look of the buildings; the typical sandstone houses of our parts had given way to the half-timbered thatched cottages of the South Midlands. This was of course before the advent of the motorway.

In London we first visited the Festival Gardens at Battersea Park and then the South Bank proper the next day: the Festival Hall (though it never entered my head that I would be singing in it a couple of years later), the 'Skylon' — a futuristic rocket shaped structure that reached high into the sky, and the Dome of Discovery, which I liked best of all, particularly the moving model of the Solar System.

Carlisle had its own celebration that year — *The Pageant* — which presented a history of the city and the border region in a series of key-moments: Hadrian and the Roman Wall, the arrival of St Cuthbert, the death of Edward I, Kinmont Willy, Bonny Prince Charlie and the rebellion of 1745, and more. Over those first two sunny weeks of August more than one hundred and twenty thousand people attended the Pageant in Bitts Park near the Eden — Mother, myself and the twins among the first — and I remember David getting lost on the way out and having to be picked up at the police station! To everyone's delight there was a very special Royal Visitor, Princess Margaret, who stayed at the Crown and Mitre hotel, where Mother happened to be working at the time. And that's not all. In the middle of all this, the Cumberland River Board was carrying out work widening and deepening the channel of the Eden and Father had been taken on as a labourer ('vacation work'). Towards the end of August, they uncovered a quantity of large stone blocks in the gravel all from the same local quarry — in Gelt Woods. Some bore inscriptions which could be dated to Hadrian's time. They had found an important Roman military bridge.

***

41

Uncle Allen had been a chorister at St Paul's Cathedral in the early '30s. Charles Groves, the celebrated orchestral conductor, was head chorister when he joined the choir; the historian Denis Mack Smith, and the comedian Jimmy Edwards were exact contemporaries of his — indeed Jimmy was Allen's best friend at the Choir School. Some of this I knew from Gran, who had photographs from the period and loved talking about it. I had a good voice, so perhaps it was natural that I should follow in Allen's footsteps. There was however stiff competition and a 'voice trial' — and for me that was a real worry.

Allen had passed on to me a 78rpm HMV recording of the Cathedral choir in his day singing Handel's well-known anthem 'Let their Celestial Concerts' and I soon knew it by heart, which was probably the intention — to get me familiar with the sound and idiom of St Paul's. At the same time contacts were made with the organist of St Cuthbert's Church in Carlisle, a family acquaintance, and I was able to join the weekly choir practices to gain a bit of experience.

At the end of October, I went down to London again with Mother for the voice trial. We stayed at the Strand Palace Hotel, not far from the British Museum. Forty other boys of my age were taking part, all looking very smart in their prep-school uniforms and I felt out of place. But by the time we got back to Hayton the letter was there, signed by the headmaster, the Revd. A. Jessop Price: I had been admitted to the Choir School. The letter is dated 1 November and shortly afterwards I went with Mother to Newcastle to get fitted at Isaac Walton's for all the clothes I was going to need, among which the Eton suit worn on Sundays. The London headquarters was on Ludgate Hill, a hundred yards from Choir House, and it was a stroke of luck that there was a branch so close to Carlisle. I've never been back to Newcastle, but I can still picture it on a rainy Monday morning, with the five bridges crossing the Tyne.

***

Meanwhile my parents had taken a major decision. We were to leave Hayton and move to Sussex. They had met in Hastings around 1936, married in 1938, and then lived in London. If Carlisle was meant to be a temporary phase and the idea was to return to London after the war was over, I'm glad it didn't work out that way! But now, having just turned nine, I was suddenly facing the dual prospect of moving to Sussex and going to boarding school at St Paul's.

I can recall little of the removal itself, only the tea-chests being taken from the outhouse and Father's books being packed carefully inside them. But I have never forgotten the night we left Hayton; the huddle of people from the village to see us off, the women in tears, and the Northern Lights flashing ominously across the sky as we climbed into a taxi and headed for Carlisle station to catch the night-train southwards.

Chapter: Two

ST PAUL'S CATHEDRAL

I could not see the Ambassador in his coach; but his attendants in their habits and fur caps looked handsome, comely men, and most with hawks upon their fists to present to the King. But Lord! To see the absurd nature of Englishmen that cannot forbear laughing and jeering at everything that looks strange...

[Samuel Pepys, the reception given to the Russian Ambassador by Londoners, *Diary*, 27 November 1662]

'He should be here at five-thirty p.m. on Saturday, 19 January 1952' the letter from the headmaster had said, rather tersely. The twins were with us too and things got off to a bad start, for we arrived at the Choir School almost half an hour late in the middle of rollcall. As we entered the room there was an audible giggle from the assembled boys.

The contrast between life at Choir House and Hayton could not have been greater. A two-minute walk from the Cathedral, the official address was *Choir House, Dean's Court, London EC4*, but only a small corner of the building was in Dean's Court — the full length of the façade with its main entrance stood in Carter Lane. The Choir School moved in 1967 to New Change, at the east end of the Cathedral, but the old building is still there, where it now serves as a youth hostel in a quiet conservation area. One might easily get the impression that time has stood still — which is not really the case; back in 1952 it was an enclave, true, but by virtue of the fact that, amidst all the destruction, it had survived the War unscathed.

Ten years after the Blitz a wide area around the Cathedral was still bomb-damage, where a kind of balance had returned and shrubs and wild flowers now thrived among the ruins. Some clearance work had been done, pathways had been laid and you would see people sitting on benches eating a sandwich at lunch time, but construction work had not yet started. The buildings that had survived in the city were often Victorian or Edwardian; banks and offices with brass plaques on polished granite or marble pillars and wrought ironwork in front of the windows. The traffic also had a pre-war look; buses designed in the late '30s, old fashioned London taxi-cabs, box-like cars (always in dark colours) that still had headlamps separate from the bodywork, spoked wheels and often with the spare tyre fixed on the rear; small trade vans with two oval windows at the back, and all the horse-drawn delivery vehicles, from British Rail, Carter Patterson, the Express Dairy and the like. A common sight in Carter Lane was to see a horse, muzzle in the food bag, chomping away next to, say, a parked Austin Princess. The pedestrians too looked rather different from nowadays; fewer tourists, more people going about their daily business. Men outnumbered women and they had a uniform appearance, with longish overcoats or raincoats, some wearing a trilby hat, and often they would be carrying a rolled-up newspaper or have one stuffed into a coat pocket, bought from the very vocal vendors outside tube stations, or at busy junctions like Ludgate Circus. The newspaper offices were still concentrated around Fleet Street and from midday onwards vans would be whizzing around delivering the latest editions of the Evening News, Star or Standard, chucking them out in bundles onto the pavement for the vendors.

Carter Lane was a busy side-street which ran parallel to Ludgate Hill eastwards to join up with Cannon Street. Between Addle Hill and Godliman Street stood the Telephone Exchange which had opened in 1902. I remember it as a factory-like building. It looked dated, but when it was built it must have been 'functionalist' with alternating layers of glass and cream-coloured tiles, criss-crossed with wrought-iron cat walks and fire-escapes. I could picture the interior, all the rows of switchboards and the operators — women, of course — yet I cannot recall much coming and going, although it must have had a large staff working in shifts around the clock. At night looking across the dormitory I could see part of the building through the window opposite, suffused in a greenish-white glow and it seemed to emit a soft zooming sound.

Straight across from the school was the Café Royal. Nothing chic about this one. It was probably named like this because it was adjacent to Wardrobe Place, where in medieval times a private department of the Royal Household had stood known as 'the King's Wardrobe'. The café served tea, coffee, and hot meals all day. There was an abundance of yellow Formica and a metallic sounding intercom between the kitchen and the serving staff, but I couldn't make out what was being said.

The buildings in Carter Lane were mostly drab Victorian brickwork. Above the café there was a furrier's business and looking upwards through the classroom window on the ground floor, you could see the furs draped over the window ledges, more like dead animals than luxury fashion items. Next door, the upper floors were occupied by the Reader's Digest. It struck me as odd that a magazine known the world over (though I never read it) should have such modest premises. There were in fact a number of printing works and publishing houses in the vicinity. At Broadway House, 67–74 Carter Lane, was Routledge & Kegan Paul, a name I knew from the covers of father's philosophy books, and at the bottom of St Andrew's Hill, turning left into Queen Victoria Street was the headquarters of the British and Foreign Bible Society. A number of evangelical publishers also had their premises in the vicinity, like the Crusaders' Union, which had a huge following in the '50s.

The City's association with publishing goes back a long way. William Caxton may have set up his first printing press close to Westminster Abbey in 1476, but a century later St Paul's Churchyard was firmly established as the centre of the London book trade. In 1557 a Royal Charter had been granted to the Worshipful Company of Stationers, who thus gained a monopoly over the trade. The Stationers' Hall was at Ave Maria Lane, on the north side of Ludgate Hill. On the night of Saturday, 1 September 1666 a fire broke out in the eastern part of the city close to the Tower. Driven westwards by a strong wind the 'Great Fire' began to threaten Cheapside and St Paul's Churchyard, at which stage the Stationers' Company intervened, granting permission to its members to store their books in the chapel of St Faith's in the crypt of the Cathedral. To no avail. On Tuesday, the Cathedral itself went up in flames, and as John Evelyn says in his *Diary*:

The ruins of the vaulted roofe falling broke into St Faith's, which being fill'd with the magazines of bookes belonging to the Stationers, and carried thither for safety, they were all consum'd, burning for a weeke following.

The Stationers' Hall itself was also destroyed. But within a few years of the completion of the new Cathedral the booksellers returned, chiefly to Paternoster Row. In December 1940, however, Paternoster Row was bombed and an estimated five million books were lost.

At the corner of St Andrew's Hill and Carter Lane was the barber's shop — 'Fosters' I think it was called — which was run by two balding middle-aged Italians. Here every three weeks the choir would pass through for a haircut — short back and sides. On my arrival at the Choir School, I had been rushed there to make me more presentable. A bit further was the 'Rising Sun', a typical Victorian London pub, and opposite in Creed Lane was the newsagents where every morning at seven forty-five, on our way back from the morning walk, we would pick up the daily papers: *The Times* for the teaching staff to read at breakfast, the *Daily Telegraph* for us to read in the day-room, and the *Daily Sketch* for the maids!

Beyond the Rising Sun, Carter Lane narrows down. Here there was an old-fashioned grocer's shop with wooden steps for the higher shelves, where the shopkeeper wore a brown overall coat — like Ronny Barker, later, in the TV series 'Open all Hours'. We often came here when rationing ended to buy sweets and sherbet; the latter we would eat (rather than mixing it with water) dipping a finger into the conical packet. Our favourite was 'kali' (pronounced *kay-lie*) which was particularly tart and turned your lips and tongue bright yellow. It was soon banned. At this end of Carter Lane, just before you got to the bomb-damage between New Bridge Street and Ludgate Hill, was a fishmonger's where the fish was stacked up outside in wooden crates packed with ice — not very appetising — and we would joke (in two minds) that this was where the fish came from which was served up at Friday lunchtime, and on Wednesdays too in Lent.

If there was one building that stood out from all the rest, it was Choir House. Built around 1875 in an eccentric Victorian-Italianate style, the façade had an inscription in large letters of biblical texts in Latin, forming a kind of frieze. Here we all lived: thirty choristers, eight probationers, the headmaster and his wife, two resident members of the teaching staff, the matron, housekeeper, and some of the domestic staff. What a different view of London I would have got if, instead, I had been a chorister down the road at the Abbey, where the choir school was set back in a secluded courtyard well away from the street. In Carter Lane we were very much part of the street scene. Every morning at eight-thirty there was a choristers' choir practice under the direction of the organist and choir-master Dr John Dykes Bower — universally known as 'DB' — and those in the café opposite would have been able to enjoy their cup of tea or breakfast to the tune of, say, Bairstow in D or Harwood in A flat! We sang for our supper. In return for our vocal services in the Cathedral, we received free board and education.

The Cathedral very much shaped our day. In all, services and choir practice added up to some twenty hours singing a week; schoolwork, sport, and recreation had to be fitted in around it. The headmaster's wife, Eileen Price, did her best to create a 'family' feeling, especially for the new probationers. She was an established artist and a council member of the SWA,[6] and she organised a weekly art class on Mondays after evensong. I joined in and not only did I enjoy it, I also learned a lot from her guidance. Superficially at least I must have adapted to this new environment, for when I returned home for the Easter holiday, I was shocked to find that the twins still had their Cumbrian accents!

Home was (to quote from the Choir School Register): *Tar Hut Cottage, Nr Plumpton, Nr Lewes, Sussex.* Not really anywhere! It was a cottage in the middle of the fields in the shadow of the South Downs. No connecting road, no running water (we had a well), no gas and no electricity. My six-year-old brothers had to walk a mile to school and back each day whatever the weather.

It was certainly a plus point having the Downs so close to us, and in the summer, family walks often followed the ridge of the Downs in the direction of Lewes. In August there was the added attraction of Lewes races. We would sometimes have a picnic sitting in the grass close to the starting line where we didn't have to pay — many people did this. Unlike the spectacle seen from the grandstand, the view here was more like going 'backstage'. I remember the jockey Gordon Richards losing his temper and swearing at his horse which was refusing to come under starter's orders. Almost fifty, at the end of a long career, he had just been knighted by the Queen — so it was all rather undignified, and greatly amused the onlookers! I would also go up onto the Downs by myself, where the numerous chalk pits and escarpments were a rich hunting ground for fossils. Exploring the possibilities, I came across an abandoned army tank halfway up to Black Cap, the highest point on our stretch of the Downs, and climbed into it. I later learned that there had been army training exercises up here at the beginning of the war in case of a German invasion.

We lived in these primitive conditions for two years and although I was only there in the school holidays, I found the contrast between Tar Hut and Choir House difficult to cope with.

***

One day in February in my first term, just before we sat down for lunch, the head announced that the King had died. I remember pudding was ginger cake with an orange, so it must have been a Wednesday. The lying-in-state of George VI was in Westminster Hall; the public patiently waiting in a long queue stretching back into Parliament Square, slowly shuffling forwards towards the coffin to pay their respects, or simply to be part of the occasion. We were treated to a 'fast-track' visit. Being a chorister of St Paul's meant you were often in touch, if not with the affairs, at least with the *trappings* of state. "The King is dead, long live the Queen!" I would be singing at the Coronation — if I was admitted as a chorister in time.

***

The latter part of 1952 was a sad time for the country, with four major disasters: the Lynton-Lynmouth flash floods in mid-August which claimed thirty-four lives; the Farnborough Air Show crash in early September killing thirty-one people; the Harrow train crash in October with a loss of a hundred and fourteen lives, and then the Great Smog of London at the beginning of December which we experienced first-hand because we were in the thick of it. 'Smog' is a word we often hear nowadays in connection with fine particle air pollution. In the '50s it was used more in its original sense of fog plus smoke. The fog was natural, the smoke was man-made — partly the result of coal-fires using low quality coal which produced vast quantities of sulphur-dioxide.

Londoners' aversion to burning coal was nothing new; the fear that smoke from 'sea-coal' used in iron smelting and in lime kilns would have an adverse effect on health is heard from the late thirteenth century onwards. Behind Ludgate Circus there was a small street called 'Seacoal Lane'. When burning coal came into more general domestic use in the sixteenth century as a cheaper alternative to wood, the health scare receded and a polemic began on the way it was corroding public buildings.

Smog was a perennial hazard in London, where it was often referred to as a 'pea-souper' because of its colour. The Great Smog was unprecedented. It lasted from Friday, 5 December till Tuesday, 9 December; a creeping mass that reduced visibility to zero, which hurt the throat and lungs, and brought the city to a standstill. But not the Cathedral. The Blitz on London claimed thirty thousand lives over a period of a year, and up to a hundred and thirty thousand casualties. Casualty figures for the Smog of 1952 vary greatly, but even taking a lower estimate, it killed six thousand in four days and a further one hundred and fifty thousand suffered lung damage.

***

I was admitted as a chorister at evensong on Saturday, 26 January 1953. The anthem we sang after I had taken my place on the cantoris-side of the choir stalls was Brahms' 'How lovely is thy dwelling-place' from his *Deutches Requiem*. The acoustics of the Cathedral seem to enhance the gentle rising and falling of the melodic lines, and I think for many old choristers this piece has a particular nostalgia.

***

The Coronation was on 2 June 1953. The dress rehearsal in the Abbey had already made one thing clear; the ceremony the wider public were to see on television (for the first time) would be rather different from what I experienced. We sat high up near the organ in temporarily constructed stands surrounded by scaffolding. My view can best be described as 'intermittent'.

The day started very early for us, as it did for all the thousands lining the streets. We were dropped at the Abbey before eight and having robed we had to stand around for quite a long time in the Chapter House before we were allowed to go to our places. Each of us had a sponge bag attached to our cassock belts hidden under our white surplices with sandwiches in case we got hungry. I don't recall any thought being given to water — bottled water was a thing of the future — and I don't think toilet facilities were talked about. We were used to services lasting a couple of hours in the Cathedral, and it never seemed to be a problem, but this was going to be a lot longer. More waiting in the Abbey. The grown-ups sitting behind me were reading the morning newspaper and they passed on the news that Hillary had successfully climbed Everest, which caused a flurry of excitement. Then the orchestra started playing a succession of appropriately patriotic pieces, and at last the moment had arrived — a trumpet fanfare leading into Hubert Parry's stirring anthem 'I was glad when they said unto me' as the royal procession entered at the West doors and moved slowly up the aisle.

Although the Coronation Ceremony itself goes back to Anglo-Saxon times, the regalia now used (crown, orb, sceptre, etc.) date from 1660. After the Civil War and execution of Charles I most of the Crown Jewels were melted down, and with the restoration of the monarchy a new set had to be made. One of those who managed to wangle his way into the Abbey for Charles II's Coronation on 23 April 1661 was Samuel Pepys, who writes in his *Diary*:

> About 4 in the morning, I rose and got to the abbey, where I found Sir J. Denham the surveyor with some company that he was leading in. And with much ado, by the favour of Mr. Cooper his man, did get up into a great scaffold across the north end of the abbey — where with a great deal of patience I sat from past 4 till 11 before the King came in….
>
> And after all had placed themselves there was a sermon and the service. And then in the Quire at the high altar he passed all the ceremonies of the Coronacion — which to my very great grief, I and most in the Abbey could not see. The crown being put on his head, a great shout begun… so great a noise that I could make but little of the musique; and indeed, it was lost to everybody. But I had so great a list to piss, that I went out a little while before the King had done all his ceremonies and went round the abbey to Westminster Hall….

***

Later that summer term we were taken on a river trip by Admiral Hotham aboard the *St Katherine*, the Port of London Authority steam yacht dating from the 1920s. Passing under Tower Bridge which was ceremoniously opened for us, we continued downstream, skirting the

Isle of Dogs (now Canary Wharf) and proceeding through the locks we entered the Royal Docks where we were given a running commentary on the ships at berth; their tonnage, their country of origin, the cargo they were carrying. Looking at their rusting hulls I couldn't help feeling that their time was up. We disembarked to get a closer view of a banana ship being unloaded. I got a shock when I saw there were live snakes in the holds and instinctively turned away.

On the return journey there was a slap-up tea and at Tower Pier as we filed down the gangplank, we were each given a souvenir copy of the book *The Royal River* which had just been published to commemorate the Queen's Coronation. Writing the above passage, I needed to check whether the *St Katherine* was with a 'C' or a 'K' and I remembered that there was a photograph of it in the book. To my surprise I also found the following:

> When King George VI and Queen Elizabeth visited Canada early in 1939, the two Royal children were left in the charge of Queen Mary who softened their temporary loss by taking them on a well-planned series of educational tours. Not the least important in this programme was a visit in May 1939 to the Port of London.
>
> The Royal Party (...) were escorted to the Tower Pier for Princess Elizabeth's first voyage down the tideway. The *St Katherine* had the honour of carrying the visitors, who cruised down the industrial reaches and through the Royal Docks. The journey was through an area where cross sections of Britain's overseas commerce are concentrated as if for inspection, and the lesson must have made a profound impression on the future Queen of Dominions and Colonies strung all over the world.

***

In late September, the choir — all thirty choristers and eighteen 'vicars choral' — some of the teaching staff and representatives of the Cathedral clergy and of course DB — took the train from Waterloo station to Southampton and boarded the *Queen Elizabeth* in time for lunch. We were on our way to America for a concert tour of two months.[7] The boys were in tourist class, but we were well looked after and given extra facilities. On board there was a swimming pool, a small cinema, table-tennis and deck-games, or simply the heavy wooden deckchairs if you wanted to relax. I sometimes sat there with the charcoal pencils Eileen Price had given me, sketching the people around me. It failed to impress one American kid of my age, who cast an eye over my efforts:

"That's no good," he said. "I don't know why you bother."

The tour involved a total of forty concerts in cities such as New York, Washington, Boston, Montreal, Chicago and New Orleans. We also sang at the White House, followed by a reception where President Eisenhower made sure we enjoyed ourselves. Any idea that we should have normal school lessons went by the board — we were simply too busy and besides the tour was an education in itself. I remember it in great detail: our arrival at New York on the morning of 29 September with the sun breaking through the early morning mist and the Manhattan skyline beginning to take shape, dramatic, modern, and still like a fairy tale; the Niagara Falls; the Powhattan Arrow — the streamlined train that took us from Buffalo to Chicago; standing on an old-fashioned observation platform at the back of the train from Memphis to New Orleans as we went through the mangrove swamps of the Mississippi Delta; the concert halls and the hotels. Most of the travelling was done by bus. On arrival our bus driver, Jim, had addressed us like a movie army officer about the dos and don'ts, on his bus; he expected no nonsense and he didn't get any. Back in New York I recall Eileen Price whisking me off to (was it?) the Whitney Museum to have a look at some huge canvasses by Jackson Pollock — I was just eleven! Our farewell concert was on 24 November at Carnegie Hall. A sell-out.

Returning to England, how green it looked, and after the automobiles in the States the cars were like something from Noddy Land. These feelings had passed by the time we got to Waterloo. In London we gave a final concert at the Festival Hall.

Canon John Collins had been one of the driving forces behind the tour. He had also represented the Dean and Chapter which, given his socialist views and outspoken criticism of racial discrimination, was a bold decision in post-McCarthy America where many states still had segregation laws. On 12 January 1954, a letter arrived:

> My dear Michael,
>
> Now that the American tour and the Festival Hall concert are over, I would like to thank you very much for your part in making the whole enterprise such a success. I'm afraid you must have been very tired sometimes, and rather exhausted by the end of term: but I hope you felt, as I did, that all the hard work was really worthwhile, and that you enjoyed it as much as

I did. I hope the whole tour will always remain with you as a very happy memory,

With all good wishes, yours sincerely

L. John Collins

P.S. next time we go you'll probably be our "David Linter"!

i.e. 'solo boy'. And there was an additional postscript to the concert tour. In February, the choir spent a week at the Abbey Road studios in St John's Wood recording a double LP for Columbia which contained much of the music we had sung in America. While it is not mentioned on the sleeve, the recording engineer was a certain George Martin.

***

At the time 1953 was seen as heralding a *New Elizabethan Age.* In retrospect it was also something of an economic watershed; rationing was coming to an end and an increasing number of households started to buy a refrigerator, a TV, a 'record player' and even a car. Austere post-war England was being transformed into a consumer society in which teenagers too were potential buyers, where pop-music and teenage fashion were gaining a foothold in the market.

In March 1954 sitting in a teashop on Oxford Street while an anti-nuclear demonstration marched by, Mother passed on the news that we were leaving Tar Hut Cottage and moving to Hove. Rutland Gardens was a wide, tree-lined street ten minutes' walk from the sea on the north side of New Church Road. The house was large, Edwardian, with black and white geometrical tiles leading up to the front door. We had the upper part of the house with our own separate entrance, and at last a proper bathroom. The furniture and smaller objects I suppose provided a sort of continuity. My father was now working as a teacher in a school for pupils with special needs near Lewes, and soon after we moved to Hove, Mother started following an extra-mural degree course from London University in Social Sciences.

I did miss the Downs a bit and the fossils, but there were a number of galleries in Brighton Museum devoted to geology and prehistory which I could go to when I felt like it. Rutland Gardens had many advantages and there was a lot to be discovered, and here my brothers had a start on me. A short walk from where we lived was a large ABC cinema on Portland Road — the Granada — and in the afternoons we would sometimes go there by ourselves. Films had to pass the Board of Censors and were awarded a U-Certificate if they were for general viewing, an A-Certificate, where children under the age of sixteen were only admitted if they were accompanied by an adult (imagine that!) or an X-Certificate if they were strictly for adults. Cinemas at that time ran continuous programmes with commercials, Pathé News, trailers, and a B-film: the starting times of the main film were of course published in the local paper, but you could buy a ticket and go in at any time, shown to your seat by an usherette with a torch — even in the middle of the film — you simply stayed sitting till you had caught up with what you had missed, or longer. I remember watching *The Charge of the Light Brigade* (starring Errol Flynn) at the Embassy on Western Road twice in an afternoon! With my parents 'going to the pictures' was better organised, and I saw my first Hitchcock film with them around this time — *Dial M for Murder*.

Living in Hove made things a lot easier. Even though it was about the same distance as the crow flies from London, it was a lot quicker to get to Hove than to Tar Hut Cottage; fifty-five minutes by train to Brighton and a short bus ride. During my first two years at St Paul's, I had regarded school and home as two apart worlds, but now I cautiously began to build bridges. I could even invite friends to come and stay. The first to come to Hove was David Driscoll, with whom I had already stayed in Guildford. Like mine, his parents voted Labour, but he at least had the courage to say so! By chance among my 'memorabilia' is the corner of a letter written by David to thank my mother — it must have been torn off for his embossed address in Guildford. Enough is preserved to allow a reconstruction of the first sentence:

"…*Windross It was awfully… me to stay for… y bit of it.*"

Even as twelve-year-olds, we could trot out the required formulas!

One of the first things my father did after we moved to Hove was to get the gramophone working again. It had not been used since Hayton. We kept the cabinet and for a while the radio too, but the old gramophone, with its little metal well for spare needles, had to make way for a new record-player with three speeds, 33, 45 and 78 rpm and an interchangeable head for LPs or the old 78s — thus marking our return to the twentieth century.

***

After all the heightened activity in the previous year things returned to a more regular pattern at Choir House — which was busy enough. The cathedral repertory included the Tudor composers such as Tallis, Byrd, and Gibbons, the Restoration composers Purcell and Blow, the Victorian and Edwardian composers like Wesley, Stanford, and Parry, and one or two 'moderns' such as Walton and Howells. We also sang selections from Haydn's Creation, Mozart's Requiem and from the Brahms Requiem too — which I loved — and of course there were the annual performances of Bach's Matthew Passion and Handel's Messiah. Three and a half centuries of musical evolution served up in the order in which it occurred in the service calendar for the year — in musical terms, at random, which we managed to internalise. Unlike the gradual process of learning a foreign language (from simple to complex), it was more akin to the acquisition of one's native language. And just as a language is handed down by one generation to the next, so the musical repertory was passed on by the choristers of one year to the next. But it was not only a collective process; there was also the individual, private journey of discovery we all experienced. Initially feelings of simply liking (or disliking) a piece, spurred on by recognition and association, and rewarded by strong emotional feelings and the sheer physical excitement of singing. And it all went quickly — it had too. I started from scratch as a nine-year-old, but by the time we were touring America (coming up to eleven) I reckoned I was quite a dab hand! Notwithstanding Canon Collins's forecast, I never quite made it to 'solo boy'. I was given the opportunity and plenty of kind encouragement by DB, and in choir practice beforehand things would go well, but in the Cathedral itself my nerves let me down.

Meanwhile I was progressing well with painting, and Eileen persuaded the head to let me occasionally skip his divinity class on Saturdays so that I could continue on an oil painting — one of which was included in an exhibition of children's art at Lambeth Palace. My easel stood next to hers in her studio on the north side of Choir House — for the best light. She was working on a commission; a series of large canvases depicting the London food markets. I have not seen the paintings since, but I remember the one of Smithfield with the rows of carcasses and especially the silvery, shimmering light of Billingsgate fish market. She wrote to my parents that summer, expressing her high hopes for me:

"He really has great talent… he draws so easily that it is awfully important that he should come into the right kind of influence… his facility for drawing could lead him into being just slickly representational which always calls forth praise from the majority of people!"

Sometimes on Mondays when the weather was good, the art class would go out sketching in the surroundings of the Cathedral, where the bomb-sites would add interesting contours to the classic views of the dome. It was about this time that construction work started in earnest, thus offering pits, lorries, diggers, scaffolding, cranes — all grist to the artist's mill. Many years later Eileen sent me a small photograph of a painting she had done in the summer of 1955 (from drawings *in situ*) of me with a sketch pad on my knee, and cranes and the dome of the Cathedral in the background.

***

In my Father's House are many Mansions
[John, 14. 2]

When Christopher Wren was appointed 'Surveyor of the King's Works' in July 1669 and given the task of designing the new cathedral, it was not simply to be a replacement for 'Old St Paul's'. He was expected "to frame a design handsome and noble, and suitable to the reputation of the city and the nation". Moreover, it had to be something that would represent the supremacy of the Anglican Church, while still providing a continuity with the English cathedral tradition. A tall order.

The cathedrals of England were built roughly in the period 1150–1450. Like all the medieval cathedrals of Europe, they were the products of an age in which each country saw itself as part of a wider Christian society. Putting it simply (if anachronistically) they had been built as Catholic churches. Some were built in a relatively short space of time in a uniform style (Salisbury springs to mind) but mostly the work was spread over several centuries, with each succeeding generation (either out of necessity or because of changing fashions) adding its own contribution. This process came to a halt around 1450. There were important places of worship built in the latter half of the fifteenth century in the late Perpendicular Gothic style, such as King's College Chapel, Cambridge and St George's Chapel, Windsor — both Royal chapels — but no new cathedral had been built in England for two hundred years when Wren was given the job. On top of this, the Reformation and the recent Civil War had put paid to any idea of continuity and tradition.

In the legislation directly following the Restoration, probably the most far-reaching was the Act of Uniformity (1662), which required all those who held office in the church or government to swear adherence to the *Book of Common Prayer* of 1662. In consequence, Catholics were barred from office and priests who refused to take the oath were driven out of the church. This marked the birth of Nonconformism and at the same time distanced the Church of England from European Protestantism. Clearly, the Anglican church had shifted away from its 'reforming' origins and saw itself less as a champion of religious zeal and more as the guarantor of social stability and an instrument of the State.

Wren was from a Royalist background, and he had family connections in the church. In his diary, John Evelyn (11 July 1653) writes that he met Wren at Oxford:

> After dinner I visited that miracle of a youth, that prodigious young scholar, Mr. Christopher Wren, nephew of the Bishop of Ely.

He was twenty-one then, and seven years later they were both among the founder members of the Royal Society. Wren, meanwhile, had built up a considerable reputation as professor of mathematics and astronomy at Oxford and he was also very good at applying his science to practical problems. It was because of this that he first became involved in an advisory capacity with the Royal Commission looking into the decayed condition of Old St Paul's. Evelyn — also an advisor — says that on 27 August 1666 he was at St Paul's Church together with Wren and a number of others

> to survey the general decay of that ancient and venerable church. When we came to the steeple, it was deliberated whether it was not well enough to repair it on its old foundation... but Dr Wren and I totally rejected it... we had a mind to build it with a noble cupola — a form of church-building not as yet known in England, but of wonderful grace....

which suggests that the dome was their shared idea. Drawings by Wren from this period showing a large dome have survived. The Great Fire a week later closed that particular chapter. Old St Paul's would have to be demolished and rebuilt anew. Having already seen some of Wren's projects on paper, the Commission knew what to expect.

The history of the building of the new Cathedral is well documented from the planning stages right through to its completion forty years later, and the story has been well told.[8] Among Wren's preliminary designs is the *Great Model Design* (his personal favourite) which has come down to us in the form of a large wooden architectural model, with an elegant dome in the centre and four transepts of nearly equal size leading off from it. In this it departed from the traditional cruciform plan of English cathedrals with their long nave and two short transepts at the crossing. The Commission took exception to this and rejected it even though Charles II had expressed his approval. The King approved of all Wren's designs including the one he put forward in a fit of pique following this rejection, with a pagoda-like construction above a squat dome — anticipating the nineteenth-century *Mole Antonelliana* in Turin! It was this so-called *Warrant Design* that was given the go-ahead. Fortunately, there was an understanding that Wren could carry out any modifications to his design that he deemed necessary and he certainly made use of this freedom; it proved crucial when it came to building the dome, where the enormous weight and the tendency for the supporting piers to settle in the London clay posed a major problem. Wren's solution was the ingenious triple structure of the dome.

It is natural to think that the dome we see from outside on the street is the same as the one we see from the floor of the Cathedral looking upwards. But this is an illusion. The inner dome is much smaller, though it certainly gives an impression of height and space. The outer dome is designed to make a bold statement whether viewed from nearby or afar; it is placed on a large drum with Corinthian columns which adds height and lends support. Surmounting it all is a stone 'lantern' with the ball and cross. To lessen its weight the outer dome was constructed of wood with a lead covering, but this could never have supported the stone lantern. To solve the problem Wren built a brick cone between the two domes, taking the thrust of the lantern but completely hidden from view.

In the later stages there were disagreements between the Commission and Wren (by which time the composition of the Commission had totally changed) — usually about the length of time it was taking, the cost, the way the money was being spent, and the final embellishments —

the paintings in the dome by Sir James Thornhill, for instance, were done contrary to Wren's wishes. But with the exception of the Great Model Design, where Wren was reckoned to have strayed too far from the English tradition, he seems to have largely got his way. Since the *Book of Common Prayer* was the focal point of Anglican dogma, it is instructive to look at the frontispiece of the 1662 edition: the portico is a semi-circle with Corinthian pillars, a shallow dome, prosperous members of the bourgeoisie socialising outside, a solitary beggar at the bottom of the steps, and above the entrance an inscription in Latin 'DOMUS ORATIONIS'. It could be Rome or even Naples! I don't know whether Wren was familiar with this frontispiece, but it is striking how much of the detail has found its way into his design of the portico to the transepts.

Wren had been asked to come up with something that would enhance the reputation of the city and the nation. Not only did St Paul's impress the outside world, but it also endeared itself to Londoners. In a small book published in 1914, G.E. Mitton writes:

"The Cathedral is part of the city life, and thus in some way *domestic.*"

It is often regarded as the National Shrine, and this can be felt when Martin Briggs remarks that St Paul's is seen at its best on some great civic occasion such as a National Thanksgiving Service.[9]

Its magnificence is very different from the religious aspirations that inspired the lofty medieval cathedrals, which in E.H. Gombrich's words, 'gave the faithful a glimpse of a different world'.[10] St Paul's is more of *this* world, as is evident in the large number of monuments to national heroes, especially war heroes like Lord Kitchener, the Duke of Wellington and Lord Nelson — admittedly placed there after Wren's time. In the vast crypt below are the tombs of Nelson and Wellington, and close by is the grave of Christopher Wren himself. Above it is a simple inscription in Latin, put there by his son:

LECTOR, SI MONUMENTUM REQUIRIS, CIRCUMSPICE
'Reader if you seek a monument, look around you'.

This brief text is not meant to inform; it serves more as a reminder of the man's modesty — which is perhaps why it is so often quoted. But what if we take it literally — and the House of God?

***

I got to know the City pretty well and could easily find my way around. Our day started early with a seven o'clock walk down St Andrew's Hill towards the Victoria Embankment via the pedestrian subway at Blackfriars, already busy with people on their way to work. This brought us to a parapet overlooking the river close to the bridge, where the river Fleet comes out into the Thames. Formerly a sewer, the smell was simply that of Thames mud. We stopped here for a while, looking across the river from the stone balustrade towards the red lights of the OXO-tower on the other side, watching the seagulls performing their early morning aerobatics and the passing tugs pulling a train of barges. At high tide they had to lower their tall funnels to get under Blackfriars Bridge. There were no staff involved on these walks; the two most senior boys took charge. Even more surprisingly, we were allowed out in pairs after evensong, on condition that one of the boys was twelve or older and that we were back in time for rollcall before supper at six. For me this meant quick expeditions to King's Cross and Liverpool Street Stations, for train spotting — these were the last days of the great steam engines — and on other occasions I would go as far as Foyles's bookshop on Charing Cross Road with Robin Holloway, to buy miniature orchestral scores published by Boosey and Hawkes and Eulenberg (Robin was already into Debussy — I tended to go for Beethoven and Brahms). These were presented to DB next morning in the few minutes between breakfast and choir practice who sight-read them on the piano with an occasional (feigned) protest that the transposing instruments were printed in a different key! Amazing. Such journeys often involved travelling on public transport — either the bus or the tube. When, in 1955, I was awarded the Macpherson Prize for the hardest working chorister (voted by the choristers themselves and therefore very special) I chose the miniature Eulenberg edition of Beethoven's Choral Symphony for the prize-giving, which I still treasure.

At the weekend, the City would become strangely quiet and deserted. In the summer we would sometimes wander down to the river after evensong, crossing Upper Thames Street to the wharves and warehouses in the area around Puddle Dock, where the air was warm and heavy with spices. In the evening after supper, we roller-skated in Carter Lane.

The summers are also associated in my mind with hours of cricket on our caged roof playground. There was just enough space, but we had to bowl off a shortened run-up as though we were in the practice nets. Leather cricket balls (which of course we used when we played matches on grass) would have become quickly scuffed and worn on the hard surface, so we used 'composition' balls, with a cork centre and a strong plastic-like covering which lasted longer and were cheaper; the bats were those retired from service and now had a protective hide covering. All our equipment came from Jack Hobbs' sport shop at the far end of Fleet Street opposite the Law Courts. In my final year, as 'sport's boy', it was my job to go there to place orders, and usually Sir Jack was somewhere in the back of the shop quietly getting on with things. One of the all-time greats of cricket he had finished his illustrious career as long ago as the late 1920s. He had recently been awarded a knighthood in the Coronation honours list.

In the summer of 1955 South Africa were once again the touring side and in mid-June they were playing Sussex at Hove. I was not the first from our generation of choristers to call himself a 'Sussex supporter', that distinction goes to Robert Phillipson — the seventh in a long line of Phillipson choristers. Listening together to the radio commentary after evensong, Sussex were two hundred and fifty for three with Jim Parks and David Sheppard approaching their centuries — which they both got. From that moment on I was a Sussex man and Parks was my hero. In the summer holidays I spent many days at the County Ground watching him and Ken Suttle notching up the runs.

That August the sun also beckoned us down to the beach. Both the twins could swim and groups of us spent hours in the sea, mucking about on a leaky catamaran raft or diving off the stone groyne to chase after pebbles. There were, I suppose, plenty of grown-ups to keep an eye on us, but we reckoned we ruled the roost. At the weekend, our parents came with us. Mother had usually taken care of a picnic which we ate sitting on our trusty blanket (the one from Cumberland) and after we kept asking "can we go in the water?" — but the thirty-minute rule stood.

Mother now had her degree in Social Sciences and had started working with the East London Family Service Unit in Whitechapel. Father got a position with the LCC as educational psychologist for the district of Wandsworth. His office was at County Hall, bang opposite the Houses of Parliament where there was a Tory government — a confrontation he would joke about. So for a while they were both working in London.

***

The long-established procedure at the Choir School had been to take what was called the 'Common Entrance' exam and to move on to one of the 'public schools'. This was still so in my time, but we also sat the 11-plus — just as a safeguard. The 11-plus was the state school exam introduced by the Labour Government after the war to ensure that good pupils would be able to benefit from a grammar school education. Hitherto this had favoured those who could afford it. Moreover, the future of the fee-paying public schools — a bastion of privilege and the class-system — was increasingly being called into question. I had passed the 11-plus and I naturally supposed I would be going to Hove County Grammar School when I left the Choir School. It came as a surprise when in early '56 I discovered that I was to try for Lancing College. I knew that my parents would not be able to afford the fees and besides my father was not in favour of the public schools. There must have been some discussion between the head and my parents about my future and quite possibly this sudden change came about through the influence of Eileen Price. Anthony Price had left the Choir School at the end of the Christmas term having been head chorister for a year and had now moved on to Lancing. In this way Eileen had contact with both John Dancy, the headmaster, and Graham Collier, head of the art department, to whom she sent a portfolio of my work. I went down to Lancing in March, and I was awarded a scholarship for music and art. Not quite home and dry as I still had to take the Common Entrance Examination in the autumn and my schoolwork was none too good.

Term always started on a Saturday, and it was Father who accompanied me up to London in early May '56. We took a mid-morning train to Victoria, and from there to Foyles, where he spent some time browsing in the philosophy section. He suggested we have lunch at the 'Kohinoor' round the corner in Soho. It was not the first time I had been to an Indian restaurant with him, and I still get a yearning for the taste of the Indian food I had in the '50s. In the afternoon we went to a matinée performance of *Porgy and Bess* — I don't recall which theatre, but it was within easy walking distance and we sat up in the gods.

Then it was back to Choir House and cricket. The 1956 season saw England again retain the Ashes against Australia. We followed the series closely, buying the evening newspapers in Carter Lane, for there were continuous updates: lunchtime scores, teatime scores, close of play scores, and of course we listened to the BBC commentaries when we could, so we heard Jim Laker get all ten wickets in the second innings at Old Trafford.

I too had a good season! We played matches against school teams in the London area and a few further afield, including one against Wycombe Abbey girls' school played in the delightful surroundings of the Chilterns with beech woods and a lake. We usually lost that match. I enclose a photograph of the St Paul's Cricket XI, taken at Wycombe Abbey on 12 July 1956 — I am the one wearing specs in the middle of the picture. There are ten of us — I presume the one missing took the photograph! I was awarded the 'Ollis' bat for topping the averages that season — a full-size Gunn and Moore signed by the Australian tourists of 1938, which included Don Bradman. Mine for a year. I wonder whether the Ollis bat survived until the 1990s when Alastair Cook was a chorister?

***

Towards the end of my time at Choir House I became fascinated by astronomy — an interest I shared with my fellow-chorister, David Thomas. We had been lent a telescope by one of the minor-canons of the Cathedral. It must have been a military instrument, beautifully made, with a brass tube encased in leather, and with a number of internal lenses to correct any colour aberration. It needed one or two minor adjustments, which we had done at Broadhurst Clarkson & Fuller on Farringdon Road. In the summer we could only make limited use of it, but we did some careful viewing of the sun, projecting the image onto a back wall, and making daily charts of the shifting sunspots. Serious business. Most of our observing we did at the top of Choir House in the solarium, adjacent to the roof playground. Originally it had been a convalescence room and it was still linked by a narrow staircase to the sickbay below. But now it was used as an additional classroom and for the Monday art classes. Looking southwards over the rooftops towards the Thames, with metal-framed 1930s windows over the whole breadth which could be opened in sections, it made an ideal spot for viewing and in the early autumn evening, when it was getting dark, we observed the cratered surface of the moon and Jupiter, which we saw as a small disk with four of its moons.

In 1956 the Royal Observatory at Greenwich was reaching the end of its time and was shortly to move to the clearer skies of Herstmonceux in Sussex. The Greenwich Observatory is very much associated with the scientific community in Restoration London of the 1660s, with astronomers like Flamsteed, Hooke, and Newton. It had been designed by Christopher Wren and the story goes that he even designed one of the west towers of St Paul's with the idea of installing a fixed zenith telescope within it — a plan that never materialised (Campbell op. cit.). On 19 August 1666, less than a fortnight before the Great Fire of London, Samuel Pepys (also a member of the Royal Society) writes:

> By and by comes by agreement Mr Reeves and after him Mr Spong; and all day with them, conversing upon opticks. We did also at night see Jupiter and his girdle and satellites very fine with my twelve-foot glass, but not Saturn, he being too dark.

He is referring to the *length* of the telescope tube — they used telescopes of such a length to limit colour aberration — he says nothing about the magnification. The one we used, had a rather modest magnification of about 30x and we too could see the moons and the band ('the girdle') on the surface of Jupiter. In fact, we saw precisely what Pepys and his friends had seen three hundred years before from the leads of their rooftop, not a mile from where we were now standing.

I also wanted to look at the stars, but the southern night-sky in October and November is rather empty, with the winter highlights only just rising on the eastern horizon. This was my last term as I was leaving St Paul's after Christmas, so there was only one thing to do; I set my travel alarm clock for four o'clock in the morning and placed it under my pillow to deaden the sound. Then putting on my dressing-gown I went up to the solarium. The sky was remarkably clear above the city skyline: Sirius, the brightest star, low in the sky, and a little higher Orion the hunter, easily recognisable with the three stars of his belt, and further to the west and even higher the Pleiades forming a faint cluster of stars, hardly discernible as such to the naked eye. The Pleiades was the furthest west and would be the first to disappear from view, so I swung the telescope in that direction. Sometimes people describe a night-sky as "thousands of stars" but the number of stars visible to the *naked eye* is less than one might expect. Even on a very clear night in a dark place it is hardly more than two thousand. As the Pleiades came into focus, I could see forty or fifty stars in my field of view — it may not sound many, but what a spectacle! Like bluish-white diamonds, a cluster that had formed when dinosaurs still ruled the earth. I then turned to the belt of Orion, moving slowly down from the centre star, and there it was, the sword, Messier 42, the Great Nebula of Orion, a gigantic cloud of gas twenty light-years in diameter — twenty thousand times larger than our entire Solar System — where stars are still in the process of being formed. In the telescope it looked like a greenish-white fan-shaped mist about the size of my thumbnail, illuminated by young stars. In one hundred thousand years from now the gas will all be used up and an observer will see an open cluster a bit like the Pleiades. After an hour or so I put the telescope away, quietly closed the window and returned to the dormitory.

***

Grandad died in Birmingham on Boxing Day. I had only seen him once since we moved south, at Eastbourne two years before. He had spent much of his life in the Royal Navy. He was a good shot and there were photographs of him with the shooting team at Bisley which Granma later kept in her sitting-room cabinet, together with the trophies he had won. He had rather a booming voice, which I put down to his having been a Chief Petty Officer; he probably put it on a bit when he called out to us:

"Where are you, you varmints? Come here!"

He once gave me a useful piece of advice. He was watching me spreading a sandwich with Shipham's fish paste:

"Take care of the sides and the centre will take care of itself."

He died of a heart-attack and he was sixty-eight.

Chapter: Three

LANCING COLLEGE

I left the Choir School on 30 December 1956. Back home, I went round to the post office in Portland Road with my father to cash the money on my savings book — money that had been paid in while at St Paul's for BBC broadcasts and special services — which would help to cover some of the initial costs at Lancing. I had first to write my signature on a form which was then compared to the one I had written when the account was opened in January 1953. My latest signature was ridiculously fancy and of course the two didn't match up at all! I don't remember how things were resolved, but a few days later we went together up to Gorringes in Buckingham Palace Road to get me fitted for the things I would need at Lancing. On weekdays we wore a herring-bone tweed jacket over grey trousers and on Sundays a clerical grey three-piece suit — not the typical school uniform. The cost was mounting up and when it came to deciding between a raincoat or a duffle coat, in spite of the member of staff advising:

"…well, sir, they're nearly all wearing the duffle coat nowadays."

My father opted for the raincoat.

I had hardly had time to reflect on the fact that I was no longer a chorister when I made the short journey by bus with Mother from Hove to Lancing College. I knew the route well, for I had often cycled along it. When we stopped at Shoreham a crowd of Lancing boys got on the bus having just arrived at the station. The double-decker drove on over the old wooden toll-bridge across the river Adur. We all got off at the 'Sussex Pad' and walked across the fields up to the College.

First there was introductory tea with the housemaster, Donald

Parsons and his wife Amanda, together with the other 'new men' and their parents. Then after the goodbyes, supper in the dining hall for the entire school — four hundred, all boarders, and all boys. The hall was in keeping with the rest of the buildings: neo-Gothic, wooden floor, panelling, beams and traditional framed portraits. The long wooden tables with benches were arranged according to houses and seating was by seniority, the new men at the lower end.

"I say, Windross, haven't your people got a car?"

I recognised one of the boys from the bus.

"Of course, they have," I retorted. "A Morris Minor."

This was the car in the neighbours' garage where I was allowed to store my bike. Luckily, the conversation fizzled out, but I regretted having said it.

There was a film-show in 'Great School' on that first Saturday evening of term: *East of Eden*, starring James Dean as the teenage rebel. The following morning after chapel the headmaster, John Dancy, gave us new men an introductory lecture which left us in no doubt that we were at Lancing first and foremost to study. He finished by stressing that outside College we were still ambassadors of Lancing and he expected us — 'men out of the top-drawer' — to behave accordingly! For a headmaster he was young — still in his thirties. He was also a socialist, though you would not have guessed it. But I do remember him wincing during a BBC television programme on the College presented by Chris Chataway (the middle-distance British Olympic runner), when one of the senior boys, asked whether Lancing should offer places to state school pupils, replied in an off-hand way:

"Good Lord, no — standards are bad enough as it is!"

In his first novel, *Decline and Fall*, Evelyn Waugh, an old boy of the College, famously described Lancing as:

"A minor public school on the South Downs of ecclesiastical temperament."

He has a point. It is built round two quadrangles with cloisters like a monastery and has a Gothic chapel of cathedral-like dimensions, intended by the founder, Nathaniel Woodard (1811–1891), to serve as a minster for all the schools in the Woodard Corporation. Although never completed as he envisaged, the huge rose window at the west-end of the chapel does at least incorporate the crests of all these schools.

While most people admire the beauty of the chapel, an early dissenting voice comes from a guidebook to Sussex (Methuen, 1900):

> The Lancing buildings are good generally, but the huge chapel is out of proportion to its surroundings and quite an eyesore.

In my time it was used daily by the whole school and twice on Sundays. Services were compulsory — and I suppose with teenagers that was asking for trouble, hence the 'bolshie' behaviour at the back of chapel. Lancing seems to have survived this and much more in the rebellious '70s, and it still regards itself as a centre for Christian worship.

Adolescence is an awkward age. In the first week or two I spent a lot of time simply staring at notice boards in the houseroom and cloisters — like the small boy ten years earlier, standing with a lump in his throat staring at the plate glass window of Binns in Carlisle as it gradually steamed up from his breath, lost and hoping to be found. Lancing was probably not the best place to have an identity crisis.

I had done rather well in the Common Entrance exam and had been put in 'Remove Science 1' which sounds like Billy Bunter's Greyfriars! It meant that I was in the fast-stream, so I would be taking physics and chemistry in my GCE 'O-levels' in eighteen months' time, when still only fifteen. The school had a hierarchical structure, and the order in the school register, contained in the little 'blue book' distributed at the beginning of each term, was based largely on form position, which in 'Remove Science 1' was heavily weighted in favour of the sciences. My preferred subjects such as history and geography were not part of my programme, let alone music or art — an embarrassing situation for a 'music and art scholar'. I had missed the first term of the academic year and never managed to catch up in physics and chemistry. It mattered little to my father that my first report said I had "settled down well" adding that I had "run a good three-mile in the inter-house competition"; what he wanted was an 'egghead' — which caused giggles of delight from my brothers!

It was an uphill struggle, but when the O-level results arrived they were not so bad. Predictably I had failed the sciences, but I passed all the rest, including French and Latin, and when I returned for the autumn term of '58 I was in a more confident mood.

***

I was now in XL-History — not 'extra-large', but 'forty' — presumably, the number of boys at some particular moment in the past. It corresponded to what is more usually known as the 'lower-sixth'. My A-level programme was History, English Literature, and Art. I would be taking the Art exam at the end of the year, History and English being reserved for the sixth form.

Lancing had a lot to offer outside the classroom. One thing we all shared from the beginning was the film club. I mentioned *East of Eden*; two other films shown in my first term were Pabst's *Kameradschaft* and Eisenstein's *Ivan the Terrible.* In the years following there were Ingmar Bergman's *The Seventh Seal*, Andrzej Wajda's *Kanal*, and more light-heartedly, *Some like it Hot* — and many, many more. The film programmes would have done credit to any arts cinema.

As one progressed to the Upper School there was a wide choice of clubs and societies to choose from, for instance the 'Cecilians' for music, the 'Lancing Group' for art, the 'Elizabethans' for literature, 'Leviathan' for history, and although, strictly speaking, it fell outside the curriculum, the 'Haverfield Society' for archaeology — named after Francis Haverfield (1860–1919), the pioneer Romano-British archaeologist who had taught for a number of years at Lancing College. Another eminent archaeologist to have taught at the school was Sheppard 'Sam' Frere (1916–2015), who was a master from 1945–54. He too was an expert in the archaeology of the Roman Provinces and he oversaw the excavation of Verulamium between 1955–61.

Sport had a high profile too. The College owned acres of land for football, cricket, and athletics; it had its own tennis courts, squash courts, fives courts, and a swimming pool, which have all been streamlined and added to since. It had quite a reputation for tennis and squash, and in *The Oxford Companion to Sports and Games* (ed. John Arlott, 1973) Lancing gets an apart entry on account of its squash — much to the annoyance of my brother David — why Lancing and not Brighton and Hove Albion? Here in the Sussex Downland, there was plenty of room for cross-country running and cycling. We were also expected to support the College in inter-school matches. Watching cricket, with the

Downs and the chapel as a backcloth from the terrace of 'the grubber' (as we called the tuck-shop) was indeed a very pleasant way of passing a summer afternoon.

At last, I got involved in the musical life at Lancing. I started learning the clarinet, and I joined the choir. When I arrived at Lancing my voice was breaking, but now, approaching sixteen, it had begun to settle into a 'promising tenor'. Our first job in the choir was to lead the rest of the school in singing the daily services, but on Sundays and feast days we always sang an anthem, often an unaccompanied motet from the English or Italian Renaissance period, and at the end of the Advent term we were the centrepiece in the traditional carol service, modelled on that of King's College Cambridge. Towards the end of the service, having waited patiently throughout, the whole school, having first warmed up in *O Come All Ye Faithful* then gave a rip-roaring rendition of *Hark The Herald Angels* and we could all go home for the Christmas vacation in a festive mood. This time not to Rutland Gardens but to Lawrence Road, just around the corner, our new home.

I liked Lawrence Road straight away. It was a fair-sized house and it needed to be. Gran had decided to move south to a retirement home at Seaford. She must have felt lonely at the Long House on the Solway and at Seaford she would be in much closer contact both with us and with Allen's family. I suppose she also felt an affinity with the retirement home environment from the years she had spent working in a private nursing home at Hastings. Because of this move some of Gran's furniture from Skinburness had to be found a place in Lawrence Road, and with it the Norton oil painting my father had bought a decade before. And there was another development. Granma from Birmingham (now on her own) had decided to come and live with us and no doubt she had contributed towards buying the house, which was considerably larger than anywhere we had lived before.

My bedroom looked southwards onto the back gardens of the even larger houses along New Church Road, and I had my own private balcony. At the coast, the clouds often seemed to retreat around sunset, leaving a clear night, and I would slip out onto the balcony with a pair of binoculars to look at the stars. In the '50s the street lighting was switched off before midnight, which meant darker skies. Sometimes I could hear the sound of the sea in the distance.

***

There were only three of us taking art A-level that year. Being such a small group, our timetable was flexible, but most mornings I would spend a couple of hours in the art school. This was situated in the rear portion of the chapel crypt, which had been modernised for the purpose while preserving just enough of the original stonework, arches and spatial divisions to keep it interesting. It was fun listening to Graham Collier's classes in the background. Approaching forty, rather tall, with an almost gaunt facial structure, aquiline nose and penetrating gaze, moustache, lank greying hair swept back partly covering his ears. He usually wore comfortable-looking tweed lounge suits and a bow tie and looked every bit the academician; but beneath it all was a Yorkshireman who had served in RAF Bomber Command in the war, and he certainly had a tale to tell. His 'office' was at the far end of the art school, surrounded by panels and storage cabinets and I remember one morning he was reciting out loud to us the starting prices in the Cheltenham Gold Cup to be run later in the day — I can picture him leaning back in his chair, newspaper in hand, feet up on the desk — blissfully unaware that the headmaster had just entered the art school with a group of American visitors.

For art A-level we were required to hand in a portfolio of work done during the year. There were also written papers on the history of applied arts, where I had chosen English architecture and the history of dress. Finally, we had to do a single block linocut and a large acrylic painting under exam conditions. I felt quietly confident going home for the summer vacation.

***

One of the disadvantages of being at boarding school was the lack of friends during vacation. It was even more difficult finding a girlfriend. When was the last time I had even spoken to a girl? Since the age of nine I had been at all-boys schools, so I was certainly coming from a deprived background. Yet around this time I became aware of their existence — Bobby Darin's *Dream Lover* was top of the hit-parade — but how to approach them was another matter. Most of the sixteen-year-old girls

I saw on the beach were knocking around with boys two years older. There was one girl I started talking to and even got so far as to put my towel down next to hers on the warm pebbles. Mother spotted this and promptly invited her to tea the following Sunday, which of course scuppered the whole thing.

I needed to find a holiday job to keep myself in pocket and possibly to get some money together to buy a clarinet. I was still playing on an instrument lent by the College and I had now progressed from the beginner's class to a proper clarinet teacher, George Garside. He had been principal clarinettist in the London Symphony Orchestra before the War — that I knew — and he was regarded as one of the finest clarinettists of his generation. By now his eyesight was almost gone and when teaching he always had his own clarinet at hand to demonstrate the point he was making. What a sound! I remember the instrument, as it was rather special — a Buffet Crampon *without* a barrel. Fifteen years later, I came across one just like it in a second-hand musical instrument shop in Antwerp — also a Buffet — which I still have. Mr Garside was another northerner and he always used an anglicised pronunciation of composers' names, so Weber became 'Webber', Milhaud 'Milawd', and so forth. He could be very blunt and I was reluctant to tell him that my father was not keen on forking out for an instrument; instead, I had resolved to save up for one myself.

I was taken on at Clarks Bakery in Hove, an industrial bakery that supplied the whole of the Sussex coast from Hastings to Bognor Regis. I worked in the buns and rolls department situated on the first floor, where there were three large ovens with heavy metal shutters and a rotating wheel system inside. In a single movement we slid the trays from the racks onto the rotating surface. The heat from the ovens was intense and when the process was reversed it meant we were handling oven-hot trays. We wore gloves for protection, but I still got plenty of burns on the inside of my arm. When I started there were two other men I had to work with, but on the second day one of them had a nasty accident on a mixer and I was left to work alone with Stu, a short, stocky Italian-looking fellow with his dark hair smarmed back.

Not only was the work hard, but it was also a long day, from seven-thirty in the morning till five-thirty in the evening, with the shortest of lunch breaks. Arriving in the morning we would first go to the changing room where we got out of our own clothes and into the white overalls provided while listening to one of Stu's monologues on how he had passed the night before. Whatever he was talking about made no difference: it was not the content that mattered, but the way he managed to get the word 'fuck' into a sentence — as a noun, verb, adjective, adverb, or expletive — any part of speech. Stu was a past master. I always made sure I was out of the changing room in time so that I didn't have to listen to him alone! Still, he was good to work with and he tried to shield me from Duggie, the Scottish floor manager, who had a habit of spending five minutes here, five minutes there, always trying to speed up production, but who had "never done a fucking day's work in his fucking life". When Duggie slipped me my wage packet at the end of the first week, Stu checked to see that he hadn't fiddled me.

***

In the Advent term 1959 there were four old-choristers of St Paul's in Lancing College choir, two from the Abbey, and a number of very gifted musicians — perhaps less noted for their voices — who went on to make international careers in music. It was great fun, but we took it seriously enough. Music was a part of the Lancing tradition. In 1948 Benjamin Britten had composed *Saint Nicolas* for the centenary celebrations. Lancing was dedicated to St Mary and St Nicolas, after the two ancient churches in Shoreham, and Peter Pears, Britten's partner, and an old boy of the College, had sung the part of Nicolas. Ten years later this was repeated. John Alston, director of music, gave me a lot of encouragement, with a bit of a push when necessary, and suggested I tackle some Lieder — Schubert and Fauré — which I performed in the concert club. A more daunting challenge was when he asked me and Anthony Price to sing the tenor and bass solos in the Mozart *Requiem* with orchestra and chorus, at the Choral Society Concert in the Chapel on 17 July 1960. This was really a job for a professional singer not a seventeen-year-old. I don't think the prospect worried me unduly, perhaps because it was taking place within the confines of Lancing, in a microcosm as it were, which made it less intimidating. On the day itself there was a slight suspicion of a sore throat and on the advice of someone (perhaps it was John Alston) I gargled with a raw egg shortly before the concert, and it can have done no harm for I coped well. It was an absolute thrill singing the tenor solos with an orchestra.

***

My history teacher was Roger Lockyer — a scholar from Pembroke College, Cambridge. He was at the outset of his career and he taught at Lancing for seven years, 1954–1961, during which time his students were very successful in gaining awards to Oxbridge. He taught us English medieval history and he had a complicated system for grading our work, using *alpha*, *beta*, and *gamma* instead of marks out of 20, and around the *beta* (a bare pass) there could be 'pluses' and 'minuses' by way of refinement. I never got a *gamma*, but I had to wait until the reign of King John before there was any sign of an *alpha*.

The meetings of Leviathan — the history society — were also held at Roger's house in the nearby village of North Lancing. We regularly came together in the evening after supper, and I enjoyed the twenty-minute walk getting there; first across 'Sixteen Acre' to Hoe Court and then a gentle climb following the edge of a wood where a Saxon burial ground had been discovered, up to Lancing Ring, below which Roger lived on the edge of the village. The return journey late in the evening was even more enjoyable; it was downhill much of the way and provided a splendid view across the Adur valley towards Shoreham harbour where the red lights on the tall chimneys of the power-station stood out against the glow of Brighton beyond. At one meeting early in 1960, two members of the upper-sixth gave a joint presentation. They had put together an audio montage purporting to give a live account of the trial of King John in Westminster Hall in the year 1215, and they had managed to get the cooperation of Richard Dimbleby (father of David Dimbleby of *Question Time*) to set the scene and describe events as they happened. Dimbleby had one of the best-known voices on the BBC, since he covered all the really big events, like the Coronation. His presence gave a verisimilitude to the supposed 'event'. As for the verdict, I'm afraid I cannot remember which way it went.

***

I was now one of a group of the 'upper-sixth' who having passed our A-levels were awaiting the scholarship exams for individual colleges at Oxford and Cambridge. It had long been assumed that I would try for a choral scholarship at either King's or St John's in March '61 but having done well in my A-levels it was suggested that in the meantime I should take part in the academic scholarship exams at King's. I was unlikely to get an award, but I might be offered a place on the strength of it. We certainly had a lot of time on our hands and I think my housemaster saw it more as a kind of 'occupational therapy'.

The exams were in early January. Cambridge was in the grip of a biting east wind blowing off the Fens. (I remember that we used to bemoan the fact that there was nothing between the Urals and Trumpington Street.) Apart from the history papers I also had two interviews. The first with John Raven, Senior Tutor at King's, who seemed more interested in my art A-level than the history — but then he was both a classical scholar *and* a botanist himself. The second was before a gathering of dons from King's, chaired by the medieval historian Christopher Morris. I received a letter from King's on 20 January offering me a definite place.

I had to return to Cambridge in March, for the choral scholarship. From an early morning preliminary round a group of us were selected to audition in King's Chapel for David Willcox and then immediately afterwards in St John's Chapel. I had chosen to sing Bach's *Ich weiss dass mein Erlöser lebt* — a tenor solo from one of his cantatas. There was only one tenor scholarship on offer at King's and listening to a more mature candidate from the Guildhall School of Music, I sensed he would get it. At John's there were two, and by now I was well sung-in and performed with more confidence. George Guest was persuaded and I was duly awarded a choral scholarship.

Having secured my immediate future, I left Lancing at the end of the Easter term. In his final report Mr Dancy wrote:

"He has had a career of varied success at Lancing."

Which left me wondering whether he meant 'in various fields' or simply 'mixed success'.

Chapter: Four

CAMBRIDGE

The weather was decidedly autumnal in early October '61 when I arrived for my first term at Cambridge. St John's College is one of the largest and also one of the best known to the general public and tourists, with its impressive Tudor gateway in red brick with all the mythical beasts and heraldic ornamentations in gold, setting off the Royal Coat of Arms.

Having travelled from Cumberland, Wordsworth was less than enthusiastic on his arrival at College.

> It was a dreary morning when the chaise rolled over the flat plains of Huntingdon… three gloomy courts… and in the first was my abiding-place, a nook obscure. [*The Prelude*]

Nor was his Cambridge career a great success, for he graduated *without* honours in 1791.

My rather cramped rooms in Chapel Court were built well after Wordsworth's time. The oriel window — a single redeeming feature — looked out across the court towards the chapel and I think its constant presence weighed a bit on me, for as a choral scholar I had to sing in the chapel every day except Monday, our day off. The music largely followed the cathedral repertory with which I was familiar — at least with the treble line. The choir was made up of sixteen boy trebles and the twelve choral scholars — really quite small. Unlike King's, where the size of the building and the resonant acoustics help create a space between the singers and the listeners, at John's it was quite the opposite. At first, I felt exposed and a little bit on trial.

An early hurdle I had to cope with was the recording we were to make for Decca (on the Argo label) of Stainer's *Crucifixion* at the end of my first term. The recording engineer was Andrew Raeburn, and the soloists were Richard Lewis, a fine Welsh tenor (a Welshman himself, George Guest tended to go for Welsh tenors on recordings) and Owen Brannigan, bass-baritone, both with a wide repertoire which included opera. Surprisingly, the whole recording was completed in two days and sometimes a single 'take' sufficed, which is perhaps one reason why it has such intensity — as in the choir's beautifully controlled 'God so loved the World'. In fact, this track was not done in one take; the first was perfect, but towards the end the microphone picked up just the slightest noise of traffic from St John's Street, and we had to redo it!

The record came out in spring 1962. I don't recall how it was received by the critics (I doubt whether I knew then) but I do know it withstood the test of time, and a later review in *Gramophone*, comparing our Argo recording with the 1978 Hyperion version under Richard Hickox says:

"When the choir is so good as that of St John's College, the sound is hard to beat."

***

The way I am describing my confrontation with this new environment says something about my general attitude. What struck me were the continuities between St Paul's, Lancing, and Cambridge; for me they were part of the same system and tradition and I simply plugged in where I had left off. I failed to appreciate the size and variety of Cambridge and all it had to offer.

It was sometimes said that choral scholars had so many musical commitments they could not be expected to shine academically. I certainly used this excuse to cover my lack of work. In my first two years, I hardly ever attended history lectures and I avoided libraries; instead, I relied very much on what I had learned at Lancing. True, the choral scholars did have a heavy load, and we were also required to be in Cambridge for the extra 'Long Vac Term' when most undergraduates were enjoying their summer holidays. This was a period of a month or so set aside chiefly for research students, and although the normal college schedule stopped, for some reason chapel services had to continue. It was also a good time for the choir to do recordings — for which we received a small fee. In July 1962 we made two records: the first for 'Musica Sacra, Klangarchiv für Kirchenmusik' consisted of unaccompanied English Motets in the Golden Age. The second, later in the month, was 'Twentieth Century Church Music' for Argo, which included Michael Tippett's *Magnificat and Nunc Dimittis*, written for the four hundred and fiftieth anniversary of the foundation of the College.

The choral duties imposed some sort of order on my day, which otherwise revolved around lunch at the Corner House at the top of King Street, a Greek Cypriot restaurant, popular with the jazz crowd and the acting fraternity, and an afternoon spent at Fenners watching the cricket or punting on the river Cam — neither of which added to my academic stature. In part I of the tripos exams at the end of my second year I scraped a 'third' — the lowest grade awarded for an honour's degree. Not the end of the world — in some circles it might even have been an occasion to pop a few bottles of Champagne, but not for me.

***

While the country was wallowing in the salacious press coverage of the Profumo Affair, I returned to Cambridge for my second long-vac term and full of resolve went round to the Labour Exchange and got a job on an archaeological dig up on Castle Hill.

I was one of a small group of student labourers. Organised by the archaeology faculty, under the direction of Dr John Alexander, the aim was to investigate a potential Roman site. A mechanical digger had removed the topsoil, and a dozen or so trenches had been marked out in a grid-pattern. We were given a brief explanation on how we were to proceed. The first stage was fairly basic, using a spade or shovel. Any object we retrieved we put into a 'finds tray' for later examination, while the rubble and soil had to be carted away by us in barrow loads. We were to proceed in gradual stages, pausing every so often allowing others to go over the surface with a trowel or hand brush. This gives the general idea.

First, we encountered broken crockery, then stems and occasionally bowls of clay-pipes, followed by layers of mussel and oyster shells. The latter are not much help in dating because vast quantities were eaten in the past: masses of them turn up on Roman sites when they were artificially cultivated and transported from the coast in barrels of salt water. Much later Pepys sometimes mentions receiving a barrel of oysters as a present from friends and they were readily available in the London taverns of his day. Generally speaking, though, the deeper you dig the further back in time you go. We did the rough work but there were others, as I said, with more experience who would supervise and make diagram sketches, brushing carefully over any traces of cobbles or masonry, looking for intrusions, for post-holes and possible rubbish tips — someone once called archaeology 'the science of rubbish'.[11]

The summer weather continued and the excavation progressed quietly. Then something unexpected happened. We came across the skeleton of a child. Immediately work stopped, the police were notified and forensic experts soon arrived on the scene. A resin was used to stabilise the surrounding soil so that it could be lifted out in one piece. It was not a crime, at least not a recent one since the skeleton turned out to be late medieval. Thereafter we had to be content with more 'humdrum' finds such as pieces of Samian Ware or *terra sigillata*, a distinctive red semi-glazed Roman pottery which, as the name says, often bears the maker's stamp. At the bottom of a deep well we found two large amphorae, almost intact.

It was on this dig that I met Ida Dequeecker, an archaeology student from Ghent University. We started a relationship and I fell in love with her. It might easily have ended with the dig and her return to Belgium, but she wrote to me in September asking me to come over to Antwerp where she lived, which of course I did.

***

From conversation I knew that Ida's parents had divorced a few years ago. She had grown up in Mechelen, but now lived together with her mother, Ida De Ridder, and her brother and sisters in the old centre of Antwerp.

Coming from the station, we took the back entrance to the house, turning up a cobbled alleyway, through a simple latched gate into a town garden. Through the shrubs I could see the tall lighted windows at the back of the house. A short flight of stone steps led to a narrow hallway dominated by a huge kilim on the wall and we went into the living room. In the fading daylight the family was sitting round a table above which hung a white opaline lampshade which lit up not only the table but also the faces of those around it. Ida's mother got up to welcome me. She was less tall than Ida and had dark features. Beyond the circle of light, I could make out oak cupboards and chests, more hanging kilims, oriental rugs on the floor, and a stove with glowing coals in the black marble fireplace. The whole setting was a throwback to the 1890s, reminiscent of the 'bourgeois interiors' which James Ensor painted as a young man, before he went off on those carnival scenes with skeletons and grotesque masks.

We had interrupted *koffie-drinken* — not simply drinking coffee (which can happen at any time of the day) but more specifically the occasion in the late afternoon when the children come home from school and the family sit together round the coffee table and chat — a bit like the traditional English 'teatime'.

That first evening, as Ida's new boyfriend, I was very much the centre of attention and of course her younger sisters wanted to know where I was going to sleep — something which Ida and her mother had talked over. Her mother felt that it would be better, taking the girls into consideration, if I were at least to sleep in her brother's room.

We had taken the back entrance to the house, which was the normal practice for the family and some of the tradesfolk. The front entrance, with a quaint old pull-bell system, gave onto a courtyard which was approached from *Venusstraat* through a rounded archway with a heavy wooden door — a bit like a college gateway. Visitors were frequent, especially in the evening — often other family members who did not have far to come since three of the seven houses on the court were occupied by family. The 'family' (I quickly discovered) had an important place in daily life in Flanders, and here this was especially so. Ida's grandfather, Willem Elsschot, was the most celebrated Flemish writer of his day and highly regarded throughout the Dutch literary world. Very much the *pater familias*, he had died only a few years before, in 1960. I suspect his person (and taste) still had a great hold over the rest of them. They certainly revered him.

Sometimes in the evening over a beer, when the conversation got more animated, I felt like a bystander and wished I could make out what it was all about. Then slowly from the stream of sounds, words began to emerge, and from repetition and gestures, came key-words or topics. It was a start.

I felt sad saying goodbye at the end of that week. Strange how things had worked out these last couple of months, as though I had been drawn into a new orbit. Braving a stiff breeze on deck as the ferry passed the jetty at Ostend and moved out into the open sea, I started to make up nonsense-utterances imitating the Flemish sounds and words that I could recall.

***

Back in College for my third and final year, I was now living in third court, opposite the Old Library. In the evening of 31 August 1654, John Evelyn arrived on a visit to Cambridge. He writes in his diary:

> We went first to see St John's College, well-built of brick… the Librarie, I think is the fairest of the University.

His fellow diarist, Samuel Pepys, had been a student at Magdalene and had graduated in that same year, 1654. His father lived near Cambridge and he occasionally returned to the city. On 15 October 1662 he went there with company:

> … and I showed Mr Cooke King's College Chapel, Trinity College, and St. John's College Library; and that being done, to our inn again.

The Old Library was held in high esteem. It dates from the early seventeenth century but retains a Gothic style of brickwork. The rest of third court is slightly later, and the inside is faced with stone — more classical — while the outside along the river Cam retains the reddish brickwork and viewed from the Wren Bridge we could almost be looking at a Dutch townscape, a view of Delft.

I checked the post at the porter's lodge. There was a note in my pigeon-hole from my director of studies, Harry Hinsley, inviting me for a glass of sherry in his rooms in the Shrewsbury Tower. I knew that it would not be just a social visit, and I had already given some thought to the courses for the coming year. 'Modern European History' was an obvious choice; Harry was editor of vol. xi (1870–98) of the *New Cambridge Modern History* and had just published a book *Power and the Pursuit of Peace* — a post-mortem on international relations from the Congress of Vienna to the League of Nations. Further, I opted for 'Theories of the Modern State', and 'David Hume, Adam Smith and the Scottish Enlightenment', which had only recently been introduced into the programme at the instigation of Duncan Forbes, a Fellow of Clare College.

I started to get some routine into my work and at long last I discovered the Reading Room at the University Library — a short walk from John's along the 'backs'. Some people have an aversion to such large rooms, but

I grew to like it, sitting at one of the long writing tables with one's own reading lamp, it put me in the right frame of mind.

I also began to enjoy tutorials, with Harry pacing slowly about the room, thumbs in lapels, pausing to look out of the window and light his pipe, listening, while I read my weekly essay. It had a relaxed atmosphere. Looking the typical Cambridge Don with his tweed suits, his horn-rimmed glasses and pipe — *all* the history dons at John's smoked pipes — Harry usually arrived at college by bike in the morning, wearing a fawn-coloured raincoat with bicycle clips round the bottoms of his trousers. I was not surprised to hear later that he had been elected Master of the College and then Vice Chancellor of the University. What none of us knew at the time was that as a young man he had been a leading figure at Bletchley Park in the War. He was one of the codebreakers!

In the Advent term I spent a lot of time studying David Hume. Some of the books we needed for the Scottish Enlightenment course were available in modern editions, such as Smith's *Wealth of Nations*, while others, like Ferguson's *Civil Society* (1767) and Millar's *Origin of the Distinction of Ranks* (1771) were not and had to be set aside in the Reading Room for us to study. These were not first editions (although those were present in the library collection) but they were *early* editions, and this gave an added dimension to the work, something that has remained with me, for over the years I have built up my own collection of early editions of works from the Scottish Enlightenment.

It was high time I started on Marx and Hegel. In my own books I regularly underlined passages in pencil, which was something John Dancy had encouraged at Lancing, and the abundant margin notes in my copy of Hegel's *Philosophy of Right* are evidence of the hard slog in the UL reading room. I also had a habit of writing the place and date on the flyleaf of books I bought. The Hegel is marked Cambridge, December 1963, indeed the receipt from Bowes and Bowes is still in the book: £1.10. The two volumes *Marx and Engels: Selected Works* were even cheaper — six shillings and sixpence each — published by the Foreign Languages Publishing House, Moscow.

My new-found enthusiasm had much to do with Ida. I missed her, and we stayed in contact with each other largely through letter writing and with visits to Belgium in vacation time.

***

In January, rehearsals started in earnest on what I initially thought was another Kings-John's joint enterprise. The idea that there was intense rivalry between the two choirs is very much overdone and we had joined forces a number of times already, notably for a performance of Bach's *John Passion* — in which David Thomas, my contemporary at St Paul's and now a choral scholar at Kings, sang the bass solos. On this occasion it was the Monteverdi *Vespers* and the conductor and musical director was John Eliot Gardiner, still an undergraduate at Kings. He was sometimes critical of our style of singing and tried to transport us away from Cambridge to that other world of late renaissance Venice. It all began to fall into place when we got to the full rehearsals with the soloists and orchestra, which was far from conventional, having for instance a section of shrill *cornetti* — a simple wooden instrument, without keys but with holes, blown like a trumpet, which produced just the hybrid sort of sound you might expect. Mother had written saying she would like to come up to Cambridge for a few days, and sensing that this was going to be quite an occasion, I suggested she come straight away. She was present at that exciting, memorable performance in Kings Chapel on 5 March 1964. The birth of the Monteverdi Choir.

A fortnight later, slipping a paperback edition of Hume's *Discourses on Natural Religion* into my travel-bag, and with Alan Bullock's *Hitler: A Study in Tyranny* for the journey, I headed off to Dover.

***

There was now just a month to go till finals. This time I was well prepared and I even found time to relax. Sometimes on these early summer evenings I walked over the Wren bridge to the backs — a perfect spot for a bit of reading, with the quiet sound of punts passing by. One of the books was Daniel J. Boorstin's *The Image: A guide to pseudo-events in America* (1962), which still sounds topical! Its central theme is that a lot of what we read and hear and accept as 'events' and 'news' is often simply manufactured by the media for the sole purpose of reporting them. The waters have recently been muddied by the appropriation of the concept 'fake news' by denialists and others who want to sow political confusion for their own ends.

In the finals I felt a bit as though I was delivering my lines in a well-rehearsed play. The main difficulty was to get it all down on paper in a coherent way in the time available. I was fortunate to find among the subjects for the general essay 'Myth is more potent than Fact', where I took Hume's views on *belief* as my starting-point, together with the public's readiness to believe in myths — related to 'pseudo-events' — which I borrowed from Boorstin. I have often returned to this essay in my mind, trying to apply it to populist trends in current politics, but I was quite pleased with it at the time.

To mark the end of term, there was the Summer Concert in hall, attended by a large audience with the Fellows of the College also present. As part of the programme the choir gave a performance of Purcell's *Welcome to all the Pleasures*, an ode for St Cecilia's day, with a small orchestral accompaniment. It is a wonderful work, melodious, full of colour and changing moods and in it I sang the quiet, reflective penultimate piece 'Beauty thou scene of love...' for tenor solo accompanied simply by the harpsichord.

***

Nowadays graduation ceremonies at English universities have become one more occasion for a public display of family togetherness. Then, I knew no one who was remotely near Cambridge when the exam results were hung out at the Senate House: you got the results from the published lists in the *Times*. Some think the universities today are too ready to hand out 'firsts' and there is talk of 'devaluation'. In 1964 a 2/1, an upper-second, certainly counted as a very good honours degree!

Returning to Cambridge in July, we made a recording for Argo of Henry Purcell's verse anthems composed for the Chapel Royal, with the Academy of St Martin in the Fields. This was the first of a series of recordings with the Academy. Not only was the record an immediate success, but years later, in 2017, it was included in a box set of forty-two CDs containing *all* the recordings St John's Choir made for Argo. It is a wonderful tribute to George Guest and to the excellence of the choir, and I find it exciting and moving to listen to. Proud too, that I participated in six of these recordings.

I bumped into Harry Hinsley in second court, who asked whether I might be interested in staying on an additional year to do the Certificate in Historical Studies — the first rung on the postgraduate ladder. This caught me a bit off guard, and I hurriedly replied that it would not really fit in with my immediate plans of moving to Belgium. He wished me luck and added that if I ever needed a reference, I could always rely on him.

So far as I can recall there were no sad goodbyes. It had been a special year, my last year at Cambridge, but now my thoughts were more directed towards the future. I packed my books, records and music in a single small trunk and had it transported to Lawrence Road, where my old bedroom was being used as a temporary storage space.

Chapter: Five

ANTWERP

I da and I married on 5 September 1964 in Antwerp Town Hall. Ida still had a year to do at university — the degree course being four years in Belgium — so initially we lived in Ghent where we rented an apartment on the second floor of a typical belle époque town house in Kunstlaan just off *Sint-Pietersplein*. This square owed its name to the medieval monastery of St Peter, which had contacts with Canterbury and the late Anglo-Saxon church. The original abbey church was ransacked during the Iconoclastic Fury (*beeldenstorm*) of 1566 and replaced by a classical basilica in the mid-seventeenth century whose interior reminded me of St Paul's, if on a smaller scale. From the balcony outside our living-room you could just see the cupola on its hexagonal base.

The old centre of Ghent is a superb example of a medieval Flemish town — a monument to civic pride. The effect is almost overpowering with three large Gothic churches and a massive Belfry in a single cast of the eye. In Sint Bavo's, the largest, is the wonderful *Lam Gods* painted by Jan van Eyck. Along the waterways and canals we see a succession of secular buildings: warehouses, guild-houses, and private residences, stretching from twelfth-century Romanesque to eighteenth-century Rococo, in no particular order and linked by small bridges, which add to the charm. I recognised the typical step gables and façades from a German book we had at home on the Hanseatic trading towns, which I had known since childhood. In recent years Ghent has been cleaned and much restored for the benefit of its inhabitants, tourists and posterity, but in 1964 this had not yet started, and in a way I'm glad I first saw Ghent when it still looked like the old brown and white photographs in the book.

"An Englishman — most certainly one who has a Cambridge degree — and who is not averse to teaching, undergoes what is almost a standard transformation upon emigrating to Belgium: he becomes a 'native speaker', one who has innate wisdom to impart to those eager to study his language and culture."

This is the rather tongue-in-cheek way in which, forty years later, my dear friend and colleague Aline Remael, described my appointment as assistant lecturer at the Higher Institute for Translators and Interpreters in Antwerp. The difficulty (at the time) was that even if I had intuitions about my own language, I had no idea how to explain things to others and I had to get hold of some standard pedagogical grammars in double quick time. I was on a yearly contract which also included teaching a couple of hours of modern European history. It was the fiftieth anniversary of the outbreak of the First World War in 1964 — for this I was better prepared.

I commuted from Ghent to Antwerp three days a week and as my classes started at eight-thirty in the morning it meant catching a train in Ghent around six. At that hour it was still dark and occasionally goods trains passed through pulled by steam engines; from the low-level 'continental' platforms it was quite a sight. I climbed into my diesel-electric train which was coming from Ostend and was already full of workers heading for the Cockerill-Sambre steel mills at Charleroi, many of whom would have cycled from the surrounding countryside of West Flanders to catch their train, so God knows what time their day must have started. Now they were sleeping in grotesque poses or if in a corner-seat, with their coats pulled over their faces. I felt very much the odd one out reading through my lecture notes.

In June, the following year we moved to Antwerp.

***

Antwerp is a large and very populous town and no smaller than our Italian Bologna. Fine streets, squares and houses, for the most part of stone, and a most beautiful church with a tower which will be almost a match for that of Strasbourg when it is finished. Running through it are a number of very wide canals. There is a fair which starts on the day of Pentecost and lasts for a month and a half... without doubt the foremost in Christendom for all kinds of merchandise.

[*Travel Journal* of Antonio De Beatis, 1517–1518][12]

English merchants had been flocking to Antwerp since the fifteenth century, drawn by the great fair at Pentecost. As Antwerp grew in importance so their numbers swelled. From seasonal visitors they became a permanent presence, profiting from the favourable trading conditions and privileges granted them by the City Fathers. The most high-profile group was the *Merchant Adventurers Company* which had recently moved from Bruges to Antwerp, and now controlled the import of coarse cloths from England for the Flemish weaving industry. Antwerp was the main port of entry and the distribution hub for the European market.

By 1500 the English were concentrated in the area around Wolstraat (wool street) where they had their warehouses and in nearby Prinsstraat where they set up their headquarters, known simply as the 'English House'. Soon more storage space was needed and approaches were made to the big land speculators for the development of a site in nearby Venusstraat, and the new warehouses were finally handed over to the Merchant Adventurers Company on 12 July 1562.

The Calvinist uprising in Antwerp in 1566 and the religious and political violence that followed scared off many of the foreign merchants in the city. The English stuck it out for a while longer. For a number of years, the city was in the hands of the Calvinists and under the leadership of Marnix of Aldegonde it became de facto the centre of the 'Dutch Revolt'. But after a year-long siege, Alexander Farnese, Duke of Parma, was able to retake Antwerp on 26 May 1585. And when Philip II of Spain reasserted his authority over the city, Sir Thomas Gresham, Queen Elizabeth's representative at Antwerp, sensed that it was all over and advised the English government to start looking for somewhere else to do business. The Merchant Adventurers left soon afterwards and in 1608 their former headquarters in Prinsstraat passed into the hands of the Jesuits who set up a college there. In 1621 their warehouses in Venusstraat became part of the *Berg van Barmhartigheid*, a charitable institution copied from Italy, where the *Monte di Pieta* still survives. For more than three hundred years it provided cheap money loans to the needy. Under its tutelage some major alterations took place and the old warehouses were transformed into eight alms-houses in 1804.

As I mentioned before, the entrance to the courtyard from Venusstraat resembled the gateway of a smaller Cambridge College. The Merchant Adventurers Company had a royal charter, hence the carved decoration on the street side of the doorway of a cupid holding a shield bearing the English Royal Coat of Arms. It was to one of these alms-houses that we moved in June 1965, and shortly afterwards our first son, Stephen, was born.

**

In early September, a postcard arrived from my parents who were on holiday in Elba — the first time they had been on holiday abroad together — and then hardly a week later there was an urgent telephone call from Mother. Father had suffered a brain haemorrhage on his first day back at work in London. He was in the Middlesex hospital and was not expected to live.

I took a flight from Brussels early the next morning. I remember every detail of the journey; the deserted departure hall at Zaventem, the cabin on board the Caravelle (it was the first time I had flown) how it looked and even how it smelled (not unpleasant), the plane banking steeply as it broke through the low cloud coming in to land, the coach journey from Heathrow to Victoria and from there the taxi. Father was still alive when I got to the hospital. His head was heavily bandaged and he was on life-support. I joined Mother and David at his bedside. His breathing was loud and irregular. We took it in turns to hold his hand. But in the early afternoon he died.

We sat there for a while longer, the curtains drawn around the bed, and then we were shown to a side-room where we were given a cup of tea. There were formalities to be completed, then we left the hospital and made our way to Victoria Station. His life had ended at the age of forty-eight. From Victoria down to Brighton it was as though we were making the journey home for him — he had done it so often.

**

The return flight from London was in a four-engine turbo-prop airliner. It was a heavy plane and seemed to climb slowly as we flew over Kent towards Dover. Looking out of the cabin window at the contours of the harbour below, I couldn't help thinking of all the war films I had seen.

**

Until now I had never really considered my moving to Belgium as emigrating. I thought of it more as 'living abroad', which leaves the door open for 'returning home'. And, indeed, my residence permit was temporary, as was my appointment. But I was now embarking on my second year of teaching. *Il n'y a que le provisoire qui dure.* Antwerp seemed to be beckoning towards the future. My son's birth naturally played a part in this change of perspective — not the first time the birth of a child had ushered in a new era, and the birth of our second son, Oliver, two years later — in Antwerp — confirmed the course.

For most people, being settled in one place is part of a normal life; it gives stability and an apparent continuity which contributes to a sense of self-identity. My formative years had taken me from one place to the other in a succession of passing stages, often part of a recognisable system and culture. But for all the benefits it had given me, it was a rather closed environment and it had left me short on down-to-earth, practical experience of normal everyday life. Antwerp was where I did some of my catching up.

***

London and Antwerp are on the same line of latitude (51°N), and the same distance from the sea — about fifty miles. The estuaries of the Thames and the Scheldt have a similar appearance and the first view of Antwerp for sixteenth century merchants arriving from London must have been a welcoming one; the Antwerp skyline with its towers and turrets and the soaring cathedral spire would have had a familiar look about it. While the appearance of central London has been totally transformed in recent decades, Antwerp has changed rather less, and one still gets something of that 'historical' view coming round the final bend in the river. The Scheldt has been of enormous historical importance to the city — still called the *Scheldestad* and *Stad aan de Stroom* (City on the River) for publicity purposes — but the river is somewhat peripheral in the daily life of Antwerpians, many of whom only go to the Scheldt promenade once a year for the firework display at New Year. The river may be a link to the wider world, but it remains a demarcation line in local terms — those from across the water are recognisable by their accent.

The Scheldt provided a base from which the city could expand outwards, fan-like, in a number of stages. Antwerp had outgrown its medieval confines by the time it entered its Golden Age. In 1542 the

Emperor Charles V ordered the building of massive defensive walls around the city, with the typical Spanish bastions and a wide moat all round.

A period of economic decline set in after the fall of Antwerp in 1585, but the arts and architecture revived a generation later in the time of Rubens, Van Dyck and Teniers, and the city certainly made a deep impression on one English visitor. In 1641 the young John Evelyn writes in his *Diary*:

> there was nothing about this City which more ravished me than those delicious shades and walkes of stately trees, which render the fortified workes of the town one of the sweetest places in Europe; nor did I ever observe a more quiet, cleane, elegantly built, and civil place, than this magnificent and famous City of Antwerp.

A hundred and twenty years later, a group of well-to-do Dutchmen decided to pay Antwerp a visit. Their trip is recorded in a little book by Frederik Cleemans entitled *Hollandsche toeristen op hun wandel in het achttiende eeuwsche Antwerpen* ('Dutch tourists in eighteenth-century Antwerp') published in the late 1940s. They set out from their home town, Alkmaar in North Holland, early on 12 June 1763. After travelling by horse and carriage as far as Haarlem, they transferred to a barge and did the rest of the journey by canal and waterway, arriving a week later:

> Antwerp is a big city, but there is very little water flowing through it.

writes Baron Van Doorn in his journal — in stark contrast to what Antonio De Beatis had said. Where had all the water gone?

De Beatis had seen Antwerp in a transitional stage; a city with a population approaching forty thousand, with a number of fine medieval churches and secular buildings, built in the late Gothic style in red brick alternating with horizontal layers of white stone, like the *Vleeshuis* ('Butchers Hall') which had just been completed.

In what appears to be a flat landscape, Antwerp was in fact built on a succession of low-lying hillocks, surrounded by swampy areas, through which a number of sluggish streams found their way before draining into the Scheldt. These waterways were still part of late medieval Antwerp, and they must have stank, for the *ruien* as they were called (*rui* is the singular, *-en* marks the plural, the pronunciation is like an Irish or Scottish 'Ryan' with a rolled 'r'!) had become little more than open sewers. Like many cities at the time, medieval Antwerp was full of such waterways, sometimes called *vlieten* or *grachten*.[13]

By 1550 Antwerp had doubled in size and was now one of the largest cities in Europe. A lot of building needed to be done to meet its new requirements. Some of it was taken care of by the city authorities, such as the erection of the walled defences, and public buildings such as the new Town Hall, and some of it was in the hands of individual land developers like the enterprising Gilbert Van Schoonbeke. Van Schoonbeke was already in the Council's good books, having taken charge of the construction of the ramparts, which speeded up the process. Now he was granted permission to develop a *Nieuwstad* beyond Venusstraat and the *Hessenhuis* in the northern part of the city. There he created a network of navigable waterways to allow goods to be off-loaded from the Scheldt and brought to newly constructed wharfs and warehouses. At the same time, he managed to gain control of the Antwerp breweries. Beer production was of major importance to the city, not only for consumption — it is estimated that *per capita* Antwerpians drank three hundred and sixty litres a year, that is a litre a day — but also because of the duties it raised. Production could not keep up with demand and beer had to be imported from abroad, notably from Hamburg and, more surprisingly, from England — for English 'ale' was held in high esteem. Beer was indeed imported from other parts of Flanders too, owing to the fact that the beer produced in Antwerp itself was inferior due to the poor quality of the water. Van Schoonbeke saw the potential gains for the city — and for himself — and he managed to persuade the City Council to give him control over beer production. The *brouwerijen* (breweries) were forced to move to the 'Nieuwstad' where he had his own supply of pure water using specially constructed reservoirs and an ingenious system of pumps and filters. In effect, he had gained a monopoly over the industry — and monopolies create enemies, but that is another story.

The works mentioned were large-scale, prestigious undertakings and took place at the perimeter of the city; but much of the building that was needed to provide housing for the swelling population was, necessarily, in the city centre, and had to be done on an *ad hoc* basis making use of the space available within the walls. One solution was to build houses over the largely redundant *ruien*. The church of Carolus Borromeus, the so-called 'Rubens Church', is built over such a waterway. The underground *ruien* can still be visited today as an attraction — seven kilometres of them. They are no longer used as sewers, for which there is now a separate network, but they still catch surplus water in times of flooding. At street level, the old *ruien* are recognisable only by the street-names. Van Schoonbeke also has a street named after him — at a considerable distance from the historical centre.

With the closing of the mouth of the Scheldt to shipping by the Dutch in 1585, a period of economic decline set in. There was a mass exodus to the North, and by 1590 the population had shrunk to fifty thousand and remained at this level for a couple of hundred years. This was the 'slumbering Antwerp' that the Dutch visitors encountered in 1763.

Napoleon gave the city a wake-up call and promptly ordered the building of a large new basin — the *Bonaparte Dock*, getting rid of most of Van Schoonbeke's earlier work. Although the *Brouwershuis* (also called the 'Waterhuis') has survived, the *Brouwersvliet* is now just another street-name. With the creation of an independent Belgian State (1830), the re-opening of the Scheldt to trade, the arrival of the railway, and the subsequent economic revival, Antwerp needed to expand once more. Between 1860 and 1869 the Spanish walls were dismantled and the moat filled in to make way for a tree-lined boulevard around the city. The 'Leien', as the wide boulevard is called, was intended for horse-drawn traffic, but within a few decades it had become a busy thoroughfare for cars and trams. In this way the foundations of the Spanish fortifications disappeared underground for a hundred and fifty years — out of sight, but not quite out of mind.

***

The Institute where I taught was situated in Schildersstraat close to the Museum of Fine Arts at the southern end of the Leien. The building (which for many years housed the *Handelshogeschool* — the School of Trade and Commerce) dates from 1897. While the façade is in that bombastic eclectic style of the period, I quite liked the semi-circular lecture theatre, with its traditional wooden tiered seats and gallery, where I sometimes taught. It was used as a filming location in *Un soir, un train* (1968) directed by André Delvaux, starring Yves Montand.

The Institute had been founded in 1961 to provide a training for translators in the busy Port of Antwerp and its commercial hinterland, while at the same time producing a smaller number of conference interpreters to work for the various bodies of the European Community. In other words, to serve a practical purpose. However, soon after its formation discussions started on setting up a State University Centre at Antwerp, and some of the staff rather fancied themselves in a Faculty of Applied Linguistics. There were, then, differing views regarding the Institute and its future, and of course in individual aspirations. Moreover, a multilingual Higher Institute in Antwerp, with parallel Dutch, French, and English sections, was almost bound to run into trouble in the charged politico-linguistic atmosphere of the mid-60s in Flanders, where there was growing pressure for a devolved Federal State. Higher education tended to be a political battleground and things came to a head with 'Leuven Vlaams!' — the demand that the University of Louvain should banish its French-speaking half to Wallonia, leaving Leuven solely Flemish. By December, the protests had turned violent, causing unease among my colleagues at the Institute, but for me it was all a bit remote.

***

In that second year of teaching, I particularly remember the history classes on Thursday afternoons — a small group of students who were almost my age: Bob Legreve, Tony Naets, Albert Gomperts — all highly motivated, which kept me on my toes and, more importantly, they remain close friends to this day. After a couple of hours of the Weimar Republic and Hitler's rise to power, I would sometimes walk up to town with Albert, to the Groenplaats — the square in front of the Cathedral — where the *Thierbrauhof* served *Dortmunder* on tap. The customers were predominantly middle-aged burghers, and while the women took off their coats, they insisted on keeping on their hats while seated at the tables. Shades of George Grosz.

There was an abundance of cafés in Antwerp at the time, catering for different sections of the public. There were the plain, traditional *volkscafés*; usually small, not much choice — just standard pils ('lager') and De Koninck van 't vat (a local brown beer), served by the landlord who sometimes displayed his *brevet van drankslijter* (licence) on the wall behind him; some still had browning copies of the 1881 *Drankwetten en Openbare Orde* ('alcohol laws and public order') on display. Many of these volkscafés were simply 'locals', but some had acquired a certain status because they were so typical of their kind — invariably Stella cafés, where the beer was served in the thin old-fashioned smooth-sided Stella glasses with a faint gold rim and faded diagonal lettering. In contrast the *taverne* or *basserie* aimed at a more bourgeois public. Here the bar was less of a focal-point and there were tables where the seating was that bit plusher, with 'garçons' in waistcoats, and often snacks would be available. The *Tierbrauhof* fell squarely into this class. Then there were the *artiesten cafés* — sometimes living up to the name, attracting a young, hip public, usually very crowded in the evening, often providing music and sometimes live jazz. Many of these were to be found in the old historical centre of the city in the narrow streets around the Cathedral — like the *Muze.*

The Muze had a reputation almost before it opened. The press announced it as a den of vice and drugs, inhabited by 'hippies' — so its fame quickly spread, attracting a horde of youngsters and older devotees from as far as Amsterdam. It occupied one of those 'high rise' sixteenth-century houses with a tall step-gabled façade, and from the beginning it put on live jazz, occasionally featuring top American musicians such as Dexter Gordon, who was living in Denmark at the time. Always popular, it is now part of the tourist route — the 'jazz-café' you simply must not miss.

Cafés had an important place in the social life of Antwerp, and since many of them stayed open long after midnight, it was quite normal to go to a café after the cinema or a concert. Meeting up with friends seemed to happen naturally with no need for prior telephone calls; indeed, useful as they are, mobile phones have taken some of the spontaneity out of life. Back in the 1960s it was not unusual to call at people's homes on the spur of the moment and this had long been so. Take Pepys's entry for 24 October 1660:

> To Mr Lilly's, where not finding Mr Spong, I went to Mr Greatorex's, where I met him, and so to an alehouse, where I bought off him a drawing pen; and he did show me the manner of the lamp-glasses, which carry the light a good way, good to read in bed by, and I intend to have one of them. So to Mr Lilly's with Mr Spong, where well received, there being a club

tonight among his friends. Among the rest was Esquire Ashmole, who I found was a very ingenious gentleman. With him we two sang afterwards in Mr Lilly's study. That done we all pared.

Maybe the size of a city plays a part. London in Pepys's time also had a population of around three hundred thousand, and he spent quite a lot of time in the pubs and coffee-houses and judging by the frequency with which he bumps into friends and other well-known figures, so did they all. This went for Antwerp too in the late '60s; a local metropolis of similar size, where in the bars you would find artists, writers, musicians, barristers, local politicians... and the odd academic.

Pepys frequently talks about making merry, or even 'exceedingly merry', especially in the earlier years before he moderated his alcohol intake. But whether he was eating, drinking, playing music, or singing, it was the *company* that really mattered — and the conversation that went with it:

23 May 1661. To the Rhenish wine-house, and there came Jonas Moore, the mathematician, to us, and there he did by discourse make us fully believe that England and France were once the same continent, by very good arguments.

11 December 1663. To the coffee-house and there, among others, had a good discourse with an iron-merchant, who tells me the great evil of discouraging our natural manufacture of England in that commodity by suffering the Swede to bring in three times more than ever they did, and our own ironworks be lost — as almost half of them, he says, are already.

Late-night cafés often went together with late-night eating in Antwerp, and Pepys too would round off an evening out with a 'take-away' — not always to his liking:

17 July 1660. ... and at night sent my wife and Mrs Hunt to buy something for supper; they bought a quarter of lamb, and so we eat it, but it was not half roasted.

The way we divide history into distinct periods encourages us to compartmentalise. Moving back to the Middle Ages we almost expect daily life to be touched by a distinctive 'medieval' quality. Yet William FitzStephen, in the introduction to his *Life of Becket* (he had been a clerk in the service of Thomas Becket, whose murder in 1170 he actually witnessed) adds the following in his description of London in his day:

Besides, there is in London on the river bank a public cook shop; there eatables are to be found every day, according to the season, dishes of meat, roast, fried and boiled, great and small fish, coarse meats for the poor... If there should come suddenly to any of the citizens, friends, weary from a journey and too hungry to like waiting till fresh food is bought and cooked... this is the public kitchen, very convenient to the city and part of its civilisation.[14]

Plus ça change...

***

The rattle of side drums and the booming of the big bass drum grew louder as the procession approached along the Meir in Antwerp. The drummer boys were making the most of their moment in the limelight and their clattering roll on the drums should have announced a loud blaze of bugles; it was in fact followed by the rather thin sound of slightly-out-of-tune lyre bells giving a tame version of *When the Saints Go Marching In* played by a company of teenage girls dressed in stocking tights and white boots in a pseudo-military uniform who looked as though they had jumped out of a Christmas panto on ice. They were followed by still younger girls doing gymnastics, under the watchful eye of matronly looking women. Then came another row of local officials and more flags and banners brought out of storage for the occasion. 'Socialist Party of Hoboken' one proclaimed. Occasionally one of the dignitaries would recognise someone in the crowd and would raise a hand in acknowledgement. And so, it went on... more drums and xylophones, banners and committee members, then... no, something was wrong... this was not part of the script... a group of women dressed in black, with hats and dark veils for a funeral suddenly appeared from nowhere moving swiftly in the opposite direction, against the flow. They were shouting slogans and handing out pamphlets to the bystanders on the pavement as they went.

It was a cleverly worked out protest action. Select an event that is going to attract a large crowd of people, like the 1970 May Day Procession in Antwerp, and you had a guaranteed audience. The Dolle Mina's were a feminist group, founded in Amsterdam, and Antwerp soon followed. Ida was one of the leading lights, fighting for women's rights across the whole spectrum: social, political, economic and sexual.

Protest actions like this were eye-catchers and they certainly caught the attention of the press and television, culminating in the disruption of the Miss Belgium contest of 1971. But there was a risk that they would remain just that — headlines — with the beneficiaries being the media and not women. For Ida and some of the others it soon became clear that a more effective way of achieving their aim was to concentrate on the social and economic structures that had produced the inequality, that is, to become political.

***

Mentioning Antwerp and Amsterdam in the same breath (not for the first time) might cause confusion, since English people seem to be in doubt whether Antwerp is in Belgium or Holland. This is understandable since the terminology — Dutch, Holland, the Netherlands, Flemish — is confusing and even in the region itself (where of course they have their own terminology!) there is some overlap and room for disagreement. Antwerp lies in Flanders, close to the Dutch border — and Flanders is the 'Dutch-speaking' part of Belgium. Historically, 'Flanders' and 'Flemish' are associated with the great economic and cultural flowering of cities like Ghent and Bruges in the later Middle Ages. Long before this, however, the word 'Fleming' crops up in the historical record; the Anglo-Saxon Chronicle entry for 1075 has *Fleminga lande*.

The generally accepted view that the Anglo-Saxons originated from North Germany and the Jutland peninsula goes back to the Venerable Bede writing in the eighth century — one of the great 'Myths of Origin'. Bede himself does not specify precisely how they crossed to England, just that they came in three boats. What support is there for such a North-Sea crossing? Their boats were more primitive than the later Viking ships; they didn't have keels and it is doubtful whether they had sails. Even with a constant rowing speed and optimal weather conditions it has been estimated that the quickest possible crossing from Jutland to the English coast would have taken fourteen days. A more realistic estimate is two months, with a high probability of not making it at all.[15]

An alternative version which crops up in late medieval Frisian and Flemish texts, claims that the coast of West Flanders and beyond as far as Calais and Boulogne, served as a bridgehead from which migrant tribes crossed the Channel to settle South-East England after the Romans had left in the early fifth century. Place-name evidence in the region gives some support to this claim. In Flanders and the Pas-de-Calais region we find *Warhem, Eringhem, Allencthun, Bellegem*, which correspond to the English names (of Anglo-Saxon origin) *Warham, Erringham, Allington, Bellingham.*

After leaving their native Jutland, the Anglo-Saxons would have sailed southwards following the coastline to beyond the mouths of the great rivers, the Rhine, the Maas, and the Scheldt, where they encountered other settlers, like the Franks. The choice is a simple one: risking five hundred miles of open sea or opting for the twenty-five miles across the Straits of Dover, never out of sight of land. Just picture it: 450 AD and *swarms* of Anglo-Saxons encamped near Calais waiting to get across. The seed of the English Nation!

But to get back to the language — to the relationship between Flemish and Dutch. With the exodus to the north and the founding of the Dutch Republic at the end of the sixteenth century, the languages spoken in Holland and Flanders went their own separate ways, just at a time when national languages in Europe were beginning to flex their muscles. Under a long period of foreign rule — Spanish, Austrian, and finally French — Flemish stagnated and no standard 'Flemish' language emerged; it remained a collection of different dialects. Even after the creation of the Belgian State in 1830 the language situation in Flanders remained much as before, since it lived under a French-speaking government. When in 1898 Flemish was given official status, it felt hemmed in by its northern neighbour; Dutch had been ticking along nicely for the last three hundred years, and hence set the standard against which Flemish could be measured.

Being so close to the border, Antwerp has a constant stream of Dutch visitors. In their dealings with the Dutch, the Antwerpians seem to lose their natural assertiveness and go on the defensive. Some try to modify their accent and even adapt their vocabulary, inserting well-known stereotype 'Dutch' words and interjections into their speech.

It is commonly held that the best way to learn a foreign language is to immerse oneself into the society where the language is spoken. The inverse holds too: speaking the language will help the process of integration into that society. I had a good understanding of Dutch — necessary for meetings, deliberations after exams, and so on. But that was in a particular setting, not communication in the normal sense of 'everyday conversation' and this was more problematical; firstly, because many Antwerpians had a bit of English and liked to practice it, and secondly, because even though they knew standard Dutch, most spoke the Antwerp dialect in their daily conversation. To avoid constant gear changes, I decided to keep things simple by becoming a fluent 'Dutch' speaker. While I largely achieved this aim, I have to say it has not made communication with the man in the street in Antwerp any easier.

Chapter: Six

BACK AND BEYOND

Late March 1994. It was six o'clock on a Wednesday evening and I had just finished my weekly class on the history of the English Language — a course I enjoyed giving, and one the students seemed to enjoy too.

Any introductory course on the history of English is bound to say something about the impact of the Viking settlement on the language and on English place names. One of its effects shows up today in *sh/sk*-pairs; the way original Anglo-Saxon 'sh' in front position alternates with Norse 'sk' as in *shirt/skirt*, and in the place-names *'Shipton/Skipton'* — only a few miles apart. Another typical Norse element in place-names is final *'ness'* referring to a headland; *Skegness* on the coast of Lincolnshire is a good example of the two together. You will remember that as a boy I often stayed at the Long House at Skinburness. I knew that Norwegian Vikings had crossed the Irish Sea from their colony at Dublin and had settled in Cumberland in the tenth century. *Skinburness* must be a Norse form too. I checked it out in the *Oxford Dictionary of Place Names*. Yes, it was Nordic, first recorded as *skinnanburh* in the eleventh century from earlier Anglo-Saxon *scinnanburh* — where *scinnan* has the sense of 'supernatural' to which *ness* was added, that is to say, 'the haunted stronghold on the headland'!

I had given a rather longer version to my student audience. That was back in January when it was already dark at this hour. Now we had got to the arrival of printing, and the low evening sun was shining through the large windows lighting up the whole room. It was the week before the Easter vacation.

As the students filed out Stan the stoker came in. He always did this, as though we were holding him up. You see, he also functioned as janitor and had to make sure the windows were all properly shut and no lights were left on before he locked the building. He was a tall man, late middle-aged, large forehead, thinning hair and with horn-rimmed glasses that magnified the size of his eyes. His physiognomy somehow did not match the brown boiler suit he was wearing. He stood there just inside the door with a fixed smile at one corner of his mouth, waiting while I cleared up my papers. I struggled trying to remove the large map of Britain from its hook, and he stepped forward to help me.

"Don't you miss all this?" he remarked.

"Sorry Stan, all what?"

"England," he said.

"Ooh… I've been in Antwerp for so long… no not really."

"You will," he replied. "You will."

I rolled up the map and we went downstairs to the main hall.

"I'll just drop this off in the office. Won't be a minute."

I was one of the few members of staff with my own office. After I was awarded my PhD at Louvain six years before, I had become chief editor of the journal *Linguistica Antverpiensia* and the office went with this new function.

He let me out and I walked along Schildersstraat, turning left at the Leien, heading for Mechelsesteenweg, where we lived.

***

Ida and I had separated in 1971, divorced three years later by mutual consent, and we have remained the best of friends ever since.

This I write with the benefit of hindsight; at the time the future seemed a lot more precarious.

I met Elly Baus in 1976. At least that was when our relationship started, for she had been a member of my English class before then. There must have been raised eyebrows among the staff, but there was little fuss or comment. Elly was still living at home and her parents can hardly have been overjoyed to hear that their twenty-one-year-old daughter was now with a divorced man of thirty-three. But they did not intervene.

In August 1978 when we were on holiday in England with the children,

Mother complained she was getting chest pains. It was diagnosed as pleurisy. Back in Antwerp I kept in close contact. In mid-September, she phoned me one evening to say she had seen the doctor again and had spent the afternoon sitting in the garden having just finished baking one of her bacon and egg pies. She was feeling a lot better, which put my mind at ease. Later that night David telephoned to say she had died from a heart attack.

Elly came to live with me at Mechelsesteenweg shortly after. In the summer of 1980, on the banks of Loch Lomond, I proposed to her and we married in 1981. For a few years Mechelsesteenweg became a 'family home' in a manner of speaking. When, in the mid-eighties, this period came to an end it left us sad and — as we admitted to each other at the time — suffering from empty nest syndrome.

***

I opened the front door to the flat and went in. It was on two floors and we had our own internal staircase which greatly added to the feeling of self-containment. From the front window of the living-room we had a view over the busy junction with the Leien, criss-crossed by tramrails and overhead wires. Until 1860, this was where the Mechelsesteenweg (literally 'the stoneway to Mechelen') crossed the defensive moat and passed through Sint Jorispoort — one of the main gateways to the city, also referred to as *Keizerspoort*. All this is shown in a mid-nineteenth century map of Antwerp — one of a series of town maps produced by 'The Society for the Diffusion of Useful Knowledge' and sold by Edward Stanford, 6 Charing Cross, London. Here we catch a glimpse of Antwerp on the eve of a major change. The Spanish walls are clearly marked and lower left is the 'route de Berchem, Malines et Bruxelles' — 'Malines' being the French for 'Mechelen'. This was all to be dismantled (sometimes using explosives) and filled in to form the 'Leien' and Mechelsesteenweg became a major thoroughfare in the expanding city. We must picture the whole of this area *extra muros* as a building site, and the population of Antwerp grew from one hundred and two thousand in 1856 to two hundred and seventy-two thousand in 1900.

Elly had said she would be a bit late. She worked in the port for Fabricom — a company specialising in electrical installations and industrial piping — and as she was taking a few days off over Easter there was work that needed to be done beforehand. I took a beer out of the fridge and went up to the roof terrace to enjoy the last rays of sunshine. The chestnut trees were already in bud and tucked in between the roofs it would have been a relaxing moment, except that I felt slightly disturbed by what Stan had said.

***

Later that evening, Elly told me she had decided to enrol at Ghent University for Arabic. She had already completed a course in Arabic at night school and had followed a summer course at the University Mohammed V at Rabat. There was, however, the practical problem of combining it with her job. Fabricom quickly agreed to her working part time, so in theory she would be able to nip back and forth to attend lectures. It would be a tight squeeze and it meant a lot of driving on the notoriously busy Antwerp-Ghent motorway, but in September she enrolled again as a student. In the long-term it proved to be a pivotal decision — but I'm getting ahead of events. For me, the period immediately following was less constructive. I felt restless and despondent, with a constant feeling that something was hanging over me.

It was around this time that we started taking short breaks, at first to the Belgian coast and, when we tired of that, to Dutch Zeeland, a collection of islands and inlets — the former arms of the Scheldt — in the south-west of Holland. Once there was a thriving trade between Zeeland and the ports on the Thames estuary. The route was sufficiently well known in the fourteenth century for Chaucer to use it in his description of the Merchant in the *Prologue*, who has:

"Upon his head a Flemish beaver hat… and would that the sea was kept free betwixt Middelburgh and Orwell."

Three centuries later the port of Vlissingen ('Flushing') was the Dutch naval base in the Anglo-Dutch Wars. Zeeland's rich past can still be seen in towns like Veere, and Zierikzee, and especially at Middelburg, where there are more historical façades than any other Dutch town, save for Amsterdam itself. But because of the Delta Works — the construction of the gigantic storm barrier after the tragic floods of 1953 — the character of the region has changed. Zeeland is now very much a recreational province, offering biking holidays, sailing and other water sports, and with its wide vistas of land, water, and sky, it attracts hundreds of visitors looking for a bit of peace and quiet.

It was within easy reach, yet very different, and we toyed with the idea of buying a place here so we could get away from Antwerp — after all, many Antwerpians had a second home at the Belgian coast and some even in Zeeland. It would have been reverting to type. Why didn't we?

We can sometimes explain *how* things happened by simply listing a train of events, in which the one seems to follow on from the other. If, however, we want to explain *why* things happened or *why* decisions were or were not taken, we need to look a little deeper. The truth is I was going through a 'mid-life crisis' — I had always been dismissive of the idea — I was beginning to feel trapped. The more I assimilated to Antwerp, the more I distanced myself from my past. After thirty years, a pent-up feeling of homesickness had at last caught up with me.

What prompted the next step was a weekend Elly and I spent in northern France at Amiens in spring '95. On the Sunday, before returning to Antwerp, we drove to Saint Valéry on the estuary of the Somme. It was from here that William of Normandy set sail for England with his army on 27 September 1066. Parking the car, we walked to the headland, where there was an observation point indicating the different directions: Hastings 100km, Brighton 140km... and that was the moment we both knew it was going to be a place in England.

***

Looking eastward from the raised position of Lancing College Chapel there is a marvellous view across the Adur Valley towards Shoreham and Brighton, and in the distance the chalk cliffs as far as the eye can see. It was a sight I knew well from my youth. True, there had been a number of changes; the wooden toll-bridge was no longer used by traffic, which now followed the A27 Brighton by-pass, cutting through the downs and crossing the Adur over a modern concrete bridge. Even from this distance you could hear the sound of the traffic. But the Adur itself had not changed; there was the same contrast between high tide, when the river was like a huge lake, spilling over the banks, and low tide when it drained into the sea through a network of fast-flowing silver streams between the mussel beds and the mudflats, leaving small boats lying at all angles, and of course the waders.

From this position Shoreham appears to be the last of the Brighton conurbation, halted as it were by the river. Yet Shoreham sees itself as a separate entity, and administratively it is not part of the new city of Brighton and Hove. Its history goes back a lot further than that of Brighton. Below Lancing College there is evidence of a Roman quayside when the Adur estuary was a wide inlet from the sea. In the Middle Ages Shoreham grew in importance, being the port closest to Normandy. Crossing the Channel from Rouen after the sudden death of his brother Richard the Lionheart, it was here at Shoreham that John landed on 25 May 1199, hurrying back to London to have himself crowned. Shoreham was sufficiently important to be granted borough status in the reign of Edward I. Notwithstanding the vicissitudes of the river and the violent storms of the late fifteenth century which swept away part of the town, Shoreham remained a shipbuilding port down to the nineteenth century. George Alexander Cooke in a *Topographical Description of the County of Sussex*, gives a lively description of Shoreham c.1810:

> Many ships are built here, both for the navy and merchant service, which renders the place full of people: ship-wrights, and ship-chandlers, rope makers and other tradesmen depending on that business… The harbour, which is safe and commodious, runs by the town parallel with the sea. It falls into the sea about half a mile east of the town. At the latter end of the year 1806 a meeting was held at Shoreham, to take into consideration an application to parliament, for an act to improve the harbour.

In the 1830s when parliament was discussing the construction of a London to Brighton railway, there was a lobby in favour of a line running from London via Horsham down to Shoreham and from there continuing eastward along the coast to Brighton. Although longer, it would require a lot less tunnelling than the more direct route, and it found support among the new citizens of Brighton who were all for a railway link with the port of Shoreham since it would put a stop to the unsightly practice of unloading coal barges onto *their* beach! In the event the direct line from London to Brighton got the nod, but a settlement was reached which accommodated the other view: a separate railway line from Brighton to Shoreham, opened with much fanfare in June 1841 — a full year before the official opening of the London to Brighton line. Later the Shoreham line was extended westward to Portsmouth and a link was made between Shoreham and Preston Park (Brighton), which removed the need to go into Brighton at all, thus providing passengers from Shoreham with a direct route to London

Shoreham-by-Sea suited our purposes perfectly, both as a town in itself and its good connections by road and rail, and we bought our cottage in Ship Street on 16 September 1996. I say 'cottage', but I should add that it was in a terrace of eight cottages built around 1830. The old census returns show that down to 1891 the terrace was called 'Cavendish Place', which sounds rather grand, but in reality, the cottages must have been very cramped, with families of five or six. The stated occupations of the head of the house are usually related to the port, to boat building or rope making. Ours had recently been renovated, while preserving much of its original character; the interior walls had been retained so that we had a separate sitting room and breakfast room (unlike all the others in the terrace); the quaint old staircase had been kept and the sash windows. There were nooks and crannies at the side of the chimney breasts, ideal for book shelves. And there was the garden. The first time we had seen the cottage in early July, the old rambling rose was in full bloom, which clinched the matter for Elly.

We had already met some of the neighbours, in particular Christopher and Linda Harris, next door to us, and their twelve-year-old son James who had kept a close eye on the progress of the work throughout. The older folk further down the street were at first a bit suspicious of the Belgian number plate on the car and curious to know when we were going to move in. I think they were disappointed when no removal van showed up. We sometimes brought things with us from Antwerp, but it was more fun scouring the antique markets at Lewes for small pieces of furniture, knick-knacks and old prints.

This, our second home, was the first place we had owned. My sense of pride and excitement also had to do with it being a shared experience. From now on England would be a part of Elly too.

***

Shoreham-by-Sea, 11 August 1999. People were walking purposefully in the direction of the footbridge. Some alone, some in groups. After a rather overcast start to the day, it was now sunny on the Sussex coast and some were wearing dark glasses or the viewers that had been on sale for days in the supermarkets. On the bridge one or two were pointing skywards. Yes, it had started — there was a little black chip on the right-hand side of the Sun's disc. Why we were all heading for the beach, I don't know, it just seemed the right place to go, even though the event would be visible anywhere in Shoreham. The path of totality was a band about 50km wide stretching from Cornwall and South Devon, skirting the Isle of Wight, across northern France, the Saarland, Munich and off towards the Balkans and the Black Sea. It began to darken. The sea became still, almost viscous. Sounds muted. Those who had been lying on the beach stood up, embarrassed, and joined the waiting throng. Then it happened. The moon passed in front of the sun, it was blacked out… a momentary pause and then the halo appeared — the corona. It was eleven-fifteen a.m. local time.

> 1135. In this year the King journeyed over the sea at Lammas. And the next day as he lay asleep on board the ship, the day darkened over all the land and the sun became like a three nights old moon and stars about it at midday. And men were full of wonder and dread and said that great things would come thereafter, and so they did, for in that same year the king was dead.

'The King' was Henry I, the youngest of the Conqueror's three sons. This is my rendering of a passage from the Peterborough Chronicle — an addition to the Anglo-Saxon Chronicle, made at the Abbey of Peterborough, which covers the period from Henry's death through the Civil War during King Stephen's reign (1135–1154). The eclipse in 1135 was strictly speaking a 'partial' one — but approaching total. Henry was on his way to Normandy and quite possibly he set sail from Shoreham. 'Lammas' was the first of August and the eclipse, we are told, occurred the day after. Taking into account the difference between the Julian Calendar used then and the Gregorian Calendar we use now, eight or nine days need to be added. The events described might well have happened on 11 August 1135.

***

Having Ship Street certainly changed my mood and outlook. I found myself taking on new commitments in Antwerp without feeling that I was compromising my future — like joining *Schola Gregoriana Cantabo*, which had been formed five years earlier by Hugo Brangers and Jan Pandelaers, bringing together a small group of singers who had been boy choristers together in the Cathedral choir. Apart from a bit of plainsong chanting, I had no experience of Gregorian music, and while it sounds effortless, it was more complicated than I had anticipated; the notation and rhythmical conventions were things I had to learn as I went along.

The Schola sang primarily at *Sint-Pauluskerk*, one of the monumental churches of Antwerp, late Gothic with richly carved choir stalls and an impressive seventeenth-century organ. It also boasts a series of religious paintings by artists such as Rubens, Van Dyck, and Jordaens — perhaps a shade too much religiosity for my taste. Only a short distance from the Grote Markt, the church is situated in the middle of the red-light district. Apparently, on the night of 2 April 1968 when a fire broke out in the roof, threatening the whole building, it was the local prostitutes (and no doubt their clients) who came to the rescue of these paintings.

We sang at the high mass on Sunday mornings. Sint- Paulus had been in the vanguard of the Counter-Reformation, yet the mass struck me as remarkably similar to the Anglican communion service; while the texts were in Dutch, they had a familiar ring to them, with the same underlying rhythm, the same cadence of speech.

After such a long gap how remarkable too that I should be singing again in another St Paul's! As choristers in London, we were often reminded that we were not just performing — it was a divine service. Once more I relished the performance side, the physical act of singing and the ritual: the lining up, a quick prayer, a ring of the bell, a shaking of the incense holder, the organ playing as we processed up the aisle through a full congregation, and then after a moment's silence the Gregorian introit.

I also enjoyed the social contact, which helped cement my relationship with Antwerp. And now one month after the eclipse — on Friday 10 September — Elly and I were welcoming the *Schola* to Ship Street. A brief visit to Shoreham combined with a bit of singing. I had been looking forward to it.

After a walk to the sea and lunch in the garden, we set off for a quick tour of the area, visiting Lancing Chapel and two of the small churches in the Adur Valley; St Nicolas close to the toll-bridge and Coombes Church a little way up the river. Coombes is mentioned in the Domesday Book and parts of the church are undoubtedly Anglo-Saxon. It is also one of a group of churches in this part of Sussex with early frescoes painted by Norman monks from the Cluniac priory at Lewes, the first and one of the largest in the country. In the evening we sang Vespers at St Mary's. What we see now is only the choir and the two transepts — yet it remains one of the most impressive churches in the county. The building dates back to c.1110 in the reign of Henry I, and the use of Caen stone shows the close links with Normandy.

Next day it was the turn of Roman Sussex. Because of the importance and popularity of Fishbourne Palace, the Roman villa at Bignor is often overlooked. In spite of its modest size there are some impressive mosaics, in particular one in the floor above the hypocaust of a Roman bathroom depicting gladiators and wild animals, a little odd here, in the shadow of the South Downs.

We had a picnic lunch at Bosham harbour, where at high tide the water ignores the harbour walls and enters the streets. It must have been like this in the time of King Canute, for Bosham is where he demonstrated to his obsequious courtiers that not even *he* could make the tide retreat. In the Bayeux Tapestry, a generation later, one of the first episodes is a depiction of Earl Harold Godwinson (future King Harold) and his mounted soldiers arriving at Bosham Church — *Harold dux Anglorum et sui milites equitant ad Bosham Ecclesia* — before he set sail on that somewhat obscure diplomatic mission to Normandy, which was to have such far-reaching consequences. Tradition has it that Harold's dead body was hastily removed by his followers from the battlefield at Hastings and brought to Bosham for burial. There is no gravestone to support this claim, but there is a stone marking where one of Canute's daughters lies.

On Sunday morning we sang at the Communion service in Portsmouth Cathedral. I had slight misgivings about singing here — it seemed like carrying coals to Newcastle. There was a large congregation and I remember the acoustics were good and at the close of the service, the Dean thanked us publicly from the pulpit:

"We in this country do not often have the opportunity to hear Gregorian singing of such a high quality."

***

My return to singing drew me into a somewhat ambitious project in Antwerp put together by my friend Freddy van der Koelen. I had known Freddy since the early '70s when he was a highly talented piano student at the Conservatory. I was an enthusiastic listener, and it was largely due to him that I got to know the Romantic piano repertoire (especially Schumann and Brahms) and the playing of pianists like Leon Fleisher and Arturo Benedetti Michelangeli. At the same time, we were great drinking companions — I believe we first met each other in the 'Sint Mattijs', one of the popular cafés in the neighbourhood of the Cathedral. A musical family, the van der Koelens: I later played in a pop band 'Prudence' with Freddy's younger brother Dirk — still an amazing bass guitarist and close friend.[16] Well, Freddy came up with the idea of tackling the Brahms *Liebeslieder Waltzes* for piano and vocal quartet. The piano part is written for four hands — which suggests it might have originated in a soirée setting — to be played by himself and his daughter, Els; the vocal quartet, which Brahms marks *ad lib*, was to be sung by four solo voices — the usual option — and I was to take the tenor part, which tends to be rather high — mirroring the soprano line, sung on this occasion by Eva Suls, a fellow-student of Elly at the Institute and a lifelong friend. The performance was on a Sunday afternoon for a largely invited audience in an informal setting with wine and snacks available, which all suited the *Ländler* style of the cycle. So much for the décor, but to bring it off successfully I had to find a relaxed lyrical style in my own singing... I seriously considered the raw egg trick I had used before the Mozart Requiem at Lancing, but no need — being a Sunday, the Gregorian singing in the morning provided just the gentle warm up my voice needed.

***

While Sir Thomas Gresham stands out as '*the* Englishman in Antwerp' during the Golden Age, it was the shadowy figure of Richard Verstegan that caught my attention. I first came across his name in connection with the emerging study of Anglo-Saxon in the late sixteenth century.

Verstegan was an Englishman of Dutch descent, a catholic activist who had fled to the Continent and settled in Antwerp round about 1580 where he continued to work as an undercover spy for the papacy. In 1605 *A Restitution of Decayed Intelligence*, was printed at Antwerp by Robert Bruney, to be sold in 'Paules Churchyard' by John Norton and John Bill. The book is a small one but covers a wide range of subjects: the origins of the English nation and its language; how languages change over time and the relations between the different languages; the earth's past and what the sea and rocks can tell us about it; the true nature of fossils — regarded by many at the time as the works of the devil. Verstegan points to the abundance of shells and sea creatures found in parts of the Netherlands and even cites the example of the remains of a sea elephant found when digging the canal from Brussels to Willebrouck in the 1550s. All of this leads him to conclude that there have been cycles of sea and land in the Low Countries, quite independent from Noah's Flood, which he says was in any case too short to account for the multitude and size of all these creatures. He even adds some of his own drawings of fossils. He dedicated the work to King James I of England, hoping thereby to receive a royal pardon that would enable him to return to England. It failed to get any response and he later wrote a Dutch version of the book (highlighting the Low Countries) which was published in 1613 with a dedication to the City Council of Antwerp. Throughout, he envisages a much longer timeframe than the Biblical one assumed by most of his contemporaries, and he comes up with ideas that were only to become part of mainstream science long after his death:

> That our Isle of Albion hath bin continent with Gallia, hath bin the opinion of divers [authors] but these authors following the opinion the one of the other, are rather content to think it somtyme so to have bin than to labour to fynd out by sundry pregnant reasons that it was indeed so.

He then gives *his* reasons: the close proximity of the cliffs at Dover to those at Boulogne, and more importantly, the similarity in composition and form of these cliffs, which after erosion reveal their true structure:

> Both of one substance; that is of chalk and flint; the sydes of both towards the sea, plainly appeering to be broken off sometime… Besides, they are formed craggy by nature or the wind and the rain having long since beaten away the earth from them, and thus have left them to appeer the very true anatomies of themselves.

I felt sorry for Verstegan having to reconcile himself to exile.[17] Thereafter, he concentrated more on Flemish literary affairs. He lived to the age of ninety and died in 1640, the same year as Rubens, indeed he was buried in the same church, Sint-Jacob's. How fitting that I was reading his *Restitution* in the library of the Plantin Moretus Museum in Antwerp — the printing house where so many important books were published in the Golden Age. You could hardly call it a forgotten book for it had never received any recognition. I concluded the article I was writing:

"His contribution is a reminder that scientific progress has not been a steady accumulation of knowledge; it is not linear, but full of loops and blind alleys, in which 'discoveries' pass unnoticed or are sometimes made twice."[18]

***

Elly's studies at Ghent were going well and she took her exams in 1999 with excellent results. She had already decided to take an extra year for her thesis, and since she was unlikely to continue working at Fabricom after Ghent she decided it was best to call it a day. This gave her a lot more time to write the thesis — *Text and Image in Arabic Political Cartoons* — a subject which combined her long-standing love of cartoons with the political, linguistic and cultural context of the Middle-East. She assembled a corpus from the cartoons appearing in three Arabic newspapers, *al-Hayat*, *al-Quds*, and *al-'Arab* in the period from 1 August to 31 October 1998. These had to be bought from newspaper shops in Antwerp as none of the official libraries had subscriptions. Inevitably there were gaps which were subsequently filled by visits to the British Library where photocopies were made. It was now a matter of persuading the faculty at Ghent that this was a suitable academic subject. The finished work impressed her jury. And shortly after receiving her licentiate degree, Elly started teaching in a secondary school in Kiel, a suburb of Antwerp with a predominantly immigrant population, where the majority of students were Moroccan and Turkish. While her studies had no direct bearing on the lessons, in discussions on current affairs her familiarity with Islamic countries and background certainly helped her relationship with the students, and her knowledge of classical Arabic was a feather in her cap. She taught at the school for the next ten years.

and then, in dreaming, the clouds methought would open, and show
riches ready to drop upon me, that, when I awaked, I cried to dream again
[Caliban in the *Tempest*]

Belgium has a number of well-known public astronomical
observatories. In the province of Antwerp, it is the *Volkssterrenwacht* at
Hove (probably the same origin as Hove in Sussex; *hoeve* is still used
in Dutch for a 'farmstead') better known as *Urania*. The dome of the
observatory is a local landmark and Urania attracts a lot of visitors on
its observing nights for events like eclipses and meteor showers. Less
well known, it also offers the public a broad educational programme.

My enthusiasm for the night sky had been rekindled by the darker skies
in Shoreham and having followed the introductory course in astronomy,
Elly and I decided to take the plunge and enrolled in the practical course
in telescope making at Urania in the academic year 2000-1. The aim was
to build our own reflecting telescope with a 15cm concave mirror. We
first made the wooden equatorial mount which would carry the finished
telescope and then the turntable which we would need for grinding the
mirror. Here we used two blank glass discs of different quality; one the
mirror-to-be and the other the tool. It was a slow process, starting with
a rough carborundum grit (almost sand-like) and proceeding through
a range of gradations till finally we were using something resembling
talcum powder. There were about ten of us attending these weekly
sessions, with three or four experts monitoring our progress.

The beautiful thing is that, although the measuring requires precision
instruments, the grinding process itself is manual and very simple,
depending on purely *random* movements — this produces the best results,
for if you start counting the strokes or try to follow a pattern when
moving the turntable things start to go wrong. After several months
of grinding came that moment when the opaque glass quite suddenly
becomes transparent. Unfortunately, it was not a lens that we wanted, but
a mirror — and after another month of polishing it was a bit of an anti-
climax when the whole thing received an aluminium coating.

We had worked hard on our telescope and had learned a lot. It
performed well, but there were drawbacks. It was big and heavy, the tube

and mount with the balancing weights together weighing almost forty kilos — impossible to cart up the stairs to our roof terrace, and far too bulky to take backwards and forwards to Shoreham by car. Moreover, while it looked sturdy enough, the optical system was so finely balanced that it was likely to go out of alignment when transported. We concluded that while it had been fun, we had built the wrong telescope. What we needed was something all the astronomy journals were raving about — almost a sign of the times — a travel scope! A small refractor, the type of telescope we normally think of, with a lens at one end and an eyepiece at the other.

I was not planning to make one from scratch — the objective lens of a good refractor usually consists of two or three separate lenses, and this is not a DIY job. I had seen a Dutch site which gave instructions on how to build a 'drainpipe' telescope, and it also offered a range of good quality Japanese lenses housed in a solid cell at reasonable prices. The only snag was that the construction involved machines and tools which were all a bit beyond me. This set me thinking, and I came up with an idea that was simple, practical, and very low-tech — applying the standard method of fixing drainpipes together to the totally unrelated field of assembling a telescope. Crucially, the diameter of standard PVC piping matched that of the lens cell. All it needed was three screws to secure the eyepiece!

After New Year 2003 Saturn was high in the south-east sky and the nights were very clear. I went out onto our terrace with my new telescope, and, having first positioned the planet in the middle of the field of vision using a low magnification, I tried a TeleVue Radian 4 mm eyepiece. This gave me a magnification of 120x — the upper limit for a scope of this size. Clear and crisp, Saturn was a small disc with its rings clearly visible and using a slightly averted vision (a well-known trick) I could even make out the 'Cassini Division' — the fine black filament between the rings. The centre of Antwerp might not sound like the best place from which to view the heavens, but there was something very satisfying and enjoyable about observing from our terrace in the city — like some medieval star-watcher on a roof in Baghdad. I have enjoyed 'deep-sky weekends' organised by Urania, observing fainter stellar objects in the much darker Ardennes. But whatever the advantages and enjoyment, they lacked that particular magic.

***

In May 2003 when I retired from teaching, I was presented with a Festschrift entitled *Configurations of Culture*, edited by Aline Remael and Katja Pelsmaekers. It contains essays written by thirty of my friends and colleagues from Antwerp, Louvain, and further afield. Elly and Aline wrote a joint article on translating *Look back in Anger* from film to poster; Ida contributed a piece entitled simply *Gender* — she had steadfastly been in the forefront of feminist politics in Belgium. My colleague Francis Thomson, whom I had known since 1964, pointed to the influence the Scottish Enlightenment had on the cultured classes in Catherine II's Russia. This presentation took me quite by surprise and it touched me deeply, and the more I return to the book the more I enjoy the kaleidoscopic view it gives.

One contribution is from my old pal Robin Holloway. We were fellow choristers at St Paul's in the '50s, you remember, and he was already composing then. He would regularly present DB with freshly composed pages before the morning choir practice to be sight-read on the Bechstein grand piano. The obvious question is where and when was he doing his composing? Clearly Robin did not need a piano; the composition was laid down in the manuscript at night — often scored for orchestra — all ready to be picked up the next morning! His contribution to my Festschrift is the other way round; a short adaptation for piano of the 'Antwerp Chorale' from his *Scenes from Antwerp*, a large work for orchestra written during his period as 'composer-in-residence' at Antwerp and inspired, he says, by the "sensory input of the city... infused with feelings and moods and the interplay of time and space". The premiere was in the Singel concert-hall, Antwerp, on 9 October 1997, performed by the Royal Philharmonic Orchestra of Flanders. Robin had asked me to come to the final rehearsal in the morning. I was full of nervous anticipation, wondering how Antwerp would be portrayed in music. A brisk fanfare-like announcement on solo trumpet, immediately taken up by other voices in the brass section, then joined by the clarinet and the rest of the woodwind, I found myself being swept along in a musical recreation of a bustling Antwerp street-scene; full of excitement, different tones and textures, shimmering light, snatches of conversation here and there, everyone butting in, knowing better… until the strings arrive and impose a bit of order, though there are still some grumblings from the baritone sax and the bass tuba. Robin was not altogether happy with the tempo and at the end of the first movement he called to the conductor, Grant Llewellyn:

"Could you crank it up a notch tonight?"

I have often listened to the work since — in effect a concerto for orchestra. When the scene changes to the river Scheldt and the slow-moving cranes in the port, we get the aquatic tones of the saxophone section. Moments of Romantic beauty too — one where the strings are reduced to a chamber trio. The final section celebrates Antwerp's architecture, not from the Golden Age, but more unexpectedly, in a soaring evocation of the pompous, flamboyant architecture of the late nineteenth century 'Belle Epoque' which is much in evidence above the fashion stores along the Meir — a finale which Robin entitles simply… *Domes*.

***

It had been talked about for some while, but the first sign of action was early one morning in the autumn of 2003 when I was awoken by the sound of a heavy thudding, repeated every few seconds and gradually getting louder. On Armistice Day at the war memorial in nearby Stadspark there is a traditional twenty-one gun salute, but this was the wrong day. I looked out of our front windows and saw what I can only describe as a huge mobile steam hammer progressing slowly along the Leien, breaking up the asphalt surface. The earth shook each time the hammer fell and there was something slightly creepy about the whole thing. It signalled the first phase in the rebuilding of the Leien.

Early victims were the huge plane trees which had to be felled, and some of the local shops did not survive the long disruption that followed. Living at the crossroads of the Mechelsesteenweg and the Leien, we had a grandstand view from the living-room windows. The work involved not only the roadway but building tunnels and the construction of a multi-level underground car park. For three years we could not cross the street. There was no street, just a deep pit, and the trams poised on make-shift ramps above all this looked like a highly dangerous big-dipper at the fairground. As work proceeded the Spanish walls and the ruins of the huge bastion at the *Keizerspoort* rose from their grave. We had several months to study them closely: the angled walls to provide for maximum artillery coverage, the outside walls faced with heavy stone masonry, inside brick and rubble which could better withstand artillery fire, neutralizing the shockwaves. For a while, proceedings were halted and the archaeologists moved in, but finally it all had to go and a convoy of lorries carted away tons of bricks and stones to some unknown destination. One particularly impressive piece of wall, however, was spared this fate; the stones were all numbered and it was reconstructed at the far end of the underground car park. Fifteen years later when the work had shifted to the area around the Opera House, another of these bastions was revealed at *Kipdorppoort* and this time every effort was made to preserve some of it *in situ* for posterity,

***

> These impressive Abruzzo ridges that combined in so special a way hard temper with soft color — as if there were steel underneath the blue silver, yet a blue so etherealized that one peak, with its pencilled veins of snow, seemed to merge into the slate-blue heavens. [Edmund Wilson, *Europe without Baedecker*, 1947]

An eventful year 2003. In November, around my birthday, Elly took me to Rome. While I had seen vestiges of the Roman Empire all over Europe, North Africa, and in Syria, I had never before set foot in Italy. On the flight there, I happened to pick up a magazine and glanced at an article on L'Aquila — a small *Citta d'Arte*. We took a day off to visit it, using the regular coach service from Tiburtina. This was our introduction to Abruzzo and the start of our Italian Adventure.

Abruzzo is the mountainous region of central Italy, with the highest peaks in the Apennine Range. Because of this it has been rather cut off from the rest and inhabited by communities that thrived on isolation and remoteness, like the Benedictine monasteries. It has cities, but not many. The largest is Pescara on the Adriatic coast, modern and unremarkable. Much more interesting is L'Aquila, which is still being rebuilt after the violent earthquake of 2009. On a smaller scale there is Sulmona, where Ovid grew up, and a multitude of hill-top towns and villages — the *borghi antichi*.

Having spent two Easter holidays in Abruzzo, we decided to look out for something of our own in the region. Many of the properties advertised on internet needed restoration and therefore time and money. We decided to look on the spot when we were next there — that was in April 2007. The whole thing was decided in a single week and the apartment we eventually bought in Barrea was the first property we had seen. Not having an Italian bank account or address the initial steps rested very much on mutual trust — helped by the fact that in Italy the buyer and seller use the same solicitor. The contract was signed on 9 June, and after a brief discussion of the various alterations we wanted doing — all the doors out, open arches in the place and a terracotta floor throughout — we left things in the hands of Giuliano, the *muratore*. It had all been conducted so amicably that we forgot to ask about the cost of the work. He phoned us in Shoreham in late July to check whether we wanted the terracotta floor tiles to be laid 'square' or 'rhomboid' and again two weeks later to announce that it was all finished: "è pieno di luce!" he enthused — like the Book of Genesis. We promptly drove down to Italy, arriving in Barrea late in the evening of 15 August, the climax of the Ferragosto festivities — hardly the moment to start unloading the car!

Barrea is one of the most striking of these hill-towns. It lies in the far south of Abruzzo within the area of the National Park and close to the border with Molise. (I always seem to go for border places!) A thousand meters above sea level, it is a fortified medieval village built at a strategic point where the river Sangro dips into a long, steep gorge before re-emerging onto the flatter plain beyond, dominated by the small town of Castel di Sangro. It was in this rugged terrain that the Germans set up the *Gustav Line* in 1943. In pre-Roman times the valley of the Sangro was home to an Italic tribe, the Samnites — related to the better-known Sabines — and excavation has uncovered burial grounds and grave goods which are displayed in the local museum. The oldest building still standing in Barrea is *Lo Studio*, the sole remains of a Benedictine monastery built by monks from Montecassino. Better preserved is the medieval castle with its two distinctive towers.

For much of its history Barrea remained a feudal fiefdom where the chief occupations were agriculture and sheep-farming — associated with the *transumanza* — and wool was a major source of profit and wealth. Compared to northern Italy, the centre and south remained underdeveloped and economically backward, so I was surprised how many large, impressive buildings one sees in Barrea — the eighteenth and nineteenth century *palazzi*. Our apartment is in 'Palazzo Victor' on Via Roma — every village and town in Italy has its Via Roma and the 'Victor' refers not to Victor Emanuel, the King, but to the local builder. Even so, our Via Roma is a stylish esplanade with wrought iron railings and lampposts, leading towards the upper gateway of the historical centre — a maze of cobbled streets, arches, and steep steps. Palazzo Victor was built c.1880 with a neoclassical façade and the typical arched shop fronts at street level. It looked far too big to be a family home and probably the family overshot the mark, because it was turned into a hotel in the 1950s and subsequently sold off as flats within a condominium.

While it had always occupied a prime position, Barrea undoubtedly benefitted from the founding of the National Park in the early part of the twentieth century, and the creation of the 'Lago di Barrea' in the Sangro valley, 5km long and almost 1km wide, with a hydro-electric dam at the entrance to the gorge. Although artificial and built for a specific purpose, the lake has a 'natural' beauty about it, and Barrea, forming an impressive amphitheatre at its head, now has superb views that change with the seasons, the weather and even with the time of day. Those who built the lake had no idea that it would give such wonderful reflections of the mountains and sunsets. From our terrace we only have a side-view of the lake, but we do look out over the typical tiled roofs towards the castle and Monte Greco, where even in May there is still snow on the summit.

Life in Barrea differs rather from the English idea of 'Italian life' — Bella Italia, la dolce vita, al fresco dining, and so forth. The Italians tend to be less extrovert, more restrained, than we picture them. The association we make between Italy, and good food and good wine, is only partly correct. They can also be abstemious: they drink Prosecco and red wine, but often only a glass or two; while the restaurant menus advertise three courses — antipasta, primo, e secondo — they are happy to take two and sometimes they even share a dish. They don't expect vegetable accompaniments to be served with the main dish; these are ordered separately (as *contorno*) and in modest portions. As for 'al fresco' dining, the phrase is not even used in Italy — it would mean 'eating in the cold' and generally when families eat in the open (*all'aperto*) it involves simply shifting the table and chairs outside onto the pavement or under the trees. Restaurants can look rather impersonal and old-fashioned, especially the *trattoria* with white table clothes and efficient waiters (there is less of the flippancy we almost take for granted in Italian restaurants in England), and some follow the old tradition of paying the bill at the till on the way out — which I like.

The coastal region of Abruzzo is Mediterranean in appearance and climate, with vineyards and olive groves and occasionally the familiar umbrella shaped pine trees. But driving inland away from the Adriatic towards the mountainous region this quickly changes as the temperature drops. It becomes more Alpine, and the change is visible in the people themselves. The men wear jeans, boots, anoraks (often with a fur collar) and baseball caps throughout the long winters, when the smell of burning wood stoves hangs in the air. When we arrived in Barrea we set out to make our apartment look as 'Italian' as possible. The *sindaco* (mayor) popped in to see how we were getting on and remarked "I can see you're not Italians". We soon realised that they make a clear distinction between 'al mare' and 'in montagna'. Barrea obviously falls in the latter category, which means that the *casa* should have been *rustica*, with a lot of dark stained wood, heavily framed wooden windows with double-glazing, and a large woodstove protruding far into the living-room — a style that seems to start in the Ardennes, south of Brussels, where the stacked log-piles against the outside of the house first make an appearance and stretches to the toe of Italy.

Barrea is largely self-sufficient for food shops, with two butchers, two mini-markets, and a vegetable and fruit shop, and twenty minutes away is the town of Castel di Sangro which has four or five large supermarkets and a weekly market. Fish is largely absent from the local menu — it is definitely a meat-eating region, though the vegetables are very good too. The shopkeepers provide for the small resident population, but at Easter (when there is a performance of the *Passione Vivente*) and even more around Ferragosto the population swells with visitors from Rome and Naples. And somewhere in between is a small group of 'quasi-Barreani' (to which we belong) who live there for part of the year — all paying council tax and utility bills, and enjoying what Barrea has to offer. A mixed group, English, American, Belgian — some with Italian forebears, not always apparent when it was on the maternal side, like Jan and Nelson Thatcher, in contrast to Steve Di Girolamo, Washingtonian, epicurist and jazz-lover, and Larry Gibilaro, Londoner and currently Professor of Chemical Engineering at the University of L'Aquila. Larry's family were from Sicily, and his father, Alfonso Gibilaro, was a composer of popular songs, two of which were recorded in 1949 for HMV sung by Beniamino Gigli. It doesn't get more Italian than that!

What everyone can enjoy is the magnificent scenery surrounding Barrea, whether it be for rock-climbing, hill-walking, or just an afternoon stroll. One needn't climb the Alpine rockface of the *Camosciara*, you can simply admire the view. There are miles of beech forests along the lower reaches of the mountains, where the silence is broken by the sound of fast flowing streams cascading over the rocks and boulders. Here you will encounter deer and foxes, occasionally wild boar and higher up the 'camosci', very rarely wolves and the large Marsican brown bear, and never the lynx — but they are there, somewhere around.

***

Travelling by car through the Alps, the Dolomites, and the flat plain of the Po Valley to Barrea must have awakened something dormant in me, and, after a gap of fifty years, I started to paint again. This time in watercolours. It was shortly afterwards that I decided to go up to London for the annual meeting and dinner of the Guild of the Companions of St Paul — the old choristers' reunion. I hadn't been for years, and the prospect of singing together with the cathedral choir and meeting some of my boyhood friends again, suddenly became irresistible.

For two and a half centuries St Paul's had been the tallest building in London. It had now been overtaken by dozens of modern skyscrapers, although it had stood up well to them, indeed the image of St Paul's regularly appears on television screens as an icon of the financial City. Now perhaps it is closer to how Wren had envisaged it in his plans for the new City than ever before.

Entering, I felt what I had always felt: the sense of space, the almost tangible acoustics, and the smell of stone — which as a chorister I noticed most when we came in from outside on a hot summer afternoon. I knew the Cathedral from top to bottom, including all those parts the public never sees, parts that Wren kept well out of sight. And like the inhabitants of a house, probably each of us choristers had our own private points of contact with the building, just as we had with the music that we sang inside it. Today it was to be Walmisley in D minor and *Ascribe unto the Lord by* S.S. Wesley — two old favourites and quickly knocked together.

On the way up from the crypt to the choir stalls, someone approached me:

"I gather you're Michael Windross."

"Yes," I replied.

"Andrew Forrest. I arrived just after you left, but I heard an awful lot about you from Eileen Price."

Andrew is an artist and photographer and, like me, he had a career in higher education, teaching history and art-historical subjects. He lives in Eastbourne, not far from Shoreham, and in the following years we were to discover how much we had in common.

Standing there in the choir stalls I quickly recognised my contemporaries David Driscoll and Francis Saunders from way back. Anthony Price and Robert Phillipson, I had of course known after St Paul's; I had been at Lancing with Anthony, and as teenagers, Robert and I had frequently stayed at each other's homes. I even joined the Phillipsons on family holidays at North Walsham on the Norfolk coast, when we would leave Blackheath, where they lived, early in the morning in the Dormobile (by its nature a *social* vehicle) stopping at Colchester for breakfast at colonel someone or other's. At home, we did not have a car, nor a 'guest book' or invitation cards on the mantlepiece. I never learned to drive, to dance, or to play tennis, and sometimes I felt as though I was lacking in the social graces (through no fault of my own!). It was therefore panic when I received an invitation to sing in an impromptu performance of the Gilbert and Sullivan operetta *Pirates of Penzance* at their home in the New Year. 'Gilbert and Sullivan' was simply not part of my upbringing! It turned out to be most enjoyable and there was a repeat the following year. Robert and I had last seen each other in Antwerp in the late 80s, around the time we were finishing our doctorates. His thesis, which he presented to the University of Amsterdam, was concerned with what he called 'Linguistic Imperialism' — a seminal work which was soon published by the Oxford University Press. Conversations at old boy's reunions tend to be somewhat fragmentary, but it certainly struck a chord when, recalling the past, Robert mentioned how much he had appreciated my parents for their openness and intellectual honesty, in contrast to the rather bourgeois conventions of his own home.

And there was Peter Chapman! Although we stood next to each other for nearly two years in the choir stalls, played together in the cricket XI, and stayed at each other's homes, we had lost contact thereafter. Peter, who had worked in the city, had kept in close contact with the Cathedral and the Guild and he had recently served as lay canon in the Cathedral Chapter — the first such appointment. In the autumn of 2011, he telephoned me in Shoreham, out of the blue, to ask whether I would like to contribute towards the cost of commissioning a new work to be sung at the sixtieth anniversary of the Coronation, at Westminster Abbey. The old choristers who had sung on that occasion back in 1953 were being approached, together with those from the Abbey and other places, and we were all to be invited to the celebration in June 2013. There were regular updates; wives and partners were also to receive an invitation.

Elly and I went up from Shoreham to London the day before and spent the night at a hotel off Bayswater Road. The morning of 4 June was bright and sunny (unlike sixty years before) and we travelled from Lancaster Gate to Westminster by tube. Parliament Square was already full of people and it was all very colourful, with hats much in evidence. The dress code was not terribly strict, but no jewellery or medals were to be worn to avoid flash, as the service was being televised — a pity since this was perhaps the one occasion when I could have worn my coronation medal! We had been warned that there would be tight security and already there was a long queue stretching back from the gates, which did not look promising.

It all went smoothly. There was a festive mood inside the Abbey and we quickly found our places, quietly chatted or listened to the organ, glancing through the service book. The form of the service followed the order of the Coronation itself, with some of the same music. While Britain's position in the world had sagged a bit in the meantime, this was to be quite a show, and to be sharing the occasion with Elly meant the world to me. The organ played *Crown Imperial* by William Walton to put us all in the right mood. Eleven o'clock. The fanfare of trumpets, and the Royal procession moved up the aisle from the west doors as the choir once again sang Parry's anthem 'I was glad when they said unto me'.

***

When we bought the cottage in Shoreham, I had naturally been looking forward to seeing my brothers more regularly. Things did not work out that way. It soon became apparent that Colin's health was deteriorating and he had to undergo major surgery several times. I saw a lot of David over this period, and we talked at great length about Colin. David even became his official carer. But after a long decline, Colin died in Brighton General Hospital on 1 June 2006, a week before his sixtieth birthday.

Elly persuaded David to become a full-time care worker in the Brighton area and for a couple of years this went well. We found time go to the cricket together and sometimes wandered around the antique shops and flea markets in central Brighton. He even went with me to Barrea in 2008, and it was there that I noticed his coughing and the difficulty he had in walking any great distance. He was stubborn about receiving medical treatment, just as Colin had been, which led to emergency situations where he was admitted to hospital, ultimately for vascular and orthopaedic surgery. David died on 2 June 2016, almost ten years to the day after his twin brother.

***

I was spending a lot of time painting. In Shoreham, I joined the Adur Art Collective, and began taking part in the biennial open-house event, the Adur Art Trail. As a member of the *Kunstatelier Horizon*, I have been able to participate in yearly exhibitions at the Kasteel van Schoten. In summer 2014, I had the opportunity to exhibit my pictures in Barrea over the festive August period — my first one-man show — at the old town hall on the main square of the historical centre, which is depicted on the poster I designed. Naturally, I was thrilled to be exhibiting in Italy and there was the added pleasure of giving something back to the community. The succession of landscapes and townscapes on show reflected our peripatetic existence and I was aware that some of the stuff from years ago had been recycled and had found its way back into these new images.

In June 2017 Andrew Forrest and I had a joint exhibition at the Crypt Gallery in Seaford. Andrew came up with the title 'Catching the Eye'. Putting on shows at such great distances raised logistical challenges, and much of the transport and organization at Seaford was done by Elly and Oliver, my younger son. The opening was thoroughly enjoyable and brought together people from different circles and places. Our good friend Larry Gibilaro was at both exhibitions — Barrea and Seaford — but for this one he only had to come down from Clapham!

***

We hear a lot about 'roadmaps' from politicians, at a time when road maps (in the real sense) are being superseded by navigation systems — a sign of the 'the retreat from literacy'. You will detect the note of disdain from a technophobic non-driver. Seated next to the driver on our way down to Italy, I like to have the road atlas at hand so that I can enjoy the journey to the full, within a wider geographical context. With an on board SatNav system, what matters is not the journey but the route and especially the present position of the car on that route — a much more restricted, self-centred view. I gather there is now an app available which allows users to follow others, thus "building up a social satnav of great experiences and memories around them" (Wikipedia). To me this sounds like posting 'selfies' on social media!

I love browsing through atlases. In bed at night, before switching off the light, I often lie next to Elly (who is reading a book) looking at my 1972 *Philips Modern School Atlas* — easy to hold and with beautiful maps. Reading a book, reading a map: both offer an escape from the here and now. An atlas can fire the imagination; it allows one to form a mental picture of areas of the world that one has never been to. Even when one does visit a new country, it is sampled in bits, never in its entirety. An atlas allows us to contemplate whole continents; it helps us grasp the geographical layout of the planet and provides important clues to its past.

On the bottom shelf of my bookcase, along with the art books are two very large atlases. Both were presents. One is the *Times Atlas of World History*, given to me by Albert Gomperts in the early '80s. It is edited by Geoffrey Barraclough, who was my tutor for medieval history at Cambridge — another pipe-smoking history don. The general conception departs from traditional historical atlases in the way it presents a changed, non-Eurocentric view. The other is the *Oxford Atlas of the World*, which was given to me in 1993 by my friend David Arden.

I have known David, a Californian, since 1972 when for a while we lived at the same address. A pianist, he had recently arrived in Antwerp as a post-graduate at the Music Conservatory, to study for his concert diploma. For him this must have been an exciting time in a new environment, meeting new people; for me, things were at a pretty low ebb — so we probably have rather different feelings about that particular period.

The first time I heard David perform was at an in-house concert at the Conservatory, where he played the well-known Scarlatti Sonata in E major, K.380 — a good candidate for 'spot the odd one out' in his total repertoire. A few years later, in 1977, I heard him perform Leonard Bernstein's *The Age of Anxiety* for piano and orchestra at the Queen Elisabeth Hall, Antwerp, to a full house. In the foyer there was a stand promoting his recently issued record — 'American Piano Music' — devoted to Samuel Barber, George Gershwin, Leonard Bernstein and André Previn. David could certainly have built up a following in Belgium with this appealing 'mainstream' American music. As it turned out, he returned to the States and devoted his energies (in so far as piano is concerned) largely to performing and, more especially, recording piano music by avant-garde composers; some American, like John Cage and Earle Brown, but also European, such as Arvo Pärt, Henryk Gorecki and Luciano Berio. Ploughing a lone furrow, you might think, yet it took him all over the world!

The funny thing is David and I hardly ever talk about music when we meet up — and we have met in some funny places! In Durrango, Colorado, for instance, where Elly, Aline, and myself went to pick him up from the small airport — more like an airstrip. Having flown from San Francisco to join us for a few days, he emerged from the turbo-prop, the lone passenger — it was like the start of a modern-day western! Another time, on his way to visit us at Shoreham, he phoned me from Gatwick Airport (I didn't yet have a mobile):

"How do I get to your place?"

"I'll meet you at the station, don't worry."

"But you don't know what time I'll be arriving…"

"That's all right, I'll just hang around."

"What, like *High Noon?*"

We even met up once at the Amex Stadium so we could watch a Brighton and Hove Albion match together (a staunch Chelsea supporter, he is very much au courant with the comings and goings of the English Premier League). Generally, however, we meet David and Sharon in London — on the steps of the Royal Academy, say, or on the grass in front of the Wallace Collection, and pick up the conversation where we left off, defying the boundaries of time and place — save for the jet lag.

The atlas too had quite a journey getting to me — five and a half thousand miles. David brought it with him from San Francisco in his suitcase. Inside the cover he has written: *To my great friend and fellow lover of geography. Have Fun Mike!*

***

One moment please…

This is the story of the English. They live on a small island near the wide land of Europe. Around the island, the sea rolls ceaselessly. This is the story of how different men came to this island, how they toiled in the fields, how they fought wars, how they sailed in ships, how they worked in towns. It is the story of farmers and poor men, townsmen and seamen, soldiers and rich men, lords and kings. All these men are the English people. [Philip Lovell, *The Story of England*, 1946.][19]

It is often said that England's history has been determined by its being an island. Here we have the beginning of my very first history book, given to me by my parents when I was eight. There is a marked difference between the tone of this passage and the well-known words put into the mouth of John of Gaunt:

"This sceptred isle, set in the silver sea… which serves it in the office of a wall, or as a moat defensive to a house, against the envy of less happier lands."

Stirring stuff, which has since been repeated in different guises to boost the national ego. *Richard II* was written in 1595, only seven years after the defeat of the Spanish Armada, and Gaunt's words would have caught the general feeling among the audience at the Globe theatre.

At present this 'island rhetoric' is part of the political dogma in support of Brexit. In my view, it presents a one-sided view of the past. As well as a defence, the sea has also served as a thoroughfare. It fostered trade and communications between the Continent and England even before the Romans arrived, and after they had left it brought a succession of Anglo-Saxons, Vikings, Norman-French, Flemish refugees, and many others, to these shores, where they gradually merged together to form the English nation, each contributing to the cultural heritage and adding a layer to the English language. Often the traffic was from the Continent, but sometimes it was in the other direction; the export of wool to the Continent for instance. An early example of cultural traffic can be seen in the missionary work of the Northumbrian monks Willibrord and Wynfrith (better known as Bonifacius) who crossed the North Sea to convert the Low Countries and a large part of Germany to Christianity around 690. A century later, Alcuin of York was appointed tutor at Charlemagne's court in Aachen, to become one of the leading figures in the so-called 'Carolingian Renaissance' which, in turn, laid the foundation of Medieval Europe. The way Anglo-Saxon England played a role in this whole process was brought home to me recently, in a rather subtle way.

It was Elly who got me interested in family history — initially through her article 'In search of my biological Baltic grandfather' which appeared in *Vlaamse Stam* early in 2018. It was like detective-work, looking beyond the official documents — which in this case served partly to cover up the facts — to the more everyday evidence of old photographs and family traditions, and then returning to the documents to tease out conclusions.

I enjoyed the places we visited in the course of her search, such as Herentals and Vilvoorde, the latter where her mother was born — and where William Tyndale was put to death in 1536. We also went together to Maaseik one early January to look into her father's maternal side — the *Meulenaars* (Millers) — who were from the region. The town, which claims to be the birthplace of the brothers Van Eyck, lies on the river *Maas* (the 'Meuse') in Limburg, the most eastern province of Belgium. There is a bridge crossing the river and on the other side you are in the Netherlands:

Nederlands-Limburg. The two Limburgs have much in common. Flemish-Limburg only became part of Belgium in 1839, while Dutch-Limburg had to wait until 1866 to become part of the Netherlands. Previously they had both been under the jurisdiction of the prince-bishops of Liège and their cultural past was closer to Germany. Limburg is a flat border-region, and two hundred kilometres from the sea, it is a strange mixture of natural quietude and maritime industrial activity.

We had managed to locate the grave of one of Elly's forefathers in the cemetery, getting very cold in the process, so we decided to call it a day and drove to the nearby village of *Aldeneik* ('Old Oak'). Once it lay on the Maas, but over time the river has shifted its bed eastwards and the village's only connection with the water now is a lake, one of the many formed by the extraction of gravel, and it is used for aqua-sports and recreational activities. The name Aldeneik must post-date the founding of the newer town Maaseik (c.1230) but the village itself is older. The present mish-mash of restored farmhouses and expensive new villas provides no clue to its earlier past — except perhaps the church, which is large for such a small village, and some of it certainly looks medieval.

This church (at least its foundations) is all that is left of a Benedictine convent founded in 728 by a nobleman, Adelhard, for his two daughters Harlindis and Relindis. It was our Northumbrian Willibrord who invested Harlindis as first abbess of the community. Willibrord had by this time finished his missionary work and had retired to a monastery at Echternach (in present-day Luxemburg) where he established an important 'scriptorium'. Journeying to Aldeneik, he had brought gifts and offerings with him, as was customary on such occasions. A parallel can be seen two centuries later in England when King Aethelstan, visiting the shrine of St Cuthbert at Chester-le-Street in 934, paid his respects with a number of precious relics and woven textiles. Willibrord too had brought textiles and an illuminated book of the Gospels (in Latin) from Echternach, both of which remained at Aldeneik until 1571, when the collegiate canons (who had replaced the earlier community of nuns) fearing for their lives during the religious wars, sought refuge within the walls of Maaseik itself, taking with them their treasures.

These have been preserved and can be seen in the crypt of the

Katharinekerk at Maaseik. The lighting is kept low, for they are the oldest surviving Anglo-Saxon textiles in the world and the *Codex Eickensis* is the oldest book in the Netherlandic region. The manuscript shows many of the distinctive Hiberno-Saxon stylistic traits displayed in the well-known *Lindisfarne Gospels* and it is every bit as beautiful.

While countless tourists visit the various battlefields of the Low Countries, those 'corners of England' fought over the last two hundred years: Waterloo, Ypres (Flanders Fields), Arnhem (a Bridge too Far), here at Maaseik, sixty miles south of Arnhem, a different message has come down to us from a much more remote past, when the English nation was still in its infancy.

Chapter: Seven

RAISED BEACHES AND AN EARLY START

Shoreham has a special relationship with its beach, which shows in its full name, Shoreham-by-Sea, not the usual 'on-Sea'. As already pointed out, the present coastline at Shoreham has been formed comparatively recently through strong cross currents and prevailing westerly winds which have caused a gradual build-up of shingle, thereby blocking what used to be the exit of the Adur into the sea, and forming a long spit of land, Shoreham Beach. To get to the beach from the town one must cross the footbridge over the Adur. This used to be a rather narrow, dilapidated concrete construction from the 1920s, but it has recently been replaced by a modern bridge which (I think) bears comparison with the Millennium Bridge over the Thames. There has also been large-scale work on the shoreline and particularly on the flood defences along the banks of the river. All this will help preserve the present landscape and fortunately it has not greatly altered the aspect of the beach.

Never very crowded, which is surprising since it is situated between Brighton and Worthing, in early June the beach is a blaze of colour from the plants growing through the shingle — the red valerian, yellow sow thistle, the white sea kale, and more — all in bloom, and it is a pleasant walk along as far as the entrance to Shoreham Harbour. At one time one would have been able to walk still further in the direction of Brighton, but in 1760 the spit was deliberately breached to create a new harbour entrance, and later, to protect it against possible French invasion, a redoubt fort was erected here in 1857. It is a walk we often take.

On one occasion I picked up a small, smooth, dark red pebble from the beach, perfectly oval and flattened on either side. I took it back to Antwerp with me and enquired at a local jewellery workshop whether it would be possible to sink my silver Edward I penny flush into the stone — partly as a way of preserving the coin. It required a small industrial diamond head to do the drilling, then a silver thread around the circumference and a simple clasp was added — and there it was, a 'medieval' pendant, combining elements from Cumberland, Sussex, and Antwerp. I gave it to Elly on our silver wedding anniversary in 2006.

***

Travelling west from Shoreham past Littlehampton, the shingle gives way to flatter sandy beaches. Collecting fossils with Elly at Bracklesham Bay brought back memories of the way we used to gather cockles and winkles with Father and Mother at Black Rock in the late '50s. 'Black Rock' — oddly enough — is where the white chalk cliffs begin at the end of Madeira Drive in Kemp Town. For many it referred simply to the popular open-air swimming pool, which was situated there, but beyond that, at low tide, a rough, rocky beach was exposed, full of pools, and it was here that we would go to collect shellfish at the end of a summer's day. Much of the area was lost when Brighton Marina was built in the early '70s.

While the activities are similar, there is an important difference. The shells we were gathering at Black Rock were living organisms whereas those in the shallows of Bracklesham had been dead for thirty million years. Both were retrieved from what is now the English Channel, but the gastropods and bivalves from the Eocene period had actually lived in another sea which just happened to be in the same place.

The geological history of the Sussex coast is complex. If we look at the chalk cliffs extending from Brighton to Eastbourne, it becomes clear that the present distribution of land and sea is (in geological terms) fairly recent. The cliffs themselves consist of layer upon layer of calcium rock deposited during the Cretaceous over a period of eighty million years and they are full of marine fossils, a hundred feet and more above the present sea level. This is also the case on the northern, inland-facing side of the Downs, where as a boy I would probe around in the chalk pits in search of fossils. The Downs once formed the seabed, subsequently uplifted, and then slowly weathered away to give their present rolling form.

There have been continuous fluctuations in sea level, particularly through the cyclical effects of glaciation in the Ice Age, where increasing glaciation (trapping the water) meant lower sea levels and retreating glaciation higher levels. During the period three hundred thousand to two hundred and fifty thousand years ago, the Sussex coastline was further inland, as can be seen from a 25km trace of sand and shingle visible at Goodwood, and sometimes referred to as the 'Goodwood raised beach'. Something similar can be seen in the cliffs along the coastline, where there are darker layers in the chalk and Black Rock itself is a remnant of one of these raised beaches. Moving forward in time, the most recent advance of the ice-sheet peaked about twenty thousand years ago and the sea level, accordingly, was considerably lower than at present. At Bracklesham we would have been standing on dry land and the nearest coastline to Sussex would have been to the south-west of Cornwall, close to the Scilly Isles four hundred and fifty kilometres away.[20]

Sand is closely connected with coastlines and even the pebble beaches at Shoreham and Brighton have an underlying sand beach which is exposed at low tide. How odd that sand should be associated with the transience of life — the 'sands of time' and that favourite renaissance *momento mori,* the hourglass — when it is one of the *oldest* things on the planet. Sand is produced by erosion and is usually deposited at continental shelves. Yet extensive deposits of sand occur hundreds of miles inland from our present coastlines — relics from the ancient shorelines of long-gone continents. Grains of so-called 'Zircon sand' go back almost to the formation of Earth's crust and are four billion years old.

Sicut erat in principio, et nunc, et semper.

***

Oliver had come over from Antwerp to watch the Albion play Everton — and our good friend Arie Aertsen was to join us with his son Diederik from Amsterdam. The fact that Arie would be flying from Schiphol to Gatwick to watch a football match, says something about the bond that exists between us — something that will be understood by devotees of the game, especially if you support a team like Brighton and Hove Albion. For as long as football is played as we know it, season after season clubs like Liverpool, Manchester City, Manchester United, and Chelsea will grab the headlines and global coverage. Like a comet, Brighton will only shine for a brief moment on the football firmament.

This appointment was a revival of an old tradition going back to the early '80s which ceased in 1983 when Brighton lost the FA Cup Final to Manchester United, and also managed to get relegated from the 'First Division' in that same season. Oliver was just a teenager then and Diederik was not yet born. After thirty years in the lower divisions of the Football League, when Albion were promoted to the Premiership in 2017 we started watching again, making it an enjoyable weekend in Shoreham.

It was still only Thursday and the idea had been to visit some of the beauty spots of Sussex. The rain put a stop to that, and with no sign of it letting up, we popped into Brighton Museum. We were in no hurry and we took our time. I used to come here as a boy to look at the archaeological and geological collections. Since then, like many museums, Brighton has modified its exhibition space and presentation, partly to make it more attractive for families with children. In the new Elaine Evans Gallery at Brighton there were now fewer objects and a different presentation using new techniques — sometimes to great effect — like the facial reconstructions that accompanied the old skeletons from the Neolithic camp at Whitehawk and other local sites. Not that they were all local residents; a number of them had arrived from the near Continent, like the pale-looking young man suffering from anaemia due to a lack of iron in his diet — he was of Flemish origin.

We stood for quite a while watching a video presentation showing the interrelation between the different phases of the Ice Age and the distribution of land and sea around southern Britain. While the planet had been getting gradually colder throughout the Miocene — a period of twenty million years - the onset of Northern Hemisphere glaciation proper, what we call 'The Ice Age', was about five hundred thousand years ago, and the most recent phase finished only eight thousand years ago. It was a process that took place in regular cycles over half a million years — indeed it is still going on and we find ourselves in an intermediate 'warm' period. Depending on the advance and retreat of the ice sheet there was either a land-bridge between England and the Continent, or open sea.

Sometimes it was a relatively narrow neck of land, but at other times the whole of the Channel and the lower part of the North Sea was land. This was the case as 'recently' as twenty thousand years ago. The animated images of the slow-moving mammoth, and woolly rhinoceros (whose fossilised remains have been uncovered at Black Rock) were of course a great success with a group of young school children, but what grabbed my attention was this repeated cycle of land and sea. As the ice sheets retreated from the maximum, so the sea rushed in, causing flooding on a catastrophic scale. The very last connection with the Continent was not at the Straits of Dover as one might suppose but further north where a large expanse of land stretched from what is now the coast of Norfolk and Lincolnshire across to the present Dutch coast. It has been named appropriately *Doggerland*, and when this was submerged by the sea at the end of the last Ice Age eight thousand years ago, Britain once again became an island.

It was impossible to watch this video presentation in Brighton Museum without relating it to Brexit.

***

> The language of the Northumbrians, and especially at York, is so sharp, grating, and unshapely that we southern men cannot understand what they say. I believe this is because they live so near to foreigners and aliens, who have a strange speech, and also because the kings of England live far from that country, being more inclined to the south, and if they go to the north country, it is always with an army and a great show of strength.

A slightly modernised version of a text written around 1380 by John of Trevisa, which in turn rests on a twelfth century text in Latin, when the Viking settlers in Danelaw would still have had an influence on the local dialect.

Brighton had beaten Everton (just) on Saturday. The others had gone back to the Continent on the Sunday, and Elly and I left early on Monday morning for the North, hoping to escape, if not the impending doom, at least the worst of the traffic on the M25. We made slow progress and it was raining heavily by the time we got to the M1. The exit signs sounded like a reading of the old First Division football sides: Coventry, Leicester, Derby, Nottingham, Sheffield, Leeds... and then we reached Scotch Corner — a name I remember from when Father used to hitchhike back from Cambridge. Here we turned off the motorway. The roar of traffic died away and we entered a different world — Teesdale — and for a full twenty miles not a single farmhouse, just hills upon hills, dry-stone walls, and sheep. This was remoteness. Eventually we got to the small town of Alston, where there was an old-fashioned road sign pointing to Brampton. Nearly there.

Me and the twins, June 1947

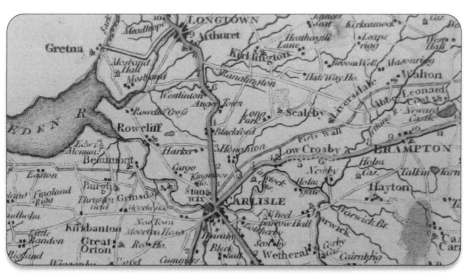

Detail from John Cary's map of Cumberland 1793.

On the wall at the White Cottage

The three of us with Mother

Father rowing on Talkin Tarn

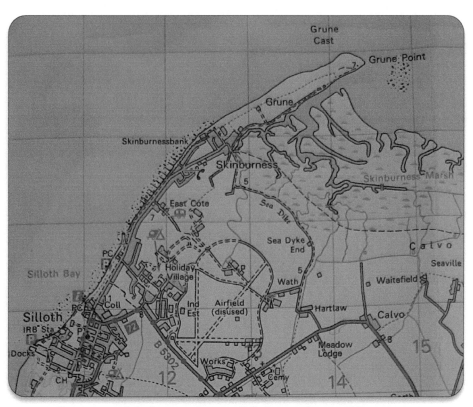

Crown copyright by permission of Ordnance Survey OS96681540

The Long House

The Happy Prince cover

Found at Grune Point

St Paul's Cathedral Choir c. 1930

Hayton school photograph 1951

CHOIR HOUSE,
DEAN'S COURT,
LONDON, E.C. 4.

_1 . 11 . 1951_

DEAR _Mrs Windross_,

　　　Your boy has been provisionally elected a Probationer for admission to the Choir School next Term. His election is subject to the receipt of a satisfactory Medical Certificate ('A'). He should be here at 5.30 p.m. on _Sat: Jan: 19th. 1952._

　　　Of the enclosed papers, 'A' and 'B' should be completed and forwarded to me as soon as possible; ' C ' and ' D ' should be brought by the boy when he comes to School; the others are for your careful attention. With regard to Form B, we are unable to keep boys in the Choir School who suffer from enuresis. It is much kinder and wiser for parents to refuse the probationership if their boy suffers from this complaint.

　　　The £10 (or £20) for Caution Money, referred to in the School Prospectus, are payable to me on or before the first day of Term. Money for "School Bank" may be deposited at the same time, and may be included in the same cheque.

　　　Please acknowledge receipt of this letter.

　　　　　I am,
　　　　　　　Yours faithfully,
　　　　　　　　A. JESSOP PRICE,
　　　　　　　　　Headmaster.

Admission to the Choir School

Tar Hut Cottage

Some of my fossils

Watercolour of Lewes race course by Mother

View of Black Cap, watercolour drawing by Father

Music for the Coronation

Coronation medal

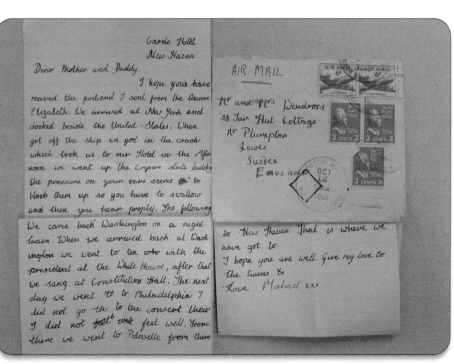

Letter home from USA

Programme for the Carnegie Hall concert

Painting by Eileen Price. Me on the right. Summer 1955

Frontispiece Book of Common Prayer 1662. Copyright British Museum

St Paul's showing dome and south transept

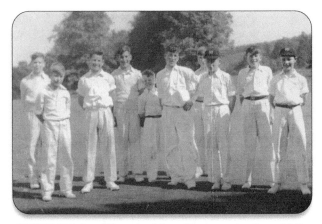

SPCCS Cricket XI 1956. Me with specs in the middle

Granma and Grandad arriving at Eastbourne 1955

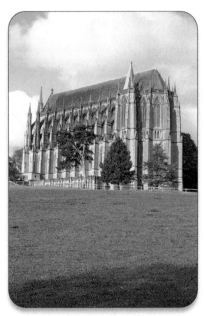

Lancing College Chapel

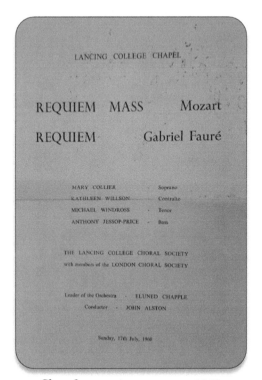

Chapel concert programme 1960

Gateway (1562) in Venusstraat

Spire of Antwerp Cathedral

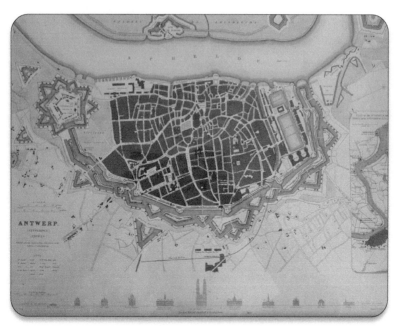

Map of Antwerp c.1850

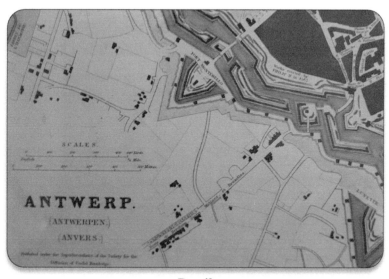

Detail

Verstegan title page. By courtesy of Museum Plantin Moretus

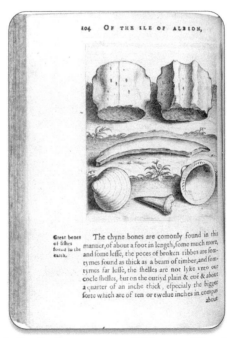

Verstegan's fossils. By courtesy of Museum Plantin Moretus

My poster for the Barrea exhibition

Trying my hand at street art. An
electricity box in Schoten

Kasteel van Schoten

My drainpipe telescope at Barrea

Edward I pendant

PART TWO

THE FAMILY CIRCLE

Chapter: Eight

THE SOLWAY FIRTH

The sense that the past is present in the landscape — that there is another world hovering just out of sight... [Thomas Williams, *Viking Britain*, 2018, p.xviii][21]

The 1861 census in Scotland was taken on Sunday 7 April. The forms had been distributed to all households beforehand and the name of each person who spent that night in the house had to be filled in, stating age and relation to the head of the house. They were to be collected on Monday morning.

"Would it be the returns you're wanting, Mr Stewart?" she said, answering the knock at the door. "I'll just fetch them for you".

The census was taken at ten yearly intervals and this was the third time she and her husband had filled them in. "How he has grown!" she thought, glancing at the small, framed photograph on the mantlepiece with James Clow her youngest child on her lap, hardly more than a baby.

"Thank you, Mrs Little. Have a good day — and don't forget to give my regards to Mr Little!"

Her husband — also a 'James Clow Little' — was born at Middlebie in 1809. She was a year younger and she was an Elliot — Barbara Elliot. The name had a ring to it. The Elliots were one of the *reiver families*, the Scottish border clans who had raided and plundered in the *debatable land* from medieval times down to the late sixteenth century, when the leaders were either exiled or executed. She was born twelve miles east of Middlebie in the village of Canonbie which lay within that small, disputed Anglo-Scottish enclave. They had married in 1834, prior to the birth of their first child. For a while they lived in Waterbeck, a small village in the parish of Middlebie, where in the 1837 county directory James Little is listed as a clog maker. In the 1841 census they were in Middlebie itself where he was both shopkeeper and clogger, together with their three children, Williamina, seven years old, John, five years old, and Mary, three. By 1851 they had three more children: Agnes, Robert and Jane, and had moved to nearby Ecclefechan, a much larger village. They were still living there in 1861, but in a bigger house on the High Street with six rooms, and eight-year-old James Clow, a bit of a late-comer, had now to be added to the list. Approaching fifty, Barbara Elliot was my great-great-grandmother.

***

I had often wondered as a boy looking out of the window at Gran's towards Dumfriesshire what the other side of the Solway would be like. Through the old pair of binoculars, I could sometimes catch the reflection of the sun on the windscreens of cars and at night the soft flickering of distant lights in the direction of Dumfries itself. This left a lot to the imagination, but Criffel was real enough — a hump-shaped block of granite nearly two thousand feet high, standing proudly after four hundred million years.

Proceeding westwards from Criffel, the landscape becomes more mountainous, and as the Solway Firth widens out into the Irish Sea so the coast grows more rugged, with a succession of rocky headlands and sandy bays. Travelling eastwards towards Annan, the shores are much more like Skinburness, with salt marshes and mud flats. Ecclefechan lies further back in a more undulating landscape, and when the light is right the narrowing Solway can be seen in the distance like a silver streak with the mountains of the English Lake District way beyond to the south.

In the early nineteenth century Ecclefechan was a bustling little town with a weekly market, a dozen or more shops, four inns, a parish school and, for those who could afford it, three fee-paying schools. It was also a stopping-place for the mail coach from London to Glasgow. Comparing Ecclefechan today with old photographs of the broad High Street, it has not changed that much over the years. The Commercial Hotel and the Bush Hotel are still there but have amalgamated into the 'Ecclefechan Hotel'. Next to it the building with the peculiar domed turret has survived, and on the opposite side of the street the two shops of Tennant and Clow are still recognisable, though the nameboards have gone.[22] Elly and I stood chatting to a young couple who were working on the front of their house further up the High Street. It had once been a tailor's shop and where they had removed the layers of paint above the front windows the shop owner's name was visible: 'Garthwaite'. We explained our interest and they kindly passed on to us a booklet with the title *Hoddom Parish memorial inscriptions*.

Ecclefechan attracts visitors as it is the birthplace of the writer Thomas Carlyle, who grew up here and attended the local school — an unlikely start for someone who grew to fame with works on a wider European canvas: *Schiller, German Literature, the French Revolution,* and *Frederick the Great.* The family home, the 'Arched House', was built by his father and uncle, and it has been carefully looked after by the National Trust for Scotland. The setting — a rather modest whitewashed building with a tree-lined burn running in front of it — had something almost central European about it.

Carlyle had moved to London long before 1853 when my great-grandfather James Clow 'junior' was born, but young James would certainly have seen the ageing writer when he paid his almost yearly visits to his home town. At the end of his life Carlyle got wind of the fact that his friends were pushing for a funeral in Westminster Abbey. He quashed this, stating that he wanted to be buried at Ecclefechan.[23]

***

As stated at the top of the 1861 census forms, Ecclefechan lies in the parish of Hoddom, so it is disconcerting to find no village called simply Hoddom. Still, you cannot miss Hoddom Castle, looming up from the woods above the river Annan — partly in ruins, boarded up, and closed to the public for safety reasons. It has a medieval aspect, though in fact it is sixteenth century, and a bit too grim to be called romantic — but perhaps that was just the weather. In the steadily falling rain we walked down the hill from the castle to Hoddom Bridge, built towards the middle of the eighteenth century to replace the ferry boat which hitherto had taken travellers across the river. With three graceful arches, it is one of a number of old bridges in these parts; the ones at Longtown (across the river Esk) and at Dumfries (across the Nith) have five and six arches, and they are all built in the local sandstone. From the bridge you can get down to the river itself, where there is a shoreline of flat stones. The water looks a dark reddish-brown and there is a swift current in midstream. There seems to be a natural harmony between the river and the sandstone, but geologically sandstone is associated with a hot, dry climate. The red sandstone used for building in Dumfriesshire (and for that matter in Cumberland too) is the result of conditions in the Permian period, two hundred and fifty million years ago, which were more like present-day Arizona — dry and desert-like. This layer of sandstone has been exposed through much more recent erosion processes and by water-courses which have eaten away the upper strata, creating the landscape we see now.

We followed a pathway along the northern bank of the river leading to a disused graveyard, known locally as 'Saint Kentigern's burial ground'. There is a tradition that this Dark-Age figure (also known as St Mungo — the patron saint of Glasgow) brought Christianity to the region and founded a monastery here around the year 600. The buildings disappeared ages ago, but the local population in the mid-nineteenth century would have been familiar with the story, and the fragments of carved sculpture and masonry that regularly turned up would have been a constant reminder of Hoddom's past, when it had been an important centre of learning.[24]

***

I had always known that Gran's maiden name was Little and that there was some connection with Ecclefechan. A preliminary search had quickly taken me to the online transcription of the 1861 census returns, which was a starting-point. Meanwhile I had also been in touch with the regional archives at the Ewart Library, Dumfries, to see if they could help me trace the Little family back to the first 1841 census and beyond. We were given an early appointment, and in the archive room, to our surprise, an envelope was handed over containing enough documentary and other evidence to draw up a family tree of both James Clow 'senior' and Barbara Elliot. Much of this evidence was in the form of photocopies of the original records, not transcriptions, so they contained additional information such as the occupation of the persons mentioned. Also present were the baptismal records from the parish registers for the pre-1841 period. Rather than going through the records bit by bit, it is simpler to start from the family trees.

There is no one 'standard practice' in drawing up family trees. Those in the history books at school — often in the appendix — were concerned with lineage within the royal family, since 'rightful claim to the throne' was an all-important factor. So, for instance, the 'Norman Line' had William the Conqueror at the top and branching from him his direct offspring — Robert, William Rufus, Henry, and Adela — and then a further branching showing their progeny, which included Maud and Stephen at the same level — rival claimants — thus helping to explain why there was a Civil War from 1135–1154. In this arrangement the top is *earlier*, the bottom *later* and the tree is intended to show the *descendants*. Another arrangement — the one we shall use here — starts at the bottom and fans out as it proceeds upwards. Again, the top is earlier and the bottom later, but the way we contemplate time is reversed; we are now looking back into the past — the aim being to show the *ancestors* of a particular person. Since it is primarily concerned with direct descent, it includes only part of a wider tree, but in our discussion, we shall sometimes include siblings and even cousins — the wider family circle.

William the Conqueror was put at the top of the tree because he was the founder of the line. Where we start in the second arrangement is a matter of choice. In fig.1 we have taken James Clow Little 'junior' as starting point. He was my great-grandfather — a concept easily grasped, and the last of the purely Scottish line. The same names occur time and again in our tree, so to avoid confusion let us call his father, James Clow Little 'senior' simply JCL:

— JCL (1809–1894) was the son of James Little (1782–1873) a farmer, and Mary Hunter Clow (1792–1872) both from Middlebie.

— This James Little was the son of Robert Little, a farmer, and Isabella Davidson, born c.1750, but no precise dates are known for either of them.

— Mary Hunter Clow was the daughter of James Clow 'in Land' (1748–?) a farmer from Middlebie and Helen Johnstone (c.1763–1839).

— James Clow 'in Land' was, in turn, the son of yet *another* James Clow in Land (1716–1805) and Mary Hunter (1723–1770).

Much of this is based on the Middlebie baptismal register where we find the following:

Fig.1

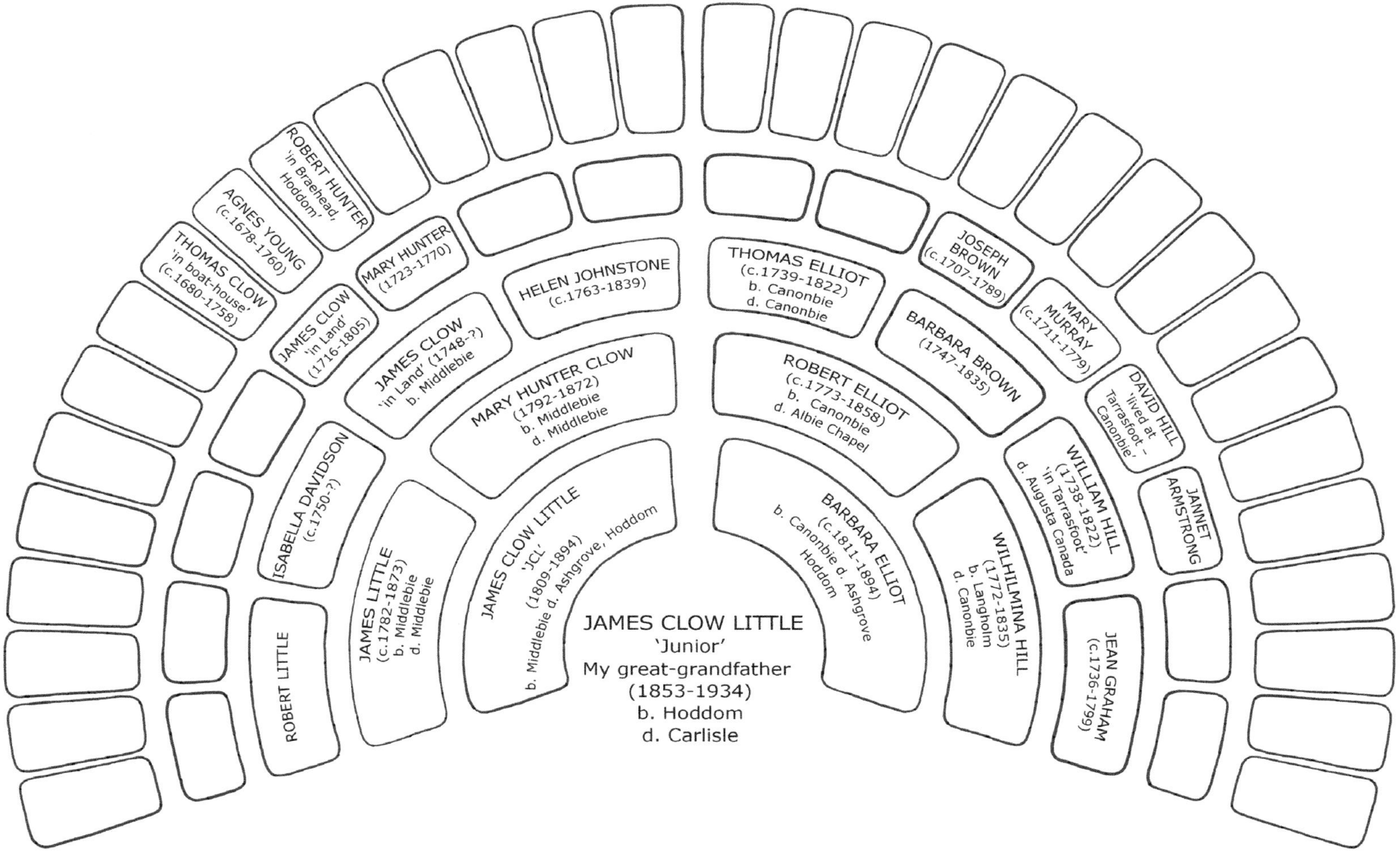

A genealogical fan chart containing the following names and details:

- DAVID HILL 'lived at Tarrasfoot – Canonbie'
- JANNET ARMSTRONG
- MARY MURRAY (c.1711-1779)
- WILLIAM HILL (1738-1822) 'in Tarrasfoot', d. Augusta Canada
- JEAN GRAHAM (c.1736-1799)
- JOSEPH BROWN (c.1707-1789)
- BARBARA BROWN (1747-1835)
- WILHILMINA HILL (1772-1835) b. Langholm d. Canonbie
- THOMAS ELLIOT (c.1739-1822) b. Canonbie d. Canonbie
- ROBERT ELLIOT (c.1773-1858) b. Canonbie d. Albie Chapel
- BARBARA ELLIOT (c.1811-1894) b. Canonbie d. Ashgrove Hoddom
- JAMES CLOW LITTLE 'Junior' My great-grandfather (1853-1934) b. Hoddom d. Carlisle
- HELEN JOHNSTONE (c.1763-1839)
- MARY HUNTER CLOW (1792-1872) b. Middlebie d. Middlebie
- JAMES CLOW LITTLE 'JCL' (1809-1894) b. Middlebie d. Ashgrove, Hoddom
- MARY HUNTER (1723-1770)
- JAMES CLOW 'in Land' (1748-?) d. Middlebie
- JAMES LITTLE (c.1782-1873) b. Middlebie d. Middlebie
- ROBERT HUNTER 'in Braehead, Hoddom'
- AGNES YOUNG (c.1678-1760)
- JAMES CLOW 'in Land' (1716-1805)
- ISABELLA DAVIDSON (c.1750-?)
- ROBERT LITTLE
- THOMAS CLOW 'in boat-house' (c.1680-1758)

1809, December 26th, James Little and his lawful wife Mary Clow born a son and baptized two weeks after — named James Clow (JCL). Entered and baptized by William Hunter, minister

1792, February 3rd, James Clow Land and his spouse had a daughter baptized Mary Hunter. (JCL's mother)

1748, October 23rd, James Clow of Land and ---Hunter his wife had a son baptized James. (JCL's maternal grandfather)

They were farmers from Middlebie, close to Ecclefechan. JCL's parents both lived long. His father's death certificate (Middlebie, 1873) states that he was ninety-one years of age. That of his mother (Middlebie, 1872) gives her age as seventy, but as we know the year of her birth, 1792, from her baptismal entry, this is incorrect. Besides, she had JCL in 1809, so she could not possibly have been born in 1802. She was in fact eighty when she died.

Longevity was something that Elly had noticed when researching her family history in Limburg. It seemed to go against the conventional view that in earlier times life was shorter than it is today. While life expectancy at the time of birth in the eighteenth century was much lower, this had largely to do with high infant mortality. Having survived infancy, the life expectancy curve rose sharply. In contrast, the life expectancy curve today is much flatter. The decline in infant mortality has been a major factor here (together with fewer deaths of women in childbirth, improved standards of hygiene, a better health service, vaccination, eradication of contagious diseases, and so forth). The early effects of medical improvement can be seen in a marked growth in the population of Britain in the late eighteenth and early nineteenth centuries, which, conveniently, helped provide a workforce for industry. Contemporary Scottish writers noticed this in the cities, though not always with optimism. Writing in 1774, the Scottish lawyer Henry Home, better known as Lord Kames, warns of the negative effects of over-population:

> The most deplorable effect of a great city, is the preventing of population, by shortening the lives of its inhabitants... The air of a populous city is infected by multitudes crowded together; and people seldom make out the usual time of life. [Lord Kames, *Sketches*, book III]

a sort of Malthusian check on over-population — mid-nineteenth century Glasgow had some of the worst slums in Europe. The families with which we are concerned lived in a rural environment and many reached the age of eighty and more. Kames divided his time between Edinburgh and his farm in Berwickshire and he died in 1782, at the age of eighty-four.

The family names (Little and Clow, etc.) were handed down via male descent, but there are two instances in the tree when a step is taken to preserve the family name of the woman. The first is in 1792 when James Clow (b.1748) gives his daughter the names 'Mary *Hunter* Clow'after his mother Mary Hunter, who had died in 1770. The second is in 1809 when James Little chooses to call his son 'James *Clow* Little' after his wife and her family. It was a fairly common practice for the family name of the wife to be used as a middle name for her offspring.

***

No feature of the landscape around Ecclefechan is more striking than the large number of kirkyards about, some of them with not a stone left of the kirk in which the dead worshipped, whose names are remembered on the mass of gravestones in each little "God's Acre". [J.M. Sloan, The Carlyle Country, 1904.]

At Hayton, the gravestones, originally clustered around the church, had spread outward until they were encroaching on the school playground, and we would sometimes watch the blacksmith digging a new grave. After that, gravestones rather dropped out of my life. I had always considered an interest in graves — even in the war cemeteries of 'Flanders Fields' — a bit quirky, nothing for me. And yet here we were, on the advice of Dumfries Library, plodding around in the burial grounds of Hoddom.

Standing there in the long, wet grass looking at these inscriptions it struck me how keen the locals had been to preserve their own family past for posterity. In St Kentigern's burial ground there were no gravestones directly related to my family, but there certainly were up the road at Hoddom Cross, closer to Ecclefechan. One gives a graphic account of the circumstances of a death of a more distant member of the family:

Archibald Little in Park, he fell a victim to the malice of William Douglas, late proprietor of Luce, who having threatened to murder him, actually perpetrated the same at Luce without any provocation, by shooting him with a pistol on the morning Friday 24th July 1795. He was 35 years, 3 months, eleven days. His corporeal remains were deposited here.

And the rather eccentric:

> Here lyes in hope of a joyful resurrection to eternal life, the body of Robert Clow, son to James Clow in Land, who died 6th September 1770 aged 33 years, one hour and a half.

One of the largest and most conspicuous memorials is a neoclassical construction in sandstone with side pillars and a triangular pediment:

> i.   This monument was erected 1779 by James Clow of Land, in memory of Mary Hunter his spouse. She was the daughter of Robert Hunter, late in Middleshaw and sister to John Hunter in Braehead of Hoddom. She was a virtuous wife, a loving mother and one esteemed by all that knew her....

which needs to be read together with a neighbouring stone:

> ii.   Here lyes Thomas Clow in Boat-House of Hoddom, who died 2nd of May 1758, aged 78 years. Also Agnes Young, his spouse who died 1st February 1760, aged 83 years. In memory of James Clow of Land, who died 8th May 1805, aged 89 years and 4 months. Also Mary Hunter, spouse to James Clow of Land, she died 7th June 1770 age 47 years and 8 months....

Delving into the family past was beginning to take on the character of an archaeological dig. We weren't digging (thankfully) but this now defunct burial ground was like a site preserving the chronology of a local community over a given period. Working backwards, Mary Hunter is the woman in whose memory James Clow of Land built the monument in (i). She died in 1770, so it was erected nine years after her death and he lived for another twenty-six years. While not stated, we can infer that this James Clow (born c.1716) was the son of Thomas Clow 'in Boat-House' and Agnes Young in (ii). Thomas was the ferryman responsible for transporting people across the river Annan before the bridge was built. He would have been born c.1680 and his wife Agnes c.1677. This is the only reference to the couple and there is no earlier record of the surname 'Clow' in the area (cf. the Regional Archives, Dumfries). What an evocative figure to have as a forefather!

***

We now turn to the maternal side. I have no record of the birth or baptism of Barbara Elliot, but her death certificate of 22 March 1894 states that she was the daughter of Robert Elliot, farmer, and Wilhilmina Elliot (maiden name Hill), and that she was eighty-three. She was born c.1811.

Her place of birth, Canonbie, is mentioned in the 1891 census returns. We do, however, have a record of her mother's birth and baptism:

> 1772. Born Aug 31 and Baptized Sept 6, Williamarmina (sic) Daughter lawful to Wm.Hill in Tarrasfoot & Jean Graham his spouse [Langholm Parish Registers]

A strange rendering of her name. I wondered whether this might have been because of its unfamiliarity. I had always thought of Wilhelmina as a typical Dutch name, but in former times variants of this name were also popular in Scotland, often 'Wilhilmina', and sometimes 'Williamina' both shortened to 'Mina' — just as in Holland.

Wilhilmina and Robert Elliot married in the parish of Canonbie:

> 1800. February 17th, Robt. Elliot and Mina (sic) Hill, Glinzierhead [Canonbie Parish Registers]

Glenzierhead is a couple of miles west of Canonbie. Barbara was their third child. From an inscription in Canonbie kirkyard we learn that there was a son, John, who died in 1826 aged twenty, and another son, Robert, who died in 1825 aged eleven. The same gravestone records the death of Barbara's mother, Wilhemina (sic), on 30 June 1835 aged sixty-two years and of her father, Robert Elliot, on 15 July 1858 aged eighty-five years.

Three years after Wilhilmina's death, Robert Elliot remarried:

> Elliot Robert and Elizabeth Beattie, both in this Parish were married 12th. October 1838 [Canonbie Parish Registers]

The new couple (not included in our family tree) are there in the 1841 census, living at Craigshaws with their daughter Mary Elliot aged three. Craigshaws is a hamlet in the vicinity of Waterbeck. Robert Elliot gives his occupation as 'farmer' and the household includes three young men, 'agricultural labourers', and two young female domestic servants.

This is confirmed in the 1851 census: still at Craigshaws, Mary Elliot, now thirteen, and again three farm labourers and one female domestic servant. On the basis of the census returns of 1851 it has been concluded that two-thirds of the farms in Great Britain were under 100 acres and the national average was 102 acres. There are regional differences. In Buckinghamshire, for instance, the average farm was 179 acres, whereas in Lancashire (close to the Pennines) it was only 41 acres.[25] In 1851 our Robert Elliot is 'a farmer of 326 acres' — roughly the size of Hyde Park.

The border region presents a very varied landscape; salt marshes around the estuary of the Esk, peat and moss bogs and ever more hilly landscape as one moves northwards from Canonbie towards Langholm and scattered in between farmland. Since the 'reiver economy' was based on stealing horses and cattle, there must have been enough around to make it worthwhile, and the castellated farmhouses in the region suggest that steps were taken to protect their valuable livestock.[26] Today, the farmland around Waterbeck looks very good. We do not know whether Robert Elliot's land was for sheep grazing, cattle, or crops like oats and barley, but farmers in the fertile region of Lowland Scotland were using more advanced agricultural methods than their counterparts on the English side of the border. There had been a remarkable transformation in Scottish agriculture in the latter part of the eighteenth century, with the introduction of fertilisers, crop-rotation and new crops, as well as improved breeds of cattle and better roads. While the 'Scottish Enlightenment' is best known for its philosophers and politico-economic theorists, transport and agriculture — a necessary basis for a state economy — were also on the agenda of discussion groups like the Edinburgh Select Society. Lord Kames (see above) was both a leading figure in the Scottish Enlightenment and a pioneer in scientific farm technology and management. In 1776, the same year that Adam Smith's *Wealth of Nations* appeared, he published a book entitled the *Gentleman Farmer*. One of those to read it and commend it to others was Thomas Jefferson, fellow agriculturalist and President of America.

Robert Elliot died in Albie Chapel, near Waterbeck, on 15 July 1858, five p.m. at the age of eighty-five, states the death certificate (thereby confirming the inscription above), so he was born c.1773. While his status is 'married' there is no mention of Elizabeth Beattie in the document, and we repeat that the gravestone in Canonbie churchyard couples him with his first wife Wilhilmina, who had died thirty-three years before. The informant is Thomas Elliot, son — with no further details — whom we have not encountered before.

Moving back a generation, Robert Elliot was the son of Thomas Elliot (c.1739–1822) and Barbara Brown (1747–1835). He appears to have been the eldest child; his three younger siblings all died in childhood according to yet another gravestone in Canonbie kirkyard:

In memory of James Elliot son to Thomas Elliot, smith in Glinzer, who died in 1786 aged 3 years. Also Isabel his daughter who died --- aged 2 years and 8 months. Also Elizabeth his daughter who died -- age ---. Also above Thomas Elliot who died January 21st, 1822, aged 82 years. And Barbara Brown his spouse who died 9th December 1835 aged 88 years.

Once again, if you survived infancy you stood a fair chance of making it to eighty and more.

From the above we can work out the years of birth, and we have the date of their marriage:

1768 Thomas Elliot and Barbara Brown were proclaimed in order to marry three several Lords Days and married November the eighteenth [Canonbie Parish Register]

We cannot go back beyond 1739 with any confidence in the Elliot line; however, Barbara Brown's parentage is recorded in the Canonbie parish register:

1747, March 15, Joseph Brown & Mary Murray in Glenzir had a daughter Barbara.

And in Canonbie Kirkyard there is a gravestone marking their deaths:

To the memory of Margaret (sic) Murray spouse to Joseph Brown in Glinzierhead who died January 24th, 1779, aged 67 years. Also above Joseph Brown who died June 27th, 1789, aged 82 years.

which means Mary (or Margaret) Murray was born c.1711 and Joseph Brown c.1707.

Turning once more to Barbara Elliot's mother's side: Williamina/ Wilhimina (1772–1835) was the daughter of William Hill (1738–1822) and Jean Graham (1736–1799). She was their third child — the two others having died in infancy shortly before she was born:

In memory of Jean Graham spouse to William Hill in New Woodhead who died May 1st, 1799. Also David their son who died April 26th, 1772, aged 8 years. Also Jennet their daughter who died in infancy. And the said William Hill, late tenant in New Woodhead who died at Augusta in Upper Canada June 20th, 1822, aged 84 years.

In the course of the nineteenth century nearly one million Scots crossed the Atlantic, and initially, the preferred destination was Canada, not the United States. Augusta lies on the St Lawrence in Ontario — a territory designated 'Upper Canada' in 1791.

We also have the baptismal record of William, which naturally gives his parents and confirms his birth date:

1738, December 19th David Hill and Jannet Armstrang had a lawful son baptised William. Witnesses Robert and John Armstrang.

Armstrang is a common variant of 'Armstrong' in the region. We pronounced the word 'strong' like that in Hayton, on the other side of the border. For us lads — always practising our 'Cumberland wrestling' — it was a word frequently used, and *strang*, once again, was the form in Anglo-Saxon times.

Notice that among Barbara Elliot's forebears there are Grahams and Armstrongs — all three reiver families. While the Elliots are well represented in the burial ground of Canonbie in the 'debatable land', there is just one pre-1855 gravestone with the name Elliot in the churchyards of Hoddom.

***

This, then, was the family into which James Clow Little 'junior', my great-grandfather, was born in 1853. His parents, JCL and Barbara Elliot, both lived to a ripe old age, and there are snippets of information which make his father, JCL, more than just a name. There had been a growing dissatisfaction towards the Church of Scotland in the early nineteenth century, leading to disruption and the setting up of 'Relief Presbyteries' which eventually merged in 1847 to become the United Presbyterian Church. JCL left the Church of Scotland at a certain point and became a prominent member in the United Presbyterian congregation of Ecclefechan. In a court case concerning the ringing of bells, he is described in May 1867, as the Chairman of the Board of Managers of the congregation, (cf. Regional Archives, Dumfries). In spite of the fact that he was a shopkeeper in Ecclefechan throughout the period, he seems to have moved house several times, although some of the changed addresses may be due to the renaming of the streets themselves. He rented all the shops where he worked. In the valuation roll of 1863, for instance, James Little, grocer, was renting a house and garden in Ecclefechan from Robert Carlyle of Waterbeck (the Carlyle family crop up all over the area): perhaps this was the six-room house mentioned in the 1861 census. Part of it might well have been used as a shop because it had previously been rented by Messrs Lothian, Parker and Co. of Carlisle, which is significant, for here we possibly have the first link between the Little family and Carlisle.

It is the moment to introduce a rather special photograph — an 'Ambrotype' on glass in a typical Victorian frame with a small oval window. In spite of its age and blemishes, the presence of the two persons is strongly felt. Perhaps this has to do with the medium — glass — which adds a certain transparency that photographs printed on card do not have, and we are accustomed to looking *through* windows and *into* mirrors. They really do seem to be looking out at us, serious and in their Sunday best. The photograph can be dated to c.1860, but, unfortunately, I was never told who the couple were. On the assumption that what is 'in the family' is 'of the family', we may well be looking at my great-great-grandparents, JCL (born 1809) and Barbara Elliot (born 1811).

My great-grandfather, James Clow Little 'junior', was the seventh and youngest child. The children's births spanned a twenty-year period from Williamina (1834) to James Clow himself (1853). It was a large family and as late as 1861 four of the children were still living at home, one being eight-year-old James. Apart from his immediate family, James Clow 'junior' would have known both his paternal grandparents Mary Hunter Clow (who died at the age of eighty in December 1872) and James Little (who died a few months later in April 1873, aged ninety-one).

***

On the other side of the Solway Firth in Cumberland, beyond Silloth and five miles inland from the coast is the village of Plumbland. It lies at the southern edge of the Solway Plain, where the countryside starts to get hilly as one proceeds towards Cockermouth and the Lake District. While Plumbland is a parish, it is the neighbouring village of Parsonby that has the church — similar to Hoddom and Ecclefechan.

Like the Littles at Ecclefechan, the Johnstones in Plumbland too were busy with their census returns on Sunday evening 7 April 1861. This was the second time and the information requested was almost the same as in 1851, the year of the Great Exhibition, when the following had been included:

John Johnstone — head of the family, aged 25, occupation — farmer of 63 acres, with one labourer, born Holme Cultram (c.1826).
Agnes — his wife, aged 35, born at Bowness (c.1816) Hannah — daughter, one month old, born at Plumbland Mary Home — servant aged 16, born in Scotby
Hannah Bateman — visitor, aged 25 from Bowness

176

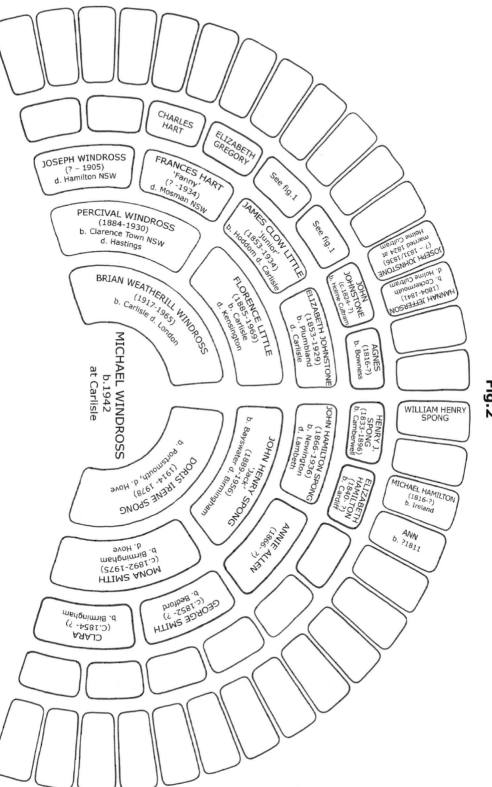

Fig.2

MICHAEL WINDROSS
b.1942
at Carlisle

BRIAN WEATHERILL WINDROSS
(1917-1965)
b. Carlisle d. London

PERCIVAL WINDROSS
(1884-1930)
b. Clarence Town NSW
d. Hastings

JOSEPH WINDROSS
(? – 1905)
d. Hamilton NSW

FRANCES HART
'Fanny'
(? -1934)
d. Mosman NSW

CHARLES HART

ELIZABETH GREGORY

See fig. 1

See fig. 1

FLORENCE LITTLE
(1885-1969)
b. Carlisle
d. Kensington

JAMES CLOW LITTLE
'junior'
(1853-1934)
b. Hoddom d. Carlisle

ELIZABETH JOHNSTONE
(1853-1929)
b. Plumbland
d. Carlisle

JOHN JOHNSTONE
(c.1824-?)
b. Holme Cultram

JOSEPH JOHNSTONE
(? – 1831/1836)
b. Cockermouth
d. Holme Cultram
married 1824 at
Holme Cultram

HANNAH JEFFERSON
(1804-1841)
d. Holme Cultram

AGNES
(1816-?)
b. Bowness

DORIS IRENE SPONG
(1914-1978)
b. Portsmouth d. Hove

JOHN HENRY SPONG
'Jack'
(1889-1956)
b. Bayswater d. Birmingham

JOHN HAMILTON SPONG
(1866-1936)
b. Newington
d. Lambeth

HENRY J. SPONG
(1833-1896)
b. Camberwell

WILLIAM HENRY SPONG

ELIZABETH HAMILTON
(1840- ?)
b. Cardiff

MICHAEL HAMILTON
(1816-?)
b. Ireland

ANN
b. ?1811

ANNIE ALLEN
(1866-?)

MONA SMITH
(c.1892-1975)
b. Birmingham
d. Hove

GEORGE SMITH
(c.1852-?)
b. Bedford

CLARA
(c.1854- ?)
b. Birmingham

John has a farm of 63 acres, a bit smaller than the national average, but still an area the size of St James's Park in London. Presumably, the land was in the parish of Plumbland, which is odd since his family was more connected to Holme Cultram — a name that has cropped up in connection with Skinburness back in the early fourteenth century. It is best known for its Abbey, part of a Cistercian monastery founded in 1150, which together with those at Carlisle and Lanercost must have formed an impressive trio. The village today is called Abbeytown. The Abbey — all that is left of the monastery — now serves as the parish church.

We do not have John's precise date of birth (see fig.2) but since he was baptised on 7 November 1824, he must have been a year older than stated in the 1851 census. He was the son of Joseph and Hannah Johnstone, who had married on 23 February 1824 at Holme Cultram. She was Hannah Maria Jefferson, born at Cockermouth on 1 May 1804 to John and Sarah Jefferson. This comes from an entry in the Society of Friends Register, where John Jefferson's occupation is 'currier' (described in John Walker's *Dictionary* of 1791 as 'one who dresses and pares leather for those who make shoes, and other things'). There are two deaths recorded in the Holme Cultram parish register under the name Joseph Johnstone: 19 April 1831 and 24 May 1836. Hannah Johnstone (née Jefferson) also died young, on 13 April 1841 at Holme Cultram and John Johnstone gave his first daughter the name Hannah after her.

His wife, Agnes Johnstone, was born at Bowness. There are two Bownesses in present-day Cumbria: Bowness-on-Windermere, in what was formerly called 'Westmoreland', which included the southern half of the Lake District, and Bowness-on-Solway, directly opposite Annan. The latter is where Agnes was born.

Now, in the 1861 returns, there are two daughters. Hannah is ten years old and her sister Elizabeth is almost eight, so she would have been born in 1853, and indeed she was baptised on 10 April of that year at Plumbland.

***

James Clow 'junior' is absent in the 1871 census, when the Little family is living in a three-room house in Academy Street, Ecclefechan. In the 1881 census he reappears, but in Carlisle, together with his wife Elizabeth and their two daughters. They live in the municipal ward of

Botchergate, at 15 Hart Street:

> James Little — head of the household, age 28, occupation 'Commercial Traveller, Groceries', born Scotland (c.1853) Elizabeth his wife, age 28, born Cumberland, Plumbland (c.1853)
> Mina - daughter, age 2, born Silloth (1879) and Agness (sic) — daughter, born Silloth (1880)

Here were my great-grandparents, and for the first time in my search I could personally relate to some of the information: Mina I had known briefly, and Carlisle and Silloth were of course both part of my boyhood. The names given to the daughters occur higher up the family tree; Mina could be named after Barbara Elliot's mother, Williamina, and Agnes after Elizabeth Johnstone's mother.

Entries in the census describe a momentary situation, but we shall try to build up a wider picture. James has moved from Ecclefechan to Cumberland; Elizabeth has moved too, though not so far. How did they meet each other? The birthplace of the two girls gives a lead, and, indeed, James and Elizabeth were married at Christ Church, Silloth, on 2 January 1878, as recorded in their marriage certificate:

> James Clow Little, age 25, bachelor, Merchant, living at Criffel Street, Silloth, son of James Clow Little, Merchant. Elizabeth Johnstone, age 24, spinster, Solway Street, Silloth, daughter of John Johnstone, Farmer.
> In the presence of Jas Smith and Hannah Johnstone.

But what had brought James Little to Silloth?

***

Lying beyond the popular Lake District, the tourist board likes to promote Carlisle as 'The Gateway to Scotland'. Carlisle was not part of William the Conqueror's England and when the castle was built by William Rufus it was to make a rather different statement to the Scots: this far, but no further.[27] From being something of an outpost in the extreme north of England, Carlisle grew to become a cathedral city and much later, a major junction in the national rail system. By 1842 there was a line from Carlisle to Newcastle, linking up with Teeside, and ten years later there was a main line both southwards to London, which fanned out *en route* into the industrial heartland of England, and northwards to Scotland where it split at the border — the eastern *Waverley Line* going to Edinburgh and the western *Caledonian Line* to Glasgow. It might have been far from London, but Carlisle was the English city closest to Glasgow — only ninety-four miles distant.

The Solway is known for its beauty and solitude — a paradise for birdwatchers — which again conceals the fact that by the mid-nineteenth century the west coast of Cumberland, owing to its mineral deposits, was also part of a regional railway network. These early railway projects were undertaken by private companies working on behalf of industrial concerns, such as the line running from the Cumbrian ports Maryport and Workington, with their coal mining and iron-ore industries, to Carlisle and beyond. In addition, a railway line was constructed from Carlisle to Port Carlisle (close by on the Solway, near Bowness) to replace an earlier canal and when a decision was later taken to build a new dock at Silloth for sea-going vessels, the railway was extended accordingly.

In 1855 a local farmer, John Ostle, had described it as "a very wild place... four farmhouses, that is all there is at Silloth" [quoted in *Solway Past and Present*, 14 August 2017]. In the detail of John Cary's map of Cumberland (1793), Skinburness is just visible under 'Wampool' — while Silloth is absent. All this changed with the building of the dock and the arrival of the railway in 1856; there was a sudden influx of people from outside — initially the labour force working on the construction of the dock and its installations, then the workers at the flour mill owned by Carr's of Carlisle, where grain brought by ship from Canada was unloaded. Thereafter, the character of the population began to change. This had to do with the rise of the English *seaside resort* — of which Brighton is the prototype.

In earlier times, no one had sought the sea for its beauty or for pleasure; the sea was something hostile and potentially dangerous, even for those who made a living from it. This was certainly borne out at Brighthelmston where heavy storms in the early eighteenth century had reduced what had been a flourishing little town to a struggling fishing village. Then in 1750 something happened — insignificant compared to the force of storms and tempests; Richard Russell, a medical doctor living not far from Brighthelmston at Lewes published a book extolling the benefits to be derived from sea-water bathing. This caught on, especially at Court with the Prince Regent and his entourage, who promptly moved for part of the year to Brighthelmston, bringing with them an army of hangers-on. His 'pleasure dome' — the Royal Pavilion — was created, and salt-water baths and even salt-water *bars* became all the rage. Soon 'bathing machines' were introduced for discrete sea-bathing, and sport, leisure, and entertainment had to be provided: horse-racing, cricket grounds, libraries, theatres, ballrooms, and gardens. Residential squares were laid out for wealthy visitors and to the east of the town, Royal Crescent, begun in 1798, was the first set of houses to be built *facing the sea*, and in the smaller side-streets there were hundreds of lodging houses to put up visitors. At the height of the season thirty-nine stagecoaches were running daily between Castle Square and London.

Then in 1841 came the railway, bringing the masses from the capital, and Brighton (as it was now called) gained the epithet 'London by the Sea'. While the train offered cheap travel to the seaside for day-trippers, it also signalled a rapid growth in the resident population. From forty thousand in 1841, it more than doubled by the end of the century, with a large lower-middle class made up of retail traders, shop-keepers of all sorts: grocers, hardware shops, printers, photographers, clothes shops, etc. as well as pub staff, restaurant staff, nurses, hospital staff, entertainers, and policemen — all providing services for the needs and requirements of this growing population.

The example of Brighton was repeated around the coast of England; Southend, Margate, Hastings, Worthing, Torquay, etc. in the South, Scarborough and particularly Blackpool in the North. Something similar happened at Silloth. With the building of the railway, it was quickly realised that Silloth too had potential as a seaside resort being so close to Carlisle, which itself was going through a period of prosperity and expansion. The railway company stood to profit if it provided passenger trains alongside its goods service. Silloth was a rather late example of the Victorian seaside resort, and a small one, but it had some of the familiar features. The town was laid out on a grid plan and construction began in 1860. It did not have the elegance of either Regency Kemp Town or Brunswick Town at Brighton, but its broad streets lined by terraced houses, stuccoed and some with shops on the ground floor, certainly breathed an air of well-being and Victorian respectability. There were salt-water baths, a church (Christ Church) and a public green taking up a large space between the town and the shoreline, and even a cricket ground. The 'wild place' had been tamed. The view across the Solway to Criffel becomes a nineteenth century landscape — like a Turner view of the Alps from some Swiss lakeside. Already in 1871 Silloth was described as a 'watering place to which many visitors resort during the summer months' — quite a difference from the earlier description by John Ostle — and many of the houses were built as lodging houses for this very purpose. But it was more than a 'watering place' — it was a town too. And as such it needed provisions. Contemporary photographs of Criffel Street show shop fronts and planted trees, with pedestrians strolling along the pavement, groups of women with hats and ankle-length skirts, and light summer blouses. There is nothing 'dour' or northern about it; could just as well be Hove or Worthing.[28]

Meanwhile work had been progressing on a final link in the railway network and in 1869 the 'Solway Junction Railway' was opened. This line ran from Kirtlebridge, a mile or so south of Ecclefechan, down to Annan and then across the narrow part of the Solway itself on a mile-long viaduct — at the time, the longest railway viaduct in Europe — to Bowness, where it linked up with the Carlisle to Silloth line. Once more, the driving force had been industry; by cutting out the loop to Carlisle it would considerably shorten the distance between the iron-ore mines of West Cumberland and the ironworks in Lanarkshire and Ayrshire. Soon a passenger service was added, and by 1870 there were four trains a day from Kirtlebridge to the Cumberland coast.

***

I think we have an answer to the question 'what was James Little doing in Silloth?' He did not come to Silloth for a change of air, nor to meet up with Elizabeth Johnstone. He would not have known her initially but given the town's small size they were almost bound to bump into each other since they were the same age and lived only a couple of hundred yards apart, in Criffel Street and Solway Street, as stated on their marriage certificate. No, the first attraction of Silloth for James Little was its commercial possibilities. He moved there to ply his trade, which he gives as 'a merchant'.

In subsequent documents (such as the 1881 census) he uses the term 'commercial traveller' to describe his job. The two, overlap. They both have to do with the movement of goods from a production source to the retailer, but historically the term 'merchant' had a wider significance referring to someone who coordinated trade, often involving the shipment of goods (wool, cloth, wine) from one country to another — hence the frequent reference to 'foreign merchants' as a distinct group. A merchant is someone who works on his own account, and he has a certain status in society, a mercantile society, in which he is the counterpart of the traditional landowner. His status is reflected in the way 'merchant' combines with a particular class of adjectives: 'a prominent merchant', 'a prosperous merchant', 'a wealthy merchant'.

In contrast, a 'commercial traveller' works for a company or a firm, from which he receives a salary, expenses, and possibly commission on top. He is involved in the movement of goods but in a narrower sense, and his job does not give him quite the same status. Hence 'commercial traveller' does not readily combine with the above adjectives; 'a successful commercial traveller', yes, but 'a wealthy commercial traveller' does not call to mind a recognisable type, and 'a prominent commercial traveller' sounds odd. The term 'commercial traveller' came into general use in the early nineteenth century and the rapid increase in the numbers of commercial travellers goes together with the expansion of the railway network: twenty thousand in 1871, forty thousand in 1881, and fifty thousand in 1891 (based on the census returns). In the public mind the job had a bit of a mixed image, and from early on professional associations were formed (notably the 'United Kingdom Commercial Travellers Association', established in 1883) to counter this rather negative perception and to establish their legitimacy and credentials against those who labelled themselves 'travellers' as a way of hiding their true identity.[29] Possibly aware of this, the instructions sent out with the forms for the 1881 census asked those who called themselves 'commercial traveller' to specify the sector or goods they were concerned with, just as 'farmers' were expected to say how many acres of land they had and whether they employed farm-hands.

This sort of information was out of place on a marriage certificate, and perhaps James felt uncomfortable with 'commercial traveller' for the occasion; it was at odds with the settled state of matrimony. We note that on the certificate James's father (JCL) is also a 'merchant' — in contrast to the earlier census returns where he is a 'shopkeeper and clogger' (1841), or simply a 'shopkeeper' (1871) and finally a 'grocer' (1881).

We can account for James's coming to Silloth, but what Elizabeth was doing there is a mystery. She might not have been in Silloth by herself. Her elder sister Hannah (who was a witness at her wedding) also got married in 1878 on 26 December, at the same church, to Robert Hutton, a farmer from Bridekirk — which in fact is much closer to her home in Plumbland. Both James and Elizabeth were present as witnesses, and the certificate states that Hannah's residence at the time of marriage is Silloth. Possibly the two daughters had left the family home at Plumbland together and lived for a while at the same address in Solway Street. Precisely where James and Elizabeth lived after their marriage is not yet known, but since Mina and Agnes were both born there in 1879 and 1880, it was in Silloth. The move to Hart Street in Carlisle would have been just in time for the 1881 census, for in *Arthur's Directory of Carlisle (1880)* we read: 'Hart Street — houses in course of erection'.

Carlisle was going through a period of growth, and especially in the area between Botchergate and Warwick Road, streets and squares were being constructed lined by terraced houses in neo-Georgian style. Hart Street was one of these. Whether James Little bought the house or rented it is not clear, but the family lived there for the next five years; *Moss's Post Office Directory of Carlisle (1884)* lists J. Little, commercial traveller, 15 Hart Street, and he is on the electoral roll of 1885–1886, at this same address. We know that in the meantime the two youngest daughters had been born in Carlisle, Jane in 1882 and Florence (my Gran) in September 1884. However, James is no longer on the electoral roll of 1887, and the family was not living in Carlisle according to the 1891 census. They had gone back to Scotland, as we can see from the census returns for the Parish of Hoddom (1891), which shows they were living on the High Street in Ecclefechan.

Among the family photographs that have come down to me, two are particularly relevant. The first is postcard size — a 'cabinet card' —

showing the whole family: James and Elizabeth behind and the four girls in front, with Gran in the middle. She is the youngest, not more than five years old. She is looking towards us, a bit camera-shy, and to reassure her, James has placed his hands on her shoulders. This is echoed by Elizabeth who has her hand on *his* right shoulder. It is a delightful family group. Judging by the age of the girls, the photograph dates from c.1890 when they were living in Ecclefechan. The embossed stamp shows that it was taken at the studio of Ovinius Davis, 52 West Nile Street, Glasgow. Why did they go all the way to Glasgow to get their photo taken?

Glasgow boasted some of the best photographers (or as they had it 'photographic artists') of the day, and Ovinius Davis, one of the longest established (1866) was perhaps the most prestigious. West Nile Street, where his studio was situated, also happened to be the centre of the tea trade in Glasgow. Recently, in 2007, the global tea trader James Finlay ended two hundred and fifty-seven years in Scotland; its headquarters were in West Nile Street. Tommy Lipton, born in the Gorbals in 1850, opened his first grocery shop in Glasgow in 1871 and in no time became a household name in Britain. Nineteenth-century Glasgow played a major role in the tea trade and the Clyde shipyards thrived on the building of the Tea Clippers, which replaced the more cumbersome East Indiamen. James Little specifies 'Commercial Traveller — *Tea*' in the census return of 1901. He clearly had strong links with Glasgow and especially with West Nile Street.

A second photograph shows four stylish young men, and on the left is a slightly younger James Little. Once again thought has gone into the way they are grouped; it comes across rather like a 'genre' painting of the period — members of a young gentlemen's club. This photograph is smaller — a 'carte de visite' — and the name of the studio is on the reverse: "By Her Majesty's Letters Patent, Turnbull & Sons, Artists, 75, Jamaica Street, Glasgow". They were at this address from 1865 to 1884. There is the additional information: "Licencees of Vander Weyd's patent process of finishing photographs". The process was patented in 1874, which gives us a ten-year window — 1874 to 1884.

By the 1880s James's route between Glasgow, Carlisle, and West Cumbria must have been well established, and there is no obvious advantage in moving back to Ecclefechan. Perhaps it was to be closer to his ageing parents (they were both in their late seventies and living at Ashgrove, just behind the High Street) but at a distance of a hundred and thirty years it is difficult to retrieve this sort of intimate information. When the parents died in 1894 — Barbara in March and JCL three months later — it was their son, James, who signed the death certificates; his mother's he signs 'James Little — Ecclefechan', but his father's (where the cause of death is 'heart disease — for several years') he signs James Little, Aglionby Street, Carlisle. He and his family had *already* moved back to Carlisle.

***

After a week in Dumfriesshire and the Solway coast, Elly and I were back in Carlisle too, where there was still work to do in the local studies room at the City Library and at the County Archives.

'Aglionby Street' I had always known, but I had never been there. Since it was only a short walk from the hotel where we were staying, we decided to take a look and make ourselves known to the present residents. We were in luck. Alan Cole and Gail Sirmais gave us a warm welcome and invited us in for a brief look around. They had tried to preserve the interiors as much as possible, so many of the original features were still there — the fireplaces, the woodwork, the plasterwork on the ceilings, and the distribution of the rooms. Furthermore, they had carefully looked after the documents related to the house — and these were bound to be of interest to us. We arranged to meet up in two days' time for morning coffee.

In the meantime, we took a breather and headed off in the direction of the museum, to check out the *'Amati Violin'* about which we had heard so much in the violin museum at Cremona on our way down to Barrea. One of the earliest violins in the world, dating from c.1560, it is kept in the oldest part of the museum, the original Tullie House, and displayed on its own in a glass case at the foot of the main staircase, but so close to the entrance that I suspect it is frequently overlooked by visitors.

Retracing our steps, we went into the Cathedral. The thing that is always mentioned about Carlisle Cathedral is that it is small in size. It has lost most of its nave through neglect, decay and very likely through deliberate damage done at the time of the Reformation and during the Civil War. Entering the building, however, it does not make this impression; the enormous bulk of the pillars in the truncated Norman nave give it an almost fortress-like appearance, and beyond the screen is the long Gothic chancel with its tiled floor and handsome choir stalls, culminating in the huge stained-glass window at the East End, which, together with that of York Minster, must be the finest in England. It is all on such a grand scale that the mind supplies what is missing.

I do not want to give a guided tour, but there are two objects in the Cathedral which I must mention. The first, in the North transept, is a finely carved wooden altarpiece — a reredos — made in 1520 by the Woodcarvers Guild in Antwerp. The second is in the chancel: a carved wooden pulpit in the 'mannerist' style dating from c.1550 which formerly stood in Sint-Andries Church in Antwerp — it was as if they had been waiting for us.

I should say straight away that there is (as far as I am aware) no special relationship between Carlisle Cathedral and Antwerp. These two objects are not part of the fabric but later imports. How objects have travelled around over time can sometimes open up historical insights, and their presence here is evidence of yet another trading link between England and the Low Countries; not one that has affected the course of events at a national economic level, like the Wool Trade, but certainly one that has left its mark on architectural design and interiors. It is what John Harris calls the trade in architectural salvages.[30]

In the 1560s, Antwerp and much of the Southern Netherlands experienced the *Beeldenstorm* (Iconoclastic Fury) with destruction of churches and monasteries and their precious works of art. Though a lot was lost, a lot could also be saved, like the magnificent *Adoration of the Lamb* triptych by Jan Van Eyck, which was dismantled and stored away and, in effect, forgotten. In this way important pieces survived. In the post-Napoleonic period, there was suddenly a market for them in England, where there had always been a lingering minority taste for the Gothic style; recycling linen-fold panelling, screens, and even choir-stalls into domestic interiors and suchlike. This became increasingly popular and fashionable towards the end of the eighteenth century, leading to the

Victorian 'Gothic Revival'.

The London salvage dealers, centred around Wardour Street, started buying from the Belgian dealers either 'for the trade' or on behalf of favoured clients. In this way the Antwerp pulpit was shipped across and installed at Hatley House, on the border of Cambridgeshire in 1826, and a large collection of continental woodwork with, most notably, the Antwerp altarpiece, ended up in St Wilfrid's Chapel, on Baron Brougham's estate near Penrith, Cumberland. Later the 'Brougham Triptych' — as it is known — was removed for safety to Carlisle Cathedral.[31]

***

We had arranged to meet up with Alan Cole at John Watt and Son's Coffee House in Bank Street, which started way back in 1865 — appropriate for the occasion. It was pouring down and Alan was carrying a hefty wad of documents wrapped in a plastic bag under his arm. It contained the complete deeds of the house.

We chatted for a while, sharing travel experiences — they had recently spent a fortnight in our part of Abruzzo. He suggested that we spend some time on our own going through the documents and photographing whatever we needed, so we retired to the Local Studies department at the Library and got on with it.

The ones that immediately concerned us were related to the purchase of Aglionby Street.

> Dated 2nd. May 1893. Mr J. Hewetson Brown to Mr James Little. **Conveyance** of a Freehold Mesouage or dwelling house situate in Aglionby Street in the City of Carlisle

There was also an indenture related to previous ownership, dated 2 November 1877, when the property is made over by the Mayor and Aldermen of the city, and John Henry Crichton (Viscount Crichton) to Henry Graham. Crichton was an Anglo-Irish peer and Conservative politician — what he was doing in the real estate business in Carlisle, I cannot say. This marks the arrival of the house on the property market.

It came back on the market in 1893 because Graham had defaulted on the repayment and Hewetson Brown exercises his prescribed powers and agrees the sale of the property with James Little, 'Commission Agent' of *Old Post Office Court*, in the city of Carlisle — for the sum of five hundred and twenty-five pounds.

Had James Little kept an address in Carlisle while they were in Ecclefechan? Old Post Office Court is tucked away in the city centre. What we see today is a two-storey brick terrace divided into four properties — at least there are four front doors. It looks mid-Victorian. Perhaps it served as a work address or for storing provisions; it certainly doesn't look like a prospective family home.

Once more we have a different term to describe his occupation — 'commission agent' — a middle-man between vendor and buyer, someone who sells the products of a firm on a commission basis (like a commercial traveller) often implying someone who operates across borders, which in a sense he was. Yet I cannot help thinking that it was used because it better suited the occasion!

The next batch of documents has to do with a loan of £400 which James Little took out on 11 January 1900 with the Scottish Temperance Life Assurance. He covenanted to pay off this sum (plus interest) at regular six-monthly intervals, during which time ownership of the property would pass to the Company to be returned to him (or his heirs) upon repayment. An indenture of 1 May 1912 recognises that the money has been fully repaid, and duly returns the property to James Little.

I made no attempt to find out what the loan was for, but it is interesting that he chose the Scottish Temperance Assurance, a relatively new insurance company founded in 1883, with its headquarters in Glasgow. Its directors had links with the Glasgow United Young Men's Christian Association and held a belief that temperance was not only good for the health, but good for business too… and it offered special terms for teetotallers!

Chapter: Nine

THE GREAT WAR

Percival Windross's War

Percival Windross arrived in Brisbane to enlist for military service overseas on 5 September 1914. Not a month had gone by since Britain's declaration of war on Germany after it refused to pull back its troops from neutral Belgium. Once the die was cast, the Triple Alliance and the Triple Entente — which had been forged to preserve the peace — committed the big powers to fighting each other.

This first stage in Percival's military service can be reconstructed from his file kept in the National Archives of Australia. Thirty years old, he was one of twenty thousand young Australian men to join up in the month of September. He filled in the attestation paper, stating his name and place of birth, nationality, occupation, and next of kin. We get a physical description: he is 5 feet 10 inches tall; he weighs 10 stone 13 lbs — so he is above average height and slim; he has a fair complexion, blue eyes, and light brown hair, and he is Church of England.

He subsequently underwent a medical examination and was found to show no sign of scrofula, syphilis, defective intelligence, haemorrhoids, unusually pendant testicle, 'or any other disease or physical defect calculated to make him unfit for the duties of a soldier' and was duly declared fit for active service and appointed to D company, 9th Infantry Battalion of the Australian Imperial Force (AIF) by the Commanding Officer, Lieutenant Colonel H.W. Lee on 9 September 1914.

Percival Windross was born in Clarence Town, New South Wales on 2 June 1884. He was the son of Joseph and Frances Windross. They had married in 1882 and had in total seven children. Percival later states that his father 'was English by birth', which might be taken to mean he was born in England, but since British sovereignty covered Australia in its entirety, all those born in Australia were automatically 'British by birth'. Joseph's parents were called William and Jane, but that is all I know about them.

Joseph Windross was a building contractor who regularly worked for the local government. From the *New South Wales Government Gazette*:

Postal and Electric Telegraphic Department. General Post Office, Sydney, 18 November 1895:

The contract of Mr W. Flannery, of Booral, for the supply of 50 ironbark poles, 46 ft. long and 25, 40 ft. long has been cancelled, and the tender of Mr. Joseph Windross, of East Maitland, accepted for the supply of the poles at a cost of £3 19s. 6d. for the 46-feet poles and £3 15s. per pole for the 40-feet poles

And again:

Department of Public Works, Sydney, 29th June 1896

Tenders have been accepted for the following Public Works: Bridges: over Sandy Creek, Road Cooranbong to Dora Creek Platform — J. Windross, East Maitland.

His early passing was announced in the *Newcastle Morning Herald and Miners' Advocate*, in March 1905:

Friends of Joseph Windross are invited to attend his funeral; to move from his late residence at Lindsay Street, Hamilton, this afternoon at two o' clock for the Church of England cemetery at Sandgate.

Frances (usually called Fanny) was born in Mudgee, New South Wales, in 1860, the daughter of Charles Hart, a 'cattle dealer', and Elizabeth Hart (formerly Gregory). After Joseph's death, the next mention I find of Fanny is in the electoral roll of the district Waratah of 1911. This has nothing to do with her being a widow or self-supporting woman; in 1901 the six separate Australian colonies had united to form the federal 'Commonwealth of Australia', and the following year Parliament passed the 'Commonwealth Franchise Act' which gave *all* British Subjects the right to vote.

Percival, the eldest of the seven children, had been working as a clerk, but he states that he is a 'mining engineer', and gives as his next of kin:

Fanny Windross 'Karnah' Waratah, N.S.W.

There was a short delay while men from different parts of Australia and New Zealand were assembled together to form the new ANZAC corps. Whatever their private reasons for volunteering — idealism, patriotism, the lure of adventure — when they finally set sail on 1 November, they had a shared idea of where they were heading: Europe, to serve on the Western Front. That soon changed. While they were at sea, Britain declared war on Turkey, and the ANZACS were disembarked when they reached Egypt, and given basic military training. The Eastern Mediterranean was soon to become another theatre of war and one forever associated with the ANZACS.[32]

The Gallipoli campaign was a disaster from beginning to end. Its aim was to secure the Dardanelles for allied shipping by destroying the Turkish army and guns positioned there, thereby opening up a second front in support of Russia. This could be achieved, said Winston Churchill, by a heavy naval bombardment on the Turkish positions; there was no need for ground troops. It failed. The Turkish troops were well positioned and much of the naval bombardment missed the targets. Moreover, they were better trained and equipped than the War Council in London had supposed and making good use of mines they sunk a number of British warships with heavy loss of life.

The response in London to this failure was a sudden U-turn. An Allied troop landing (British, French and ANZAC) at different beaches at Gallipoli, advancing separately on the Turkish positions, and having knocked them out, linking up again to advance further. But the Turks were professionals, whereas the Allied troops had virtually no combat experience.

The troops embarked for Gallipoli on board HMS *Queen*, *Beagle*, and *Colne*, and under cover of darkness, they were brought close to the beaches where they were transferred to smaller landing craft. The three battleships lay a mile or so out at sea ready to open up with their heavy guns in support.

The 9th Infantry Battalion — that of Percival — was on board HMS *Queen* and was among the first ashore at dawn on 25 April 1915. The men were quite unprepared for the horrors that confronted them. The terrain favoured the Turks, positioned high above the beaches; it was impossible for the Allies to advance on them, and any retreat was bound to be a bloody affair. All they could do was dig in where they stood. The command took a heavy toll and failed to re-order the troops under them. The commanding officer of the 9th, Lieutenant Colonel Lee, was carried from the beach, apparently with a badly sprained ankle, but others say he lost his nerve at the landing. In any case he was relieved of his command and transferred to London. The heavy casualties continued, particularly in June and July, when there were sustained Turkish attacks on their positions. On top of everything, there was sickness and disease to contend with due to the appalling conditions; contaminated food and water, the hot weather, rotting corpses and flies, resulting in dysentery, paratyphoid, bronchitis, and finally physical and mental breakdown. The Allies had four hundred and ninety thousand troops at Gallipoli: a hundred and eighty-seven thousand were killed or wounded, a hundred and ten thousand were evacuated sick. There were similar losses on the Turkish side.

Private Percival Windross survived three months at Gallipoli. He was evacuated on 5 August 1915 having suffered a 'total breakdown' and was taken on board the hospital ship *SS. Devanha* to Malta where he was admitted to the hospital at Valetta. From there he was transferred aboard *SS. Ascania* to London and was admitted to Fulham Military Hospital on the 23 September, suffering from a 'general breakdown' and 'dysentery'.

Among a total of sixty thousand ANZAC troops, there were twenty-six thousand battle casualties. The administration of the Defence Department in Melbourne must have been swamped with work, but they were prompt in notifying Fanny Windross by telegram about the whereabouts and condition of her son. Two telegrams were sent: the first on 16 August informing her that he had been invalided to Malta; the second on 22 September to let her know that he had now been sent to England, which is the day *before* he was actually admitted to hospital. I include a photographed copy of one of the letters that Fanny wrote to the Secretary of the Defence Department in return.

Another letter in the AIF records is dated 21 October 1915 from W.J. Weatherill of Courier Building, Queen Street, Brisbane addressed to Sir George H. Reid, Commonwealth High Commissioner, London. It is worth quoting in full:

> My dear Sir George,
>
> My cousin Private Percival Windross, has been invalided from Malta to a hospital in England, but which hospital I do not know. I had a sheepskin vest ready to send to him when I saw in the paper that he had been sent to

England from Malta. I have therefore taken the liberty of addressing the parcel containing this vest to your care, and I beg that you will be good enough to notify him that the parcel is at your office, or if possible, forward same to him, and I would therefore ask you to be good enough to complete the address and send the enclosed letter to him.

Apologising for troubling you in this matter, but I really did not know to whom else to apply, with kindest regards and trusting you are well, etc.

W.J. Weatherill

Sir George Reid (1845–1918) was born in Scotland, and his family had moved to Australia when he was a boy, where he later had a distinguished career as a politician. He was leader of the Free Trade Party from 1891–1908 and became the fourth Prime Minister of Australia from 1904–5. He was appointed Australia's first High Commissioner to Britain in 1910. But who was W.J. Weatherill?

We find an answer in the obituary that appeared in *The Week* (Brisbane, Friday, 23 March 1928):

Commander William J. Weatherill died on Sunday, 18 March, at his residence in Butler Street, Albion. The deceased gentleman who had been in failing health for some time, found an outlet for his abilities and energies from his profession as an accountant in many ways; but he never sought to enrich himself by any of these means. The good of the community was his great concern and the youth appealed to him strongest of all.

Commander Weatherill was a son of the late Captain W. Weatherill, who after his sea-going days, settled down at Newcastle, New South Wales, where for many years he was secretary of the marine board. Commander Weatherill was educated at Newcastle and Sydney. He began to earn his living in a colliery company's office. It was only natural that a love of nautical things would be strong in him. He therefore joined the naval brigade at Sydney. After a few years of travelling abroad he returned to Australia, where he came to Brisbane and joined the local marine brigade in which he rose to the position of Commander.

When the movement to establish the Institute of Social Service was afoot, Commander Weatherill took a keen interest in it, and it was due to him that the naval cadets were linked to that Institute. He also filled the responsible position of secretary of the Chamber of Commerce for years — and a most courteous official he was. At the same time, he was vice-consul for the United States here, and the Imperial Government honoured him by making him His Majesty's Trade Correspondent for Queensland… The late Commander's favourite pastime was yachting and of late years, motor boating. He had a fine motor yacht of his own.

I have still not discovered the family connection; the only clue seems to be in his early employment in a colliery company's office, which links him possibly to Joseph and Percival at Newcastle, NSW. Since he states that he is family, we shall add a little more detail. He was the son of William Foxton Weatherill (1819–1906) and Lucy Dorton Cole (1827–63). His father was born on 31 August 1819 at Whitby in Yorkshire, and his mother on 1 September 1827 at Plymouth, Devon. The two married, however, at the Cathedral Church, Gibraltar on 14 May 1846. (I have heard of MCC teams stopping off to play an unofficial cricket match at Gibraltar *en route* to Australia!) One can imagine all sorts of scenarios around this event — he was twenty-six while she was only nineteen, so they might have eloped; they could have met on the boat, or even in Gibraltar itself; they might have decided it was a wise thing to do for immigration procedures, but then again, we don't even know whether they were on their way to Australia in 1846.

Their first child, William John Weatherill, was, however, born on 23 August 1854 at Hexham, Newcastle, New South Wales — a full eight years after their marriage — and over the following eight years Lucy gave birth to seven more children, the last being Annie Laura Weatherill (1862–1941). Lucy died on 31 October 1863, 'after a short and painful illness, deeply regretted by a large circle of friends', says a death notice. William Foxton remarried in 1864 to Hebe Chippendall (1835–99) but they had no children.

The 'Institute of Social Service', highlighted in Weatherill's obituary, was founded by the Revd. Loyal Lincoln Wirt, born in Michigan on 3 March 1863.[33] Wirt had spent three years in Alaska, from 1898–1901, attending to the pastoral needs of miners in the Klondike Gold Rush where he suffered a physical breakdown, followed by a period of convalescence, mainly at sea. Arriving at Brisbane in 1905, he described it as 'a roaring frontier city with all of a city's problems': poverty, poor housing conditions, poor health, alcoholism, disease, vice, crime…' conditions we know from Charles Dickens and Henry Mayhew's Victorian London. I was surprised to find them here in burgeoning Australia, but then Brisbane had seen a spectacular growth in population from thirty-seven thousand in 1881 to more than one hundred thousand by 1900.

Wirt believed that physical deprivation produced moral depravity. The solution lay, not in a programme of moral reform, but in providing sufficient physical space and back up as an alternative to the 'sordid streets', 'the unhappy homes', and the 'pubs and drunkenness'. Having found a vacant four-storey factory building owned by the British Australian Tobacco Company, he set up the Institute, starting with a crèche for working mothers, and a free kindergarten, a working girls' guild, a young men's club, a gymnasium and a swimming pool. It advertised itself as 'Humanitarian' and in contrast to the YMCA, it did not provide any form of religious instruction. For financial backing Wirt turned to leading citizens, known philanthropists, one of whom was Commander William J. Weatherill. He was to take a leading role, becoming Treasurer, Honorary Secretary, and finally Managing Director of the Institute from 1909–12. Clearly a prominent figure in Brisbane of the time, he would have known the Commonwealth High Commissioner, Sir George Reid.

***

The London hospitals in the Great War were not able to cope with the vast numbers of casualties arriving back from the front. As we have seen, war casualties were not only the sick and wounded but also soldiers suffering from mental breakdowns. Initially the latter were discharged from the army and sent to lunatic asylums — but public protest put a stop to that. Private Windross did not stay long in hospital, two months at the most, just long enough to have started a relationship with Florence Little, who was a nurse at Fulham.

Soon after his admittance to hospital he filled in an application form (MT/393) seeking a commission in the British Regular Army for the period of the War. There is no date on the form, but a written date on the covering letter to the secretary at the War Office says 29 September, and it is stamped 1 October. (Note that this pre-dates Weatherill's letter to the High Commissioner, so the application seems to have been made on his own initiative.) The form asks whether he is of *pure European descent*. He also affirms that his nationality is 'British by birth', and that his father was an 'Englishman by birth'.

On 28 November, after a medical examination, Percival is declared fit for military service by Major John Robert Lee of the Royal Army Medical Corps, a reputed orthopaedic surgeon. Shortly after, on 6 December, he receives a certificate of good moral character, signed by none other than Lieutenant Colonel H.W. Lee — relieved of his command of the 9th Battalion in Gallipoli and now sitting behind a desk in London!

In a letter addressed to Lieutenant Matthews at the Furlough Department of the AIF in London dated 25 December 1915, Percival confirms that he has applied for a Commission in the Tunnelling Company of the Royal Engineers and that the War Office has assured him that the Commission would go through within four weeks — but not before the expiry date of his present furlough. He asks for an extension, to be posted to Aglionby Street, and adds: 'my fiancée lives in Carlisle, and I want to avoid the expense of travelling to and fro'. He and Florence married in Carlisle at New Year.

On 10 January, a letter arrived for Percival from the War Office, written in an impersonal, oblique style:

> I am directed to inform you that Private P. Windross, 9th Batt, AIF, has been appointed to a temporary 2nd. Lieutenancy in the Royal Engineers... and this will shortly be gazetted. He should proceed to Chatham and report to the Commandant, School of Military Engineering, with a view to proceeding overseas with a draft of Royal Engineers.

He was discharged from the AIF with a certificate of conduct and character — 'very good' — and on 16 January 1916, was duly gazetted. The profile of him in uniform, taken by 'T.E. Howe — Chatham' must date from then.

In a letter dated 8 March 1916, written from Aglionby Street and addressed to the same Lieutenant Matthews regarding correspondence intended for Percival, Florence writes:

> My husband, Percival Windross, was gazetted on Jan 16th. 1916 and is now with the BEF in France... It is difficult for me to get into direct communication with my husband as he is continually on the move and my letters are not reaching him....

He had embarked to join the British Expeditionary Force in Northern France on 5 February 1916. His subsequent service record — reg. no. 121608/13 — is kept at the National Archives at Kew [ref. WO 339/1069]

He was in 184th Tunnelling Company of the Royal Engineers (nicknamed 'the Moles') which was formed in February 1915 to counter German mining activities. They carried out underground work for mine placement and maintenance under German lines, digging trenches and subways for troop movement, for cables and for medical supplies. To ensure basic safety there was a need for men with experience in this kind of work and many coal miners from the South Wales coal fields were enlisted. A mining engineer like Percival Windross was in the right place. In spring 1916 the 184th were active along the Vimy Ridge situated midway between the towns of Arras and Lens, and in May they had to withstand a heavy German infantry attack. By September, they had largely completed this network of tunnels.

It was also at this stage that Percival Windross, now Captain, finished his active service in France due to sickness. He was diagnosed with 'neurasthenia' — similar to chronic fatigue syndrome — but after all he had been through it is more likely he was suffering from post-traumatic stress, then known as 'shell shock'. He embarked at Le Havre on the 20 August and arrived at Southampton the following day on the hospital ship HMS *Lanfranc*. Eight months later on the night of 17 April 1917, doing the same crossing from Le Havre to Southampton, the *Lanfranc* was torpedoed and forty lives were lost. He returned to Carlisle on leave of absence until 12 October, when his case was to come before a Medical Board. In a letter to the War Office on 29 September (written from Aglionby Street) Percival asks whether he might perhaps be examined by a medical board in Carlisle. Whether this took place or not, on 2 October 1916 he assumed duties with the Ministry of Munitions.

The rallying call in August 1914: 'Let's get this over and done with!' proved to be hollow rhetoric. Far from being home for Christmas the lads were very much stuck in their trenches in Northern France and Flanders. Reality began to take hold and news of a shortage of munitions led to a public outcry. In response to this the Government passed the 'Munitions of War Act' (1915) which called into being the new 'Ministry of Munitions' with the Chancellor, David Lloyd George as Minister in charge. This had far-reaching consequences: private factories were brought under state control and trade-union regulations suspended; health and safety conditions were investigated and improved — particularly in relation to the handling of dangerous chemicals. By the end of the war the Ministry was employing three million workers in over twenty thousand factories, the largest of which was close to Carlisle, at Gretna Green — the biggest munitions factory in Europe. The sudden arrival of thousands of navvies (mainly from Glasgow and Northern Ireland) in 1915 for construction work and the additional thousands of munitions workers — both men and women — in the small community of Gretna, had an enormous impact on neighbouring Carlisle.

Carlisle had a lively pub trade, and the workers from Gretna would descend on Carlisle after working hours and at weekends to make the most of it. It was feared that things were getting out of hand; drunkenness, sickness and absenteeism were beginning to affect output, thus undermining the war effort. Lloyd George stated, "we are fighting the Germans *and drink*" and in an effort to keep munition workers off the booze he introduced state management of brewing and pubs in Carlisle (and also in Gretna and Silloth) — three hundred and sixty-three licensed premises were taken over. The new pub managers were no longer landlords but civil servants on a fixed salary, the strength of alcohol was reduced, the sale of spirits restricted, buying 'rounds' was forbidden, hot drinks and food were encouraged and social table games were introduced. The effect was not immediate, nor was it achieved solely through the Government measures. Not surprisingly in a city with a long-term alcohol problem, the Temperance Society maintained a high profile throughout. But it definitely worked, judging by the steady decline in police figures for drunkenness, after a peak in 1916.[34]

Percival worked for the Ministry for more than two years, during which time he and Florence had a son — Brian Weatherill Windross — who was born in July 1917 at Carlisle. I had always associated my father's second name with the village Wetheral near Carlisle. It was only from reading the records that I realised he must have been named after W.J. Weatherill of Brisbane.

I mentioned above that Percival was the eldest of seven children. He had a brother, Brian, whose file I came across in the AIF records.

Private B. Windross enlisted on 15 May 1916 and was assigned to the 20th Battalion, light trench mortar battery. On 17 June 1918, the AIF contacted Fanny Windross, to inform her that her son Brian had been gassed in northern France, and again three days later to say he had been admitted to the Southern General Hospital Birmingham, England, 'gassed — severe'. Once more Fanny wrote a letter in reply. Brian survived and died much later in Taree, NSW, in 1964. I never heard his name mentioned at home, nor that of William Weatherill.

The Armistice came at eleven o'clock, 11 November 1918, and the guns fell silent on the Western Front. At St Paul's, the 'Great War' was still a living memory for many. In the British Legion parade at St Paul's on Remembrance Day there were as many veterans from the Great War marching past as there were from the Second World War. As choristers, we were daily reminded of it by the wooden panelling in the prayer-room bearing the names in gold lettering of the thirty-five old choristers who had fallen on the battlefields, and above it '*And all the trumpets sounded for them on the other side*' from Bunyan's 'Pilgrim's Progress'. Among them there were siblings and some had only recently left the Choir School. We were told to remove our caps as a sign of respect when we passed the Cenotaph in Whitehall on the number eleven bus. The number eleven was also the bus I took to get from St Paul's to Victoria station when I went home at the end of term, but I cannot remember whether or not I doffed my cap when I was sitting alone on the top deck.

***

I had expected Percival's military service to come to an end with the Armistice in 1918. His service record [WO 339/1069] shows that this was not the case. He continued working at the Ministry until 9 April 1919, and then he embarked for North Russia, the northernmost tip — Murmansk — on the Barents Sea, within the Arctic Circle. The Murmansk Deployment was part of the Allied intervention in the Russian Civil War after the collapse of the Eastern Front and the October Revolution. Troops had already been sent there in 1918, ostensibly to prevent the ice-free port of Murmansk with its installations and munitions depot from falling into the hands of the advancing Germans. But after the Soviets had signed the Brest-Litovsk treaty with Germany, the Allied troops remained in position to support the White Russian cause against the Bolsheviks. Another failure. Undermanned and with defections of White Russians to the other side, the best they could do was to cut their losses and beat a hasty retreat. On 12 October 1919, Murmansk was abandoned.

Percival Windross's military service officially came to an end on 9 November, almost a year after the Armistice, when he relinquished his commission, retaining the rank of Captain. He was mentioned in despatches from North Russia 'for valuable and distinguished services' (see *the London Gazette*, 3 February 1920). The photograph of him seated in his captain's uniform with swagger stick and the three pips clearly visible, from Wykeham Studios, was probably taken around this time.

Jack Spong's War

We had been listening together to an episode of *Pepys's Diaries* on the radio. Mother remarked to me:

"We're related to Mr Spong, you know."

The 'we' because she was a Spong. I never followed this up which I now regret, for it would be quite something to be related to Mr Spong: optical instrument maker, musician, and above all, a dear friend of Samuel Pepys:

> 17 January 1669: Thence to Whitehall, and there parting with Spong, a man that I mightily love for his plainness and his ingenuity.

The documentary evidence I have managed to assemble on this side of the family dates mainly from two hundred years later.

***

Jack Spong joined the Royal Navy in 1904. I have two documents relating to his years of service: one the Passing Certificate of Qualification in Seamanship for a Warrant Officer — the original, signed 6 May 1918; the other a copy of his entire naval record down to 1928, when he finally left the service. [National Archives, ADM363/271/70].

He was only just sixteen years old when he presented himself at Portsmouth. He had been working as a 'stable boy'. He was 5ft 3in tall, brown hair, with hazel-coloured eyes and a fresh complexion, and, even at that early age, he had a tattoo of an Eagle on his left arm. Two years later he had grown a bit and was now 5ft 6in — not very tall by today's standard, but average for the time.

John Henry Spong, my Grandad, was born on 18 July 1888, in Bayswater, London. He was baptised on 25 September at St Peter's Church, Bayswater. I refer to him as 'Jack' for that is what everyone called him, and it will save confusion because 'John H. Spongs' abound in the records.

The 1891 census shows his parents, John Spong and Annie Spong, at 17 Southwark Buildings Road, which should probably read 'Southwark Bridge Road'. His father is twenty-five, born in 1866 in Lambeth, occupation 'carriage driver'; his mother is also twenty-five and she too was born in Lambeth. Jack is of course included as is an elder sister, Amelia, born c.1887.

The 1901 census states that his father, John H. Spong, is thirty-four, born in Newington and his mother is thirty-seven — neither of which tallies with the previous returns. They are living at 102 Neate Street, in the parish of Camberwell. While the census aimed to be as accurate as possible, there are sometimes discrepancies in age and locality, since the enumerators were very much relying on what their informants told them. Moreover, the same locality can be referred to in different ways depending on whether we are talking about boroughs, districts, parishes, or simply some 'local' demarcation. Lambeth, Newington, Walworth, and Camberwell, all lie just south of the Thames and are adjacent to each other. Lambeth is itself a London Borough, while the other three all fall under the London Borough of Southwark. Add to this the fact that the busy roads crossing the river — Lambeth Bridge, Westminster Bridge, Waterloo Bridge, Blackfriars Bridge, Southwark Bridge, and London Bridge — converge here to form a junction commonly known as the 'Elephant and Castle'. Not surprisingly everyday usage finds its way into the census returns. Neate Street, by the way, lies between The Old Kent Road and Camberwell Road, on the edge of Brixton, which falls within the Borough of Lambeth.

Amelia is now thirteen and Jack eleven (which does not tally with his date of birth) and the names of six more children are included. Their father is working as a 'coachman — not domestic'. If we move on to the 1911 census, we see there are four more children, which means that in the space of nineteen years Annie Spong has given birth to twelve children, from Amelia 1888 to Elsie 1907. There was indeed another girl born on 6 August 1905 — Doris Victoria — but she died shortly after birth.

They are living at 4 Beaconsfield Mansions, Avenue Road, Camberwell. By this time Annie is forty-eight and several of the children have already left home; Jack had left seven years earlier and he is listed separately in the 1911 census: 'HMS *Bonaventura*, Portsmouth'. On 25 December (sic) 1910, at Clapham Parish Church, his elder sister Amelia Spong got married to Alexander William Cook, aged twenty-five, a 'motorman' and Jack was one of the witnesses. I remember 'Auntie Mill'. We visited her several times in Clapham and once she told me she was born 'when ducks wore drawers and Hyde Park was in a flower-pot'. In the sixties, her two sons, Len and Stan, were regular visitors at Lawrence Road. Len was, I believe, production manager at the *Daily Worker*.

***

Jack's service record shows he started at on-shore training stations before serving on warships. His first naval vessel was HMS *Edgar*, a cruiser launched in 1890, on which he was 'boy 1st class' for the period 1 February to 12 May 1906. This was followed by several months on land and then a longer period on HMS *Euryalus* — another armoured cruiser — on which he served from 14 February 1907 to 21 December 1909, first as 'ordinary seaman' and later as 'able seaman'. Then a shore establishment for five months, followed by a long spell on HMS *Bonaventura*, a second-class cruiser launched in 1892, from 27 May 1910 to 14 October 1912 — he was serving on this ship at the time of the 1911 census. The next, his first battleship, was HMS *Duncan*, from 24 May to 31 December 1913 on which he served as 'able seaman'.

On 3 September 1913, Jack Spong and Mona Smith married at Portsmouth Register Office. The marriage certificate states that he was twenty-four years old, and she twenty. His address is HMS *Duncan* and hers is 25 Albert Road, Southsea. His father's profession is now 'Royal Mail — Van Driver'. Until the turn of the century, the Royal Mail used horse-drawn carts — thousands of them — operated by private contractors. Experiments had been made in the 1890s using steam powered vehicles and in 1904 they began to use the internal combustion engine. It is quite possible that he had worked longer for the Royal Mail — that the 'carriage driver' of 1891 had simply become the 'van driver' of 1913.

On the marriage certificate Mona Smith's father is given as George

Smith, a 'Hydraulic Engineer' — and presumably Albert Road was where he lived too. However, I had always known that Granma's family was from Birmingham and in the slightly earlier 1911 census, we find mention of a Mona Smith, born c.1892 at Aston, Warwickshire, England, the daughter of George Smith and Clara Smith, who were then living at 20 Jardine Road, Aston, Birmingham. Her father is fifty-nine years old, born at Bedford c.1852, and he works as a 'Labourer in a Vinegar Brewery'. Her mother is fifty-seven, born in Birmingham c.1854. She had ten children: Leah, Beatrice, Olive, Nellie, Mona, Ethel, Winnie, Lenard, Bertie, and George — one child died in infancy. Many of these names I knew from my visits to Birmingham — indeed I can almost put a face on some of them. Mona is nineteen and works as a 'garment maker'. While the census return and the marriage certificate differ on the father's occupation, I am confident that the two documents refer to the same Mona Smith. There remains the question: why did the Smiths move from Birmingham to Portsmouth?

Jack Spong returned to HMS *Duncan* from 1 January to 3 June 1914 as 'leading seaman' — the period leading up to the outbreak of war. It was on his next ship that his war service proper began.

HMS *Queen* was one of the London-class 'pre-dreadnought' battleships delivered to the Royal Navy in 1902, with a main battery of four 12-inch guns (305 mm) and a top speed of eighteen knots. Jack Spong joined HMS *Queen* on 4 June 1914. In the weeks following the declaration of war she was part of the Dover Patrol, deployed off the coast of Belgium to bombard German forces attacking French positions.

It was in this first period of the war — just as the men of the 9th Battalion of the AIF in Brisbane were embarking for overseas service — that my mother, Doris Irene Spong, was born in Portsmouth, on 22 October 1914. Her first name recalls the baby girl who had died ten years earlier. On her birth certificate Jack Spong is mentioned as leading seaman on HMS *Queen* and it was her mother, Mona Spong, who on 13 November acted as informant. The address and place of birth are both 31 Waterloo Street — presumably, Mother was born at home.

***

While the official records provide a primary source of evidence for a family history, they do not exclude other types of evidence — oral traditions, letters, pictures and photographs. The latter — often interesting in themselves — sometimes need to be 'read' like documents and in turn, they may influence the way in which we read the documents themselves. Let us turn to two items that bring some respite from all these warships and official papers: two miniatures which belonged to Mother and have — as far as I know — come down through the family.

The first is a portrait of a young man in profile (on card) surrounded by a golden ring within a red velvet, circular frame. The high collar, side-whiskers and hair brushed casually forward give him that Regency look with a hint of the dandy about him — a Beau Brummell! I also have a larger photographic reproduction of this miniature in a plain wooden frame. Someone obviously thought it was worth going to the trouble of having a copy made, and fortunately the two have stayed together. The mount shows that the copy was done at Hudson Studios Ltd, Birmingham. They were a photographic firm with premises in the city centre in the 1890s — specialists in the enlargement of miniatures. Examining the back of the original miniature, I found handwritten 'Smith' and a row of numbers and letters. Probably this has to do with the placing of the order — that is, with the family rather than the identity of the sitter. But it could very well be both!

The second is of a young woman, almost front on, probably in her twenties, with dark curled hair in a style reminiscent of the Napoleonic period, which was again popular in late Victorian times. The miniature is oval and painted on ivory placed on what was is now very worn green velvet, with a decorative bronze frame around it. It bears a name, 'Eve Hamilton — 94', presumably the sitter, and not the artist. It was not a name I knew. The date (if that is what it is) is puzzling; the style does not look quite right for 1894, but 1794 would surprise me. When portraits are handed down from generation to generation, it is natural to assume a family connection.

If I had not known this second miniature and hence the name 'Eve Hamilton', I might well have missed something in Granma and Grandad's marriage certificate, where it is also stated that Jack's father is John *Hamilton* Spong — not 'John Henry' as I had supposed. 'Hamilton' is not a common first name. (The only example I can come up with is Hamilton Harty, the orchestral conductor who died in 1941, whose name I heard in childhood.) Could it have been passed down from an earlier surname in the family — in the same way as 'Clow' on the Scottish side of the family?

***

English census returns never mention the wife's maiden name, but marriage certificates do, and on 14 November 1886 in the Parish of St Mary's, Lambeth, John Hamilton Spong and Annie Allen were married. Her father is Thomas Allen, 'Carman' — a traditional name for a driver of horse-drawn vehicles, while his father is Henry James Spong, 'Coachman'.

We find an earlier reference to this John Hamilton in the census of 1881, where he is aged fourteen, son of Henry James Spong aged forty-seven and Elizabeth Spong aged forty. They are living at 50 Palatinate Pollock Road. John Hamilton is the second of five children and he has an elder brother, Henry, who is nineteen and works as a 'Carriage Driver'. His father, Henry James Spong, is an 'Omnibus Driver' and he was born 25 October 1833 and baptised at St George's, Camberwell on 1 December of that year. The 1881 census also states that Elizabeth Spong was born in Cardiff.

Could she have been a 'Hamilton'? To find out we chased up her marriage certificate, and there it is: Henry James Spong and Elizabeth *Hamilton* were married on 4 January 1860 at the Church of St George the Martyr, Southwark. This church has strong associations with Charles Dickens who lived nearby when his father spent time in the adjacent Marshalsea debtor's prison, and some of *Little Dorrit* (which appeared in serialised form between 1855 and 1857) is set here. The bridegroom, Henry James, is a 'Coach Driver', and his father, William Henry Spong, is a 'porter', while Elizabeth's father is Michael Hamilton, a 'mason'. In the 1861 census these two jobs come in the top twenty-five; there were one hundred and twenty-five thousand masons (or 'paviers/paviours'), and sixty-six thousand porters.

Henry James Spong and Elizabeth Hamilton had seven children born between 1862 and 1880, the second of whom was my great-grandfather John Hamilton Spong, born on 20 July 1866 in Newington. His birth certificate confirms that the original name of Elizabeth Spong was

'Hamilton' and that his father's occupation is 'Omnibus Driver'; they were living at 2 Havelock Cottages, Victory Place, Newington. Henry James passed away at Lambeth in 1896 at the age of sixty-three. John Hamilton, his son, died on 30 June 1936 at 46 Flaxman Road, Loughborough Junction, aged sixty-nine. He was apparently still working as a van driver for the GPO at the time of his death. I have no record of the death of either Elizabeth Hamilton or Annie Allen.

I can find little on the earlier generation mentioned in the 1860 marriage certificate. Nothing, in fact, on William Henry Spong, and just a little more on Elizabeth's side. Her father was Michael Hamilton, born in Ireland c.1816 and he had a brother, Thomas, born c.1813, also in Ireland. Young Michael appears to have fathered three children: John, born in 1833; a daughter, Ann, born in 1835; and Elizabeth, born in 1840 — all three born in Cardiff.

Elizabeth Hamilton turns up in the 1851 census for the parish of St George the Martyr, Southwark:

52 Webber Row:
Thomas Hamilton, head, 38, b. Ireland
Sarah Hamilton, wife, 51, b. City of London
Elizabeth, niece, 11, b. Wales, Cardiff

Elizabeth must have been living with her uncle and aunt — Thomas being Michael's brother. She could of course have been visiting, but the fact that she marries in this same parish nine years later makes this unlikely. One reference (in a transcription) mentions that Michael Hamilton's wife was called Ann (b. 1811) but nothing more about her is known; nor can I find out when and where Michael died. The Eve Hamilton in the miniature is proving very elusive.

In the 1861 census for Newington/Lambeth, shortly after their marriage, Henry James ('coach driver') and Elizabeth were living as 'lodgers' at the house of Thomas Quaife and his wife Elizabeth. Quaife is also a 'coach driver' (his wife is 'a servant'!), and another lodger, William Watson, is listed as 'coach driver' too — three coach drivers under one roof. A recurrent thread in the documents is the male occupation; there is a line running from before 1860 to 1911, starting with Henry James Spong who is an 'omnibus driver', through his sons Henry James, 'coach driver' (1861), 'carriage driver' (1881) and John Hamilton, 'carriage driver' (1891), later 'cabman' (1910) and 'cab driver' (1911). Furthermore, young Jack Spong prior to joining the Navy had been working as a stable-boy, and when John Hamilton's daughter Amelia marries in 1910, her husband, Alexander Cook is a 'motorman', while her sister Alice Louise marries Henry Smith in 1915, whose late father, Isaac Smith, was a 'horse keeper' — all related occupations.

***

The population of London had grown from one million eight hundred and seventy-three thousand in 1841 to four million two hundred and thirty-two thousand by 1891 and the boundaries expanded accordingly as more and more of the outlying parishes were sucked into the metropolis. Just as the Industrial Revolution depended on a nationwide railway system for the transport of raw materials and goods, so London needed an internal transport network for it to function efficiently. To give just one illustration: the railways would transport passengers and parcels, dropping them off at one of the major railway terminals — Paddington Station, Euston, King's Cross, Victoria, etc. — but from there they needed to be picked up and taken to a final destination; sometimes, indeed, this journey might be from one of the main stations to another, and in this way the London transport system performed a 'feeder' role for the railways. As far as transport within London itself is concerned, while there were innovations like the opening of the Metropolitan Underground Line in 1863, which certainly caught the public's imagination, on the whole it continued to depend on that time-honoured mode of transport: the horse-drawn carriage and its variant the horse-drawn omnibus.[35]

The Victorian Hansom Cab was a considerable improvement on the traditional four-wheeler Hackney Carriage in terms of speed and comfort. It also had two major advantages over the omnibus and tram — it did not work to a timetable nor did it follow a specified route; it was flexible and admirably suited to the requirements of customers who simply had to 'to hail a cab'.[36] Cabs were of course only for those who could afford them; most Londoners were pedestrians, and it is estimated that one hundred thousand people walked over London Bridge daily and seventy-five thousand over Blackfriars Bridge, but cabs were immensely popular, becoming almost emblematic of London. During the peak period 1884–1906, an average

209

of ten thousand licences were issued annually for Hansom Cab drivers. By 1914 this had dropped to only one thousand three hundred and ninety-one for horse-cabs, the other eight thousand were now for motor-cabs.[37]

The area where the Spongs lived was ideal for a cab-driver. Elephant and Castle was a hub from which the major roads across the Thames all radiated, giving ready access to the West End and the City. We do not know whether John Hamilton Spong had a personal contract with Royal Mail or worked for a firm who operated on their behalf, but the private cabby would have had a considerable outlay for the horse (or horses), the cab or carriage, and the running costs for stables, fodder, repairs and replacements. Keeping the job in the family would have alleviated the costs.

While writing these pages, my mind kept returning to the painting of Piccadilly (1890) by W.E. Norton, which I grew up with. The painting has three essential elements: Hansom Cab, horse-drawn omnibus and the London policeman in his cape. The policeman is more than just 'staffage' in the composition. Initially the job of the police was to maintain law and order, but by the period with which we are concerned, regulating the traffic had become the responsibility too of the Metropolitan Police.

***

On 3 March 1915 Jack was promoted to Petty Officer — a non-commissioned officer in charge of crew discipline and a crucial link between the men and the command — a responsible position on a battleship in wartime. HMS *Queen* was ordered to the Dardanelles. She left England on 13 March, arriving at Lemnos on 23 March, by which time the British had lost two battleships in the naval offensive against the Turks, and it was at this stage that the War Council in London had decided on an infantry landing. HMS *Queen* played an important part in the Gallipoli landings on 25 April, transporting, among others, the 9th Battalion of the AIF. Completely unknown to each other, my two grandfathers were on board the same ship at this juncture! Under the cover of darkness, the ANZACS were brought to within a couple of miles of the beaches. There as planned they clambered down the ropes into smaller landing craft and headed for the shore.

HMS *Queen* and the other battleships spent the next month off the coast in support of the forces ashore, bombarding the Turkish positions with their heavy guns. It made a deafening racket, but as in the earlier Dardanelles offensive, it had limited success. In late May she was withdrawn to bolster up the Italian fleet in the Adriatic.

Jack continued to serve on HMS *Queen* until 20 November 1916 — a total of two years one hundred and sixty-one days. After such a long time at sea, the next two years were mainly at onshore stations in Portsmouth. Olive, Mother's sister, was born during this time.

As a regular in the Royal Navy there was no reason for his naval career to finish when the War ended. The Armistice of 1918 was, as has often been pointed out, more a statement of intent than a final settlement; the details had still to be worked out in separately negotiated treaties, notably the Treaty of Versailles (1919). While hostilities had ceased on the Western Front, the situation was very different in Russia which had seen the collapse of the Eastern Front, the mutiny of the Russian army, and the Bolshevik Revolution in quick succession. The North Russian Expedition of 1918–19, showed how Britain was keen to exploit the situation so as to nip Bolshevism in the bud. In the Black Sea, a combination of factors came into play. While Turkey had been eliminated from the War, it remained a strategic focal point. French, British and Italian troops — fifty thousand of them plus heavy artillery — were sent to Constantinople to ensure that the Black Sea was kept open to international shipping and to prevent the Bolsheviks from gaining control of the Dardanelles.

Meanwhile, the White Russian Volunteer Army was positioned in Crimea, the Kerch Peninsula, and around the Sea of Azov, and it had to be given military support. At the same time, there were thousands of Russian refugees pouring into Crimea, waiting to be picked up and transported to safety, including, supposedly, members of the Russian Imperial Family — a cause of some personal concern to King George V of England.

Jack Spong's file shows that from 12 January 1919 to 30 September 1919 he was in the Black Sea serving as Petty Officer on HMS *Caesar*, a Majestic-class pre-dreadnought battleship, in support of naval operations against the Bolsheviks. In a letter from the High Commissioner, Admiral Somerset Calthorpe, to the Admiralty on 18 January 1919, there is mention of the arrival of HMS *Caesar* at Constantinople, but he adds that an additional battleship is needed 'to give a greater display of force'. HMS *Caesar* was mainly used as a depot-ship at Crimea, since the shallow water, especially in the Sea of Azov, prevented the operation of any ships bigger than a destroyer. But the Royal Navy certainly gave active support to the Volunteer Army; Crimea was recaptured in June, followed in August by Odessa, and in the autumn a White Russian army got two-thirds of the way to Moscow, before it was halted at Orel and forced to retreat.

By this time Jack Spong was serving as Chief Petty Officer on HMS *Emperor of India* — most likely the 'additional battleship' that Calthorpe had requested. Built by Vickers at Barrow-in-Furness and launched on 27 November 1913, she had served in the North Sea 4th Battle Squadron based at Scapa Flow and was active in the Black Sea from 1919–1921. She was the most up-to-date and the most heavily armed battleship Jack served on.

By a quirk of fate, my two grandfathers had both been on board the same battleship at Gallipoli, and now — two thousand miles apart — both ended their war service fighting the Bolsheviks. They never knew each other.

Chapter: Ten

THE INTER-BELLUM

James Little was in his sixties when the Great War broke out. He and Elizabeth continued to live at Aglionby Street with their two middle daughters, Agnes and Jane. Their eldest daughter Mina had married Thomas B. Hetherington, a master plumber and sanitary engineer, in 1909. The 1911 census shows they were living at Stanwix Bank, on the other side of the Eden bridge where the Scotland Road begins, with their two-year-old daughter Margaret. The Little's youngest daughter Florence was no longer living in Carlisle. In the 1911 census she is listed as a nurse at Huntingdon County Hospital where she is one of nine resident nurses: born in Carlisle, aged twenty-six and still single. Subsequent editions of the *Nursing Register* show that Huntingdon was where she did her training from 1908–12. Later, as we know, she worked at Fulham Military Hospital where she met Percival Windross, and the two married in January 1916.

In November 1919 James made a will in which he appoints his wife Elizabeth as the sole trustee, executor, and beneficiary, stating that after her decease the property should pass to the surviving daughters.

In March 1923 he makes a revised will in which he appoints his wife Elizabeth *and* his daughters Agnes and Jane as trustees and executors. Elizabeth Little died on 1 December 1929, aged seventy-five.

In February 1930, James adds a codicil to his will whereby Station Master Nicol Campbell and solicitor Horace Wills Mawson also become executors and trustees in the place of Elizabeth. Mr Campbell had been superintendent of the Citadel Station throughout the War and was a well-known figure in the city of Carlisle.

On 13 December 1934, James Little dies, aged eighty-two.

These are the bare facts. An obituary appeared in the *Cumberland News* on Saturday, 15 December 1934:

Mr James Little, Carlisle

We regret to announce the death, which occurred on Thursday at his residence in Aglionby Street, Carlisle, of Mr James Little, one of the oldest and most respected commercial travellers in the North-West.

Mr Little, who was 82 years old, had been in failing health for several months, but his end came suddenly. He had represented Messrs J. Robertson and Sons Ltd, preserve manufacturers, in Dumfries, Cumberland and the Furness district for 45 years, and retired about eight years ago. He was a man of very kindly disposition and took the keenest interest in helping young men who were beginning their careers 'on the road'.

Having been born at Ecclefechan, he was greatly interested in the works of Thomas Carlyle, and he was also very fond of Burns. His recreation was bowling, and he was one of the oldest members of the Carlisle Subscription Bowling Club. He was also an active Churchman, and at one time was a sidesman of Christ Church, Carlisle. His wife predeceased him five years ago. He is survived by four daughters.

The funeral will be at Carlisle Cemetery on Monday afternoon, following a service in Christ Church.

Michael French (2005:op. cit.) has discussed the contrast between the public's image of the 'commercial traveller' and their own self-image in the period 1860–1930. It remained an exclusively man's world (unlike, say, clerical work) and by the nature of the job it clashed rather with generally held views on the family unit and domesticity. To compensate for this, they developed a strong sense of professional identity and fellowship both on and off the road. There was a marked participation in what might be termed 'middlebrow' culture: whist drives, bowling, golf competitions, children's parties, and suchlike; there was an interest in literary culture too, but highly regional. Their professional associations were generally not political and were more often linked to Christian associations. Judging by his obituary, James Little was an embodiment of these principles.

The obituary also provides a little more information about his job. We knew that he was a commercial traveller in tea — which, by the way, explains the supply of tea-chests at Hayton — but not that he was representative for Robertson's Jam in the North-West. James Robertson had set up a factory in Stevenson Street, South Glasgow, producing marmalade in 1864. Tea and marmalade go well together and although neither uses home-grown products, each has its commercial roots in nineteenth-century Glasgow. James Little was connected to both.

***

What about Florence, Percival, and young Brian? In my preliminary search through the AIF file, I had come across a slightly later letter from the Base Records Office at Melbourne, 27 June 1922 to Fanny Windross, still living at Waratah, NSW:

> Dear Madam,
>
> I shall be much obliged if you will inform me whether communications forwarded to your son ex-AIF, subsequently served with Commission in the Imperial Army, addressed — 86 Victory Avenue, Gretna, Scotland, will reach him, as it is desired to forward the 1914/15 Star in respect of his services with the AIF....

At that stage I knew nothing about his subsequent service with the British Forces. The Gretna address was explained when I found he had been seconded to the munitions' factory at Gretna. After his service in North Russia, his demob papers [Officers Dispersal Unit 17 Nov 1919, London] also confirm that his permanent address is Victory Avenue, Gretna Green.

For the duration of the war normal family life for many had been put on hold and the 'war effort' had taken over. This was obviously so for the young men serving on the battlefield; less obvious perhaps is the way governments, with emergency powers, took over the lives of ordinary people (as at Carlisle) regimenting civilians as they did soldiers — all to serve the national cause. Family life had been disrupted and putting it back together again was not going to be easy — if indeed there was any going back to the way things were. Having relied on women to fill the men's places in factories, hospitals, schools and shops during the war, they could not simply turn the clock back.

Florence was one of those who had served as a nurse in the London military hospitals. She now had two small children: Brian four years old, and Allen two. And here we come to one of the more puzzling episodes in the family past. The two boys were brought up apart. Brian remained in Carlisle at Aglionby Street, where he was raised by his aunts, Agnes and Jane, while Allen went South with his mother Florence. It was not really talked about at home. Passing references were made, but no reasons were given. What about Brian's father, Percival Windross? I was always aware

215

that I had an Australian grandfather who was invalided out of the First World War, had been nursed by Gran, and had died shortly afterwards. But he was hardly ever mentioned and I was tactful enough not to bring it up.

A War Office communication giving the particulars of his Military Service. Dated 22 June 1927 is addressed to:

Captain P. Windross, 27 Cambria Road, Loughboro Junction, S.E.5.

I was surprised by this and somewhat disturbed — as far as I knew Gran had moved south to Hastings. Had they separated? The evidence is a bit thin, but I think we can conclude that they were at this address together.

In 1909, King's College Hospital moved to a new site at Denmark Hill. In WW1 it was requisitioned by the War Office to treat military casualties and after the war it served the mainly poor areas of Camberwell, Peckham and Brixton in South London — close to where the Spongs had lived. When I was a chorister, twice a week — on Monday mornings and Thursday afternoons — we took the train from Blackfriars station to Bellingham, a journey of some twenty minutes, where there were playing fields owned by the Federation of Boys' Clubs. Here we played football and cricket. I remember the elevated view we had of South London from the train, with the dome of St Paul's in the distance, and after all those years, the stations we stopped at on the way still roll off my tongue: Elephant and Castle, Denmark Hill, Crofton Park, Peckham Rye, Nunhead, and Catford. As we slowed down approaching Denmark Hill, we passed the hospital, and in sunny weather the patients would be sitting outside on their balconies. I did this journey with Mother and Gran in June 1956 when they came up for Sports Day — which would have taken Gran back to the late '20s when Allen was a chorister — and I remember her waving to the patients as we passed by. The hospital was only a couple of hundred yards from Cambria Road. She must have worked here.

**

As well as death and destruction, war also generates paperwork — mountains of it! The line of command on the ground is reproduced in reams of official documents, attestations, medical reports, appointments, promotions, reports, appeals, etc. This is what fills the archives and enables historians to reconstruct events. Not surprisingly there is a lull in the period following the Great War, as far as the daily life of the average citizen is concerned. All I have of my father from the period c.1920–35 when he was a boy in Carlisle, are a few photographs.

The earliest shows Brian and his younger brother Allen together as small boys. Brian, not more than six years old, takes a rather protective, brotherly pose. The photograph lacks a background and was taken in a studio.

There follow two family photographs taken in the backyard of Aglionby Street — neither very distinct. The first shows my father, about twelve years of age, astride a black Labrador with his mother (Gran) standing behind him. It must have been a snapshot and no one has taken the trouble to remove the stockings from the washing line! In the second, I cannot identify the boy on the left, but Brian is standing on the right — now in long trousers. The elderly gentleman in the middle is his grandfather, James Little, which makes this photograph rather special. It must date from c.1930.

The final photograph from the group shows my father standing alone in the street (literally!) in front of a parked car. Because of the sporting associations of the plus fours — golf in the 1930s — I always think of it as a convertible sports car, although this is not visible. He looks rather serious and he would have been sixteen or seventeen when it was taken.

These photographs amount to just a few fleeting seconds in those sixteen years. I knew he attended Carlisle Grammar School, but not much more. He talked about Jim Hetherington, his cousin, and Tommy Jones, who must have been his best friend, and how he collected stamps and bird's eggs. My urge to collect things was possibly stimulated by his enthusiasm and I was probably following in his footsteps when I started to visit Tullie House Museum. I never heard him talk about his grandparents — it was always 'my aunts'. His grandmother, Elizabeth Little, died in 1929 when he was twelve (which perhaps explains the presence of Florence on the photograph), and he would have been seventeen when James Little died in 1934. The photograph with the car must have been taken around this time. There is nothing in these images to suggest anything other than a comfortable middle-class upbringing. Which leaves me wondering: where did he get his love of jazz, his modernist taste in art and literature, and his left-wing political views?

It is not clear whether his heading South was to make a break with Carlisle or simply part of a regular pattern — visiting his mother and brother in Hastings (or to be precise, St. Leonards) where she was now a nurse in a residential care home. Allen was a chorister at St. Paul's Cathedral from September 1928 till the end of December 1933. He describes his time there in a memoir he wrote when he was ninety-two, shortly before his death, of which I have a copy. One of the amazing things is how *similar* life was at the Choir School in his time and mine. The cycle of events around the Cathedral and its music, the sports calendar, the daily round... everything, even the morning walk to the embankment, and the roller-skating in Carter Lane, notwithstanding the twenty-five years that had intervened, which of course included the Second World War. Perhaps that was it! Life returned to normal after the war, and in order to move on people moved back, they returned to the *status quo ante*. The choristers had been evacuated to Truro for five years, then it was back to Carter Lane, to the same building. Like cities, buildings help to create and preserve a particular pattern of life.

Allen kept strictly to his subject, but he does talk briefly about the end of term when he travels by train from Charing Cross down to Hastings for the holidays, and he mentions the return journey to London with his 'recently widowed' mother, and here we have a second piece of evidence suggesting that they had remained together: Percival Windross died at Hastings in 1930.

One thing is certain, by March 1937 Brian was a 'Young Communist', as we see in the photograph of him reading the *Daily Worker* of Saturday, March 6, 1937. It is a striking photograph with clever use of shadow, and its size (12 x 9 in) makes me think it might be a press photograph, or at any rate one taken by a press photographer. The day and month are legible, but not the date itself, though it can be worked out from the headlines: the holding of the Arganda Bridge, near Madrid, by an Anglo-Irish battalion in the Spanish Civil War, and the Labour gains in the London Council elections which were held on 4 March that year.

Brian arrived in Hastings somewhere post-1936, and it was here that he met Doris Spong.

***

We last heard of Jack Spong in the Black Sea region. While his ship, HMS *Emperor of India*, continued to operate in the Mediterranean Jack returned to Portsmouth, to HMS *Victory I* and *Excellent*, both shore establishments, until 14 October 1925, when he was transferred to HMS *Egmont*. There had been a number of ships of the line with that name. This one, however, was the Naval Headquarters at Fort Saint Angelo, Malta. The impressive hexagonal fortification still stands and commands the entrance to the grand harbour at Valetta. Medieval in origin, it was rebuilt in the sixteenth century and reconstructed in the 1690s. He was stationed here from 15 October 1925 until 26 February 1927, when he returned to Portsmouth — once again to *Victory I* and *Excellent*, where he served until July 1928. Throughout the entire period from 1914–28, Mona Spong and the two daughters had lived at Portsmouth and there will have been long periods when their father was away from home.

Mother had received a good education and her progress is evident in the school prizes which she received. From Trinity College of Music, December 1925, Doris Spong was awarded 2nd prize for 'Preparatory Theory' — no doubt a course organised by the school she was attending — Portsmouth Secondary School for Girls. The prize itself was Robert Schumann's 'Album for the Young' — a delightful set of piano pieces for young learners. Mother could play the piano, and although Allen and the St Paul's connection played such a major part in my childhood, I feel I never gave enough credit to Mother for awakening my musical instincts; the way we hummed and sang together from when I was small, in a simple everyday way, popular songs, folk songs, and things like *O for the Wings of a Dove* and *Jerusalem*. From the same school she received First Prize for form IVB for the school year 1927–28, when she was fourteen years old; a slim green, leather-bound volume of Palgrave's *Golden Treasury* of English poetry, with an embossed golden crest of the city of Portsmouth on the cover. There is yet another prize for music, but this time from Hastings High School on 30 October 1929, when she was fifteen; two volumes of *Studies in Modern Music* (from Schumann to Brahms) by D.H. Hadow — which I still love reading. Another little book from Mother is *At the King's Table* from the time of her confirmation in the church of St Ethelburga, St Leonards on 4 December 1930, when she would have been sixteen. She passed it on to me when I was confirmed at St Paul's in 1955.

These little books can be linked to a train of events. The Spongs moved from Portsmouth to Hastings in 1929. After twenty-four years, Jack Spong left the Royal Navy and joined the Royal Fleet Reserve (RFR) on 25 July 1928. This allowed a man to carry on in a civilian job provided he trained with the Fleet once a year, and with the added condition that he could be recalled to service in times of national emergency — which indeed is what happened in 1941. Their moving to Hastings might have to do with the fact that in June of that year Earl Jellicoe (Admiral of the Fleet) had opened the new British Legion headquarters at Hastings, for I remember references to both Granma and Grandad being involved with the bar there.[38] And lastly, the new Hastings High School for Girls was opened in 1929.

As a child, I often heard about Hastings both from my parents and from Gran. For me it had a kind of aura about it. Hastings in the '30s doubtless had its attractions, with its Art-Deco buildings along the seafront and the 'cricket week' — a regular part of the Sussex calendar — but it also had poverty, and in November 1934 slum clearance began in the Old Town disrupting the lives of hundreds. In late 1938 the Hastings branch of the Communist Party published a pamphlet called 'The Other Hastings' — pointing out there were two Boroughs of Hastings: one for the rich and one for the poor. There seems to have been a marked political polarisation in the town. On 14 April 1934, a local branch of the British Union of Fascists was set up and on 12 February 1936, Sir Oswald Mosely, leader of the movement, addressed a fascist meeting at the White Rock Pavilion while there was an anti-fascist protest going on outside [see *Hastings Chronicle*, 1900–49].

Brian Windross and Doris Spong were both members of the Young Communist League at Hastings. They married in Hastings in December 1938 [marriage certificate: 2b.56.] although they were no longer living there, as is shown by a number of letters addressed to Brian connected with work and employment.

The first is a letter of recommendation from the Associated Garage

Company Ltd. 242/246, Commercial Road, E.1., dated 9 November 1938:

> To those whom it may concern,
>
> This is to certify that Mr. B. Windross, of 134 Tollington Park, Stroud Green, N.4. has been employed by this company as book-keeper since May last, and that he now seeks other employment with a view to advancement. His work has been most satisfactory, and he has proved himself to be a diligent worker with a sound grip of his job. He is strictly honest, punctual, willing and reliable, and has gentlemanly manners and address.
>
> In his quest for advancement he carries with him my very best wishes, etc.

This letter just predates their marriage, and it makes clear that he has been living and working in London since May 1938.

The second is a letter to him personally (at the same address) from Taylor Staff Bureau (Employment Agents) of Chiswell House, 133-139 Finsbury Pavement, London E.C.2. dated 12 July 1939, informing him that they have received an inquiry from the Rom River Company (Westminster, S.W.2.) for a bookkeeper. They strongly advise him to apply, and to mention specifically Taylor Staff Bureau. The letter is signed by Mr. Taylor himself.

He applied and was promptly asked to come for an interview:

> We shall be glad if you will arrange to call and see Mr Bruce on Monday the 17th instant, as soon as possible after 6 o'clock at his private flat, 402 Grenville House, Dolphin Square, S.W.1. You should bring with you any original references you have. Yours faithfully, etc.

Dolphin Square — Europe's Greatest Residential Landmark on London's Riverside Drive is how it announced its opening on 25 November 1936. It attracted a wide range of persons, from minor royalty and politicians to opera singers and writers — "Not all tenants were respectable or well behaved", says Terry Gourvish in his *History of a Unique Building* (2014) — but most were well-off. Mr Bruce, with whom Brian had the interview, was one of the directors of the Rom River Company.

There was an immediate response from Head Office, Old Queen Street, Westminster:

> We confirm our interview and your appointment as a book-keeper in this office, at a salary of £3. 10 per week to start as from the 31st July next.

The outbreak of war was only six weeks away.

***

One of the measures introduced by the government to cope with the new situation was rationing, and with it came more paperwork — ration books. The first commodity to be rationed was petrol, immediately after the outbreak of the war in September 1939. Food rationing was officially introduced on 8 January 1940 by the Ministry of Food, nevertheless, I have a ration book issued to Doris Windross on 23 October 1939 — "on His Majesty's Service". The address was 134, Tollington Park, N.4. and pinned inside the book are the counterfoils of coupons in their two names, which confirms that both were living at this address at the time, although it has later been scratched out and replaced by 50 Florence Road, which was adjacent to Tollington Park.

A later 'ration book supplement' has also survived. It was issued at Carlisle by the Ministry of Food on 7 July 1941 to Doris Windross, Aglionby Street, Carlisle. It states: 'This is a Spare Book — you will be told how and when to use it' which does not seem to have happened since the book looks unused — except that the address has been changed to 10 Chatsworth Square — which, as we shall see, was where Gran was now living.

Other than these ration books, I have no record of Doris and Brian between 23 October 1939 and 7 July 1941 — indeed, the last date only indicates that Doris was living in Carlisle, which raises the question *why* she moved there.

The Blitz on London had started on 7 September 1940 and lasted until the following spring. The East End was particularly hard hit due to its proximity to the docks, but the rest of London suffered too, including the Finsbury Park-Stroud Green area of north London where they lived. From late October onwards cities like Birmingham and Coventry in the Midlands were being bombarded. Bristol and Southampton followed and in March 1941 Cardiff and Portsmouth suffered, as did Liverpool, Hull, Glasgow and also Belfast. The South-East of England, in the path of the bombers, did not escape either, and the first bomb to fall on Hastings was on 26 July 1940 — before the Blitz even started. The casualty figures give an overall picture; almost thirty thousand civilians died in London and slightly more than thirty thousand in the rest of Britain. If Doris left London for Carlisle in July 1941, it will not have been to escape the Blitz, for by then the greatest danger had passed.

As I said, the Carlisle ration book is only in Doris's name; we have no record of where Brian was over this period. He would certainly have fallen under the Armed Forces Act (1939) which introduced male conscription — more often than not into the infantry. The new conscripts were not ready for fighting yet, nor for being sent abroad, indeed there was no immediate plan or strategy for a large-scale offensive against Germany. A million and a half young men found themselves in army training camps up and down the country, and I assume that this was the case for Brian. If he was stationed somewhere 'up North', this would have been a reason for Doris to move to Carlisle.

By 1941 there had also been a change in the family circumstances. When James Little died in 1934, Aglionby Street had been left to the two daughters, Agnes and Jane, and this is where they were living according to the 1939 Register. But within a year they were both dead; Agnes died on 12 May 1940 and Jane on 24 November 1940. As we saw just now, Gran had also moved back to Carlisle around this time — to Chatsworth Square.

Perhaps these various strands each played a part in the move to Carlisle.

Chapter: Eleven

BRIAN WINDROSS'S WAR — FULL CIRCLE

Among the family papers that have come down to me are the letters my father wrote to my mother during his time of active military service from 1943–45. There are fifty letters in all, mostly written under strictly imposed conditions. Many have a declaration on the reverse:

'I certify on my honour that the contents of this letter contain nothing but private and family matters. B. Windross' and sometimes they were passed by a superior officer — 'the censor'. I hesitate to use the term 'war correspondence' because that awakens certain expectations about their content. There are few battle scenes as such, but there is a store of material that gives an insight into how one soldier experienced the war in Italy.

Naturally, he thinks about 'home' too; reflections on the past, thoughts about the present situation in Britain and what the future might bring. Every so often there are glimpses into the family past and occasionally comments linking up with some of my very earliest memories, for these letters were written after I was born. The more intimate side of his correspondence with Doris remains private.

These letters were passed on to me after Mother's death in 1978 by my brothers, who reckoned that I was the one most likely to do something with them. They lay for many years in a small compartment in the writing desk that Gran had given me back in 1964. At least they were kept in a safe place. It is only recently while working on this book that I have read them properly.

***

225

The earliest letters were written from infantry training camp in the UK. The first is from Fort George, Inverness-shire. He gives his number — 7672904 — which he kept of course throughout the war, and he is in a signals platoon. There is no reason to regard this as the 'first' in any sense other than it is the earliest letter to be preserved — he writes as though picking up the conversation again:

> What on earth are you going to do now Michael can crawl — suspend the bookcases from the ceiling?

It must have been early summer 1943. Then down to business:

> It seems that we are not to be posted without special War Office instruction — meanwhile we have to stay here.

His next letter is from Barrow-in-Furness, where he starts with routine domestic matters:

> The Rom River letter has not arrived yet. This letter is becoming a constant source of worry to me….

Four years later and he is still on the books of the Rom River Company.

> … but let's leave the sordid subject of finance. I think the army has developed my sense of beauty. Before I liked the 'Lake District' and the soft rolling curves of the Sussex Downs. But in both cases, the attraction was mainly associative. The 'Lake District' was my boyhood and my hopes of being a journalist. Sussex is linked up with holidays, during which I lived in a way in which I thought nature had really intended me — a cook, two servants & Mrs Beauchamp's super-something etc. etc. car. Now it's different with Furness Abbey and Inverness-shire — they are not connected with anything pleasant, yet Christ! How I like them.

A flippant backward glance at youthful expectations; but it does provide a rare glimpse into his boyhood which indeed sounds carefree and comfortable, especially Hastings, which he must have visited regularly. He goes on to mention St Paul's Cathedral as a building that he loves — quite apart from its associations:

> I used to see the dome from Clerkenwell Hill every morning when walking to work.

It is a long, rambling letter (written on paper with the logo of the YMCA 'with His Majesty's Forces' top left). Later he turns more to the immediate present:

> On Friday I shook up a brains trust during the Padré's Hour. Was congratulated by the Padré and one of the Signal's Officers — he is on the permanent staff and is a party member. We discussed world revolution over

a beer and waxed enthusiastic over the ignoble collapse of Fascist Italy.

The Brains Trust was a popular BBC radio programme in the '40s, where a panel of experts replied to the audience's questions. The reference to the collapse of Italy means the letter must have been written after 8 September 1943.

> Am I to go overseas? To me, it is not a Faulkneresque menace (after *three years* in the army one resembles rather one of Hemmingway's dumb oxen)

The time reference tells us that he has been in the army at least since autumn 1940, and two years later, my birth certificate mentions: '*Brian Weatherill Windross: Private, Royal Army Pay Corps*'.

The next letter is from Edinburgh and there is a rather more urgent tone to it:

> I'm to be transferred to a Primary Training Wing. The major had 16 of us in and said that we'd all have to go overseas or out, and that he wanted 8 volunteers. As I liked the other blokes who stepped forward, I volunteered. One bloke said I was a bloody fool & that I ought to have sat tight for the sake of my wife and child — but I don't think that's true. If I were to go back to civvy street now I don't think I'd be very much good to you and Michael. It's no good my calling for a Second Front in Europe, if I'm sitting in a soft job myself — and what the hell is a communist doing in a soft job in times like these!

At Barrow-in-Furness, (now from the HQ Coy Signals, Seaforth Highlanders, 10th Batt.):

> We've been issued with our tropical kit (but no topees — which means that we're not going to the Far East)… we don't really know much about what's happening. I feel okay and a bit excited.

After more delay and uncertainty:

> We are really off now — I wonder where? The Seaforths in the hut are as nice a bunch of blokes as I've met in the infantry. I hope we are able to keep together.

I was somewhat surprised to read this — 'comradeship' was not something I had associated with Father.

> We are now at sea, and I'm enjoying the voyage. I do four hours police duty each 24 and that's about all. (I bet some of my ancestors are turning in their graves). After coming below in the morning, I have a hot salt-water bath. Luxury! — it's quite my favourite bit of the ocean. There's not much more I'm allowed to say….

I am puzzled by the aside: which 'ancestors' and why would they be turning in their graves? Was it a reference to the hard-working farmers in the border country, perhaps to the diligence with which James Little had pursued his occupation? Could it have been a passing reference to his own father, Percival, who had also sailed to war and to the horrors of Gallipoli — while he, in contrast, is taking it easy? There are parallels in the course of events which overtook the two of them, as we shall shortly see. As to the likely destination, even for someone like Brian who read the newspapers and kept abreast of events, it would have been largely guesswork.

For Britain, the first eighteen months of the War had been fought mainly on the sea and in the air. There had been engagements on land — so badly coordinated that they cannot be called 'campaigns'— and they had all been military failures, leaving Germany in full control of the countries it had invaded: Poland, the Baltic States, Denmark and Norway, the Low Countries and France. As yet there was no plan for an infantry attack on Germany, and for its part, Germany had a mixed attitude towards a military invasion of Britain. For that to happen, the Royal Navy and Royal Air Force would have to be defeated first. This they failed to do. During the 'Battle of Britain' in August and September 1940, the RAF fighter planes gained the upper hand and inflicted heavy losses in both lives and planes on the German Luftwaffe, and the subsequent Blitz — the heavy bombing of London and other cities — though causing damage and suffering, did not lead to surrender.

Two things happened in the second half of 1941 that were to alter the course of the War. Hitler attacked Russia, as he had always planned to do, and the United States entered the conflict. From then on, the final outcome was never really in doubt. For the time being, however, Roosevelt and Churchill decided to postpone any cross-channel invasion of Western Europe and to turn their attention instead to the Mediterranean and North Africa. There was a lot of political and military disagreement about this. The British had a long-term interest in the Mediterranean — political, economic, and strategic — and in military terms it would help divert German forces away from the Eastern front, thereby stretching their resources to breaking point. That was the theory at any rate. A re-equipped Eighth Army (most of the materiel had to be sent via the Cape) fought and won the battle of El Alamein in late '42, and the Allied army, with air and naval support, had defeated the Axis forces in North Africa by April 1943 when two hundred and fifty thousand German and Italian troops surrendered. The attack on Italy ('the soft under-belly of the axis') began on 9 July 1943, with the invasion of Sicily.

***

I have arrived here in N. Africa… after disembarkation we had a 72-hour train journey in cattle trucks — 30 men per cattle truck….

From an 'airgraph' (I borrow the word from him). This is the first official letter bearing the stamp 'passed by the censor' on it. It gives name, rank, Seaforth Highlanders, 6th battalion and then BNAF ('British North African Force'). It is dated 30/12/43 and addressed to Mrs D. Windross, 2 Montreal Street Carlisle.

2/1/44: I've sent off an airgraph, but as this may reach you first, I repeat myself. I am now in a camp in N. Africa, miles from anywhere — from our tents we have a fine view of the mountains and the Med. I like the blokes in our tent. The chap next to me has just written something bloody funny — but as this is a 'family letter' I'd better keep it to my next one. I'll alternate 'family letters' with 'not for publication' ones! I haven't received any mail yet, but I'm longing to hear about your Christmas and the development of the infant prodigy.

Three weeks later, his battalion, part of the 5th Army, sailed from North Africa to the heel of Italy, in the vicinity of Taranto:

25/1/44: I have now started the 'Grand Tour' — Italy being my starting point. There is so little I am allowed to say, that I must confine my remarks to generalities. It's interesting to be treading on the soil which bred Fascism and it gives me a good deal of satisfaction — so much for the 'New Roman Empire'! Incredible when one looks at the peasants and the civilian population. The peasants are much as Silone has described them in 'Fontamara'. Poor, friendly, hospitable. Our lads mix well with them and, in turn, they like us. Last night we called on a wood worker and sat round his fire for a short time. His four buxom daughters stood round the bench and giggled at us. Their teeth flashed in the firelight and we were glad of the warmth. The fire soon died down and the lamp needed oil — when this happens in a poor family it is time for bed — so, as we had nothing to give them and they nothing to give us, we shook hands politely and went out into the cold, clear night.

I would like to paint one more picture for you. In the background hills capped with snow, at the foot of which gleam the white houses of a village. A fertile valley in the hot midday sun, the fields misty as the dew is lifted. Along the road come carts drawn by splendid white oxen followed by a lighter cart drawn by sprightly looking horses. The drivers swear and crack their whips. At the side of the road are women working in the fields, two standing with baskets on their heads, a third is hoeing. They are barefooted and big breasted, they wear bright-coloured scarves and shawls; they seem as old as time; a classical frieze.

The war news keeps me cheerful, but a letter from you would complete my happiness.

And there is an added P.S. at the top of the page:

Just received my first letter!

Notice he writes 'Italy being my starting point' — as though he were expecting events to move on at a steady pace.

Here I must recapitulate. Having secured Sicily, the Allied invasion of Italy in early September went well at first and the Italian army quickly surrendered. A landing by U.S. forces at Salerno further north on 9 September, however, soon ran into trouble. Hitler was determined that the German troops, under the command of Field Marshal Albert Kesselring, should hold out. Their defence forces had been set up along three lines: the Bernhard Line, the Victor Line, and the Gustav Line. Together, the military fortifications and the Apennines constituted a major obstacle to the Allied advance, while favouring the defensive positions of the Germans, and by winter the offensive had ground to a halt.

The planning of the Anzio landings (code-named 'Operation Shingle') began on 1 January 1944.[39] The idea had been championed by Winston Churchill, who was getting frustrated by the failure of the Allied army to capitalise on its initial successes. It was argued that, provided the troops were landed in the correct place, a surprise attack should do the trick; the German field defences were thinly manned and would offer nothing too difficult for the American Major General, John Lucas. Some of the General Staff in London had serious misgivings, however, and it had not escaped them that it was the same Churchill who had proposed the Gallipoli landings in 1915.

Later, Lucas's doubts, coupled with a feeling of responsibility towards his men, led to delay and inertia on the beachhead when a quick advance was called for, and he was removed from his post in late February (Clark op. cit. p.199). By then Anzio had become a death trap, with conditions resembling the trenches of the Great War and persistent artillery bombardment.

16/2/43 [44!] CMF 'Central Mediterranean Force'

It must be at least a week since I wrote — here one tends to lose track of time. I have been amongst some of the fireworks — our life resembles that of foxes rather than of human beings. I am getting the experience straight and undiluted as a private on the line. Here the sur-real *is* part of the real. A night patrol. An artificial arm lying in the bushes, the flash and cracking of artillery, a lamb, lost and frightened crying like a child (someone picks him up), the village on the hill gleams white in the moonlight, cold and silent and classical (we have been there before with Chirico), there are figures lying on the path, but one doesn't look too closely, their posture is strange (one remembers Spencer's 'Resurrection Morn') and, of all things, a dead donkey! Waiting to be lifted onto a grand-piano by Dali.

In the middle of the night the mind plays strange tricks — I feel that I am actually tiptoeing downstairs to the kitchen to make myself a hot, sweet mug of cocoa. I wonder if when I arrive at Carlisle station, I'll brew up tea on the platform from force of habit!

In the morning, at dawn, the snow-caps on the hill seem to be floating in space. Then as it gets lighter, the outlines of the landscape fill in. Then someone shouts 'breakfast'. The porridge, cooked the Scots way with salt and no milk, tastes grand.

This last paragraph is reminiscent of the description of Abruzzo by Edmund Wilson quoted earlier, but Brian's pre-dates it by three years. What he says very much matches something I have noticed myself in Abruzzo when we are driving back northwards from Barrea early in the morning. At a certain point having crossed a high alpine plateau (the 'Altopiano delle Cinquemiglia') a wide plain opens up three thousand feet below, giving an almost aerial view with Sulmona in the foreground and way beyond — fifty kilometres or more — floating in the pale blue sky above the early morning haze is the outline of the snow-capped summit of the *Gran Sasso* (the 'Big Pebble'), the highest peak in the Apennines.

Not normally on the front line, Brian writes that he is getting the full experience of war 'undiluted'. It is also evident in a press cutting from one of the Carlisle newspapers, where Brian himself is the source:

TAKING UP THE RATIONS
Carlisle Soldier's nightly job on the bridgehead.

Every night after dark a party of men leave their 'B' echelon area on the Anzio bridgehead and travel up to the infantry companies in the line to deliver food, water, and ammunition. They go in trucks part of the way, then climb out of their vehicles and carry the rations through shell bursts and German machine gun fire, through a wadi which has been called 'Death Valley' to deliver the goods.

Pte. B. Windross, of 2 Montreal Street, Currock, Carlisle, describing one of the journeys of the 'human mules', as they call themselves, said: "We debus from the three-tonners without any incident other than the usual gun flashes from both sides which you see driving down the road. Then we walk quietly along the one-and-a-half-mile track to the ration point. Here you pick up sandbags full of rations, or two tins of water (about 64lbs. weight). Sometimes you get a handcart for the heavier stuff, and then its five to a handcart. The handcart keeps falling in the ditch, and you have to man-handle it out again. On one occasion Jerry heard the handcart after we'd made fifty yards, and his tracer from machine guns came over. When that happens we go flat and, naturally, the handlebars of the cart go up. You then start being afraid first of it being seen and secondly of being hit by bullets.

The trip with the rations is about 500 yards, and sometimes, owing to mortars and shells, it takes three-quarters of an hour to do it. When you reach the company's H.Q. you hand over the rations, pick up the empties, and come back. We have one volunteer that comes with us every night. It is a black and white cat. It hops into a truck at 'B' echelon and comes right up with us. No one knows how it gets into the truck, but it comes... for luck."

***

He finds it difficult to write letters because of the restrictions, which irritates him:

> I must admit that my letter writing is somewhat dilatory. The main trouble, I think, is this — what is really interesting I must not mention as it would indicate my present whereabouts. By the time I can mention anything, the impression is much less vivid or has been eclipsed by some more recent one. I have always to write in the past. So far as the present is concerned, I'm living in a society where a crease in the pants is more important than the Labour theory of Value!

It is only in late May that he feels able to say something about his whereabouts:

> 20/5/44: I think it is O.K. to tell you that I'm in the 5th Army and was on the Garigliano front.

The Garigliano is a river on the border of Campania and Lazio. It flows westward towards the Tyrrhenian Sea, and the mouth is just south of Gaeta. Following the breakout from Anzio, the crossing of the Garigliano on 11 May turned the tide in the Allies favour, for in breaching the Gustav Line it opened up the possibility of an advance through the Liri valley and on to Rome. And soon after the liberation of Rome on 4 June, Brian was promoted from Private to Lance-Corporal:

24/6/44: from L/Cpl Windross B.: Do you notice from what rocky, unpaid, unwanted eminence I now address you?

***

A major topic in his letters is 'reading matter' — even on the beachhead at Anzio:

I found an old, battered copy of 'the Last of the Mohicans' in a cleft of rock. I'm enjoying reading it. I suppose all early American literature (apart from the pseudo-European stuff of Poe and James) is of a heroic character — the perfect boy's adventure story. I guess the times were too tough to be written about truthfully.

7/3/44: Your letters are beginning to roll up now... I generally have plenty of cigarettes, so will you tell Mother etc. not to send me any... I long for reading matter. Will you ask mother to collect any money she might get for fags and buy me Herbert Read's anthology for soldiers instead... It's a selection of prose and poetry and it will really help to sustain me (as much as a bible might some other person)... It's March now and Max Weiner in Reynolds [News] said Hitler would be finished in March. Let's hope he's right!

Among the writers and books Brian has been reading are: O'Neil, W.W. Jacobs, Jack London, Graham Greene, Evelyn Waugh, and Thomas Hardy:

6/4/44: — I had been reading Under the Greenwood Tree as a charming, harmless, English Country-Life novel, when I suddenly thought 'here we have a modern novel indeed! — the forerunner of Huxley, Joyce, and Virginia Woolf.

and to his reading-list can be added George Moore's *Confessions of a Young Man*, Hemingway, Proust, Tolstoy, Malreaux, Dos Passos, etc.[40] He is an avid newspaper reader too:

[no date] The Observer and N(ew) S(tatesman) are arriving very regularly now and are always welcome.

17/3/44: We see the 'Union Jack', which is a damn sight better than I would have expected — not a bad little newspaper at all — much better than its trans-Atlantic counterpart 'The Stars and Stripes'

12/4/44: Did you receive the 'Stars and Stripes' and 'Union Jack' I sent?

They indeed arrived and have both been kept with his correspondence!

233

There are moments of nostalgia too:

17/3/44: Though I don't think Carlisle is a particularly interesting town, I have often thought of it with longing during the past month... It must be years since I was in Silloth — would it be a good place to spend a leave when I get home? I suppose that really depends on the time of year. However, we should have plenty of choice within a reasonable distance from Carlisle, and I would still like to keep our appointment at that hotel in Alston sometime.

9/6/44: The days are really hot, the countryside is a mass of flowers, but I have not noticed the freshness one associates with Spring in England — we seem to have gone straight from winter to summer... I've seen just about every butterfly I ever had in my collection flying about.

One of the few references to his boyhood. Occasionally there are references to other family members:

12/4/44: So Jim Is back in Blighty! He's had a long spell and I bet it feels grand to be back home.

25/4/44: I haven't heard from Allen at all and am not very hopeful. Let me know if he has any interesting news.

9/6/44: Will you thank Uncle Tom for his letter

24/6/44: I got a letter from your father — which was almost embarrassing in its warmth.

[No date, but early in '45]: I got a letter from Mother, will you thank her for it. Is Allen really a Captain at last?

Jim was a cousin of Brian's — the son of Uncle Tom; Allen was Brian's brother, who had been at St Paul's and was now serving in the Far East. These are just some of the examples, and usually they are just passing remarks.

Sometimes we are only getting one side in a dialogue:

26/5/44: Re miniatures, I think they come into the category of 'beautiful things' — like say, dress materials or silver ware — that are pleasant, but do not produce the higher type of aesthetic thrill. I prefer a crude bit of Congo sculpture....

but, of course, we ought to be surrounded by both; each can be appreciated on a different level.

which would seem to follow from something Doris has said about miniatures. It is not a very likely topic of conversation and there must have been something that set it off. No more than a guess — could it have to do with the two 'family' miniatures in her keeping?

**

I repeat here what Brian had written back in Edinburgh shortly after volunteering:

'It's no good my calling for a second front in Europe, if I'm deliberately sitting in a soft job myself.'

He was of course referring to a second front in *North-Western Europe*. An Allied invasion of the European mainland had long been on the table — and long expected by the Soviet Union, which had borne the brunt of the biggest military invasion in history. The Anzio landings, in contrast, had been planned at short notice and the invasion of Italy was criticised by some because it diverted men and armaments away from where they were most needed. Now the moment had arrived:

> 20/5/44: Things seem to be hotting up for Mr Adolph (sic); here we are waiting for the whole works to start. We run sweepstakes on the date of the second front.

It was a carefully guarded secret precisely *when* and *where* the invasion would take place, and the Allied command had done its best to put the Germans on the wrong scent by feeding them clever disinformation.

Brian is still in Italy:

> 26/5/44: Here things have certainly hotted up — and we all thought Italy was in the bag nearly a year ago!

where the afterthought might be compared to the letter written when he first landed in Italy.

On a different note:

> I don't blame Michael one little bit for crying at the bagpipes — they are definitely an acquired taste — they're OK at Fort George but here in Italy, I'm not sure….

I acquired the taste before long, for I had ample opportunities to hear the pipes in Carlisle and even sometimes in the evening on the quayside at Skinburness. Though the Scottish pipes are the ones I know best, I have recently heard a solitary piper in Barrea, producing a stirring sound on the large Abruzzo bagpipe (*Zampogna Abruzzese*).

Sometimes he refers to places he has been to on leave from Italy:

> 28/4/44: Beirut is another place I've visited during my travels. Another festering sore — but my God! In what beautiful surroundings. The hills around it are the grandest and most impressive sight I have ever seen… As one climbs the air gets cleaner and one enters the abode of the very, very rich… Here, in these villages, Hollywood becomes true.
>
> But alas, I met up with a Palestinian soldier and we got drunk on neat Arak — an Arab drink like Pernod.

Brian's reference to 'another festering sore' might be taken as something an Englishman *would* say confronted by a hot, overcrowded Middle Eastern city, with a heterogenous population of Arabs, Christians, and Jews. But I think it refers more to the present situation in the region and particularly in Beirut.[41]

At the Paris Peace Talks in 1919, the League of Nations had given Britain a mandate over Iraq, Palestine and Trans-Jordan, and France over Syria and Lebanon. A 'mandate' was seen as a transitory stage leading to full statehood, based on the principle of the 'nation-state'. But applying the principle was bound to be difficult in an area of mixed ethnicity, religion, and language; moreover, there were no fixed guidelines about when a mandate territory was ready for full statehood and nothing that compelled the caretaker government to implement such proceedings. In short, the whole process was fraught with difficulties, and as the historian Elie Kedourie pointed out, increasingly led to political rows wrapped in layers of equivocating, legalistic jargon.[42]

The discovery of rich oilfields in Iraq made it essential to remain on good terms with that country, and Britain was even prepared to trade in the mandate in return for such a friendship. In 1930 the Anglo-Iraqi treaty was signed, with provisions for a common foreign policy, use of Iraqi air bases, and a British military presence to train the Iraqi army. Iraq, in turn, became a member of the League of Nations in 1932.

France, on the other hand, took a more conservative, colonial approach in Syria and Lebanon; if there was to be a new constitution, it would be on France's terms. In the period 1941–43, the British tried to apply pressure on the French to speed up national elections for a Lebanese parliament, but De Gaulle, head of the so-called 'Free French' government, was not going to act simply to satisfy Britain's self-interests. Not for the first time he prevaricated: the Free French movement had no international recognition, hence he as its leader had no authority to implement proceedings for renouncing the mandate over Lebanon – that was a matter for a future French Government (Barr op. cit. p.242). He had a point. This set the stage for a protracted period of Anglo-French rivalry, diplomatic subterfuge and violence. The stand-off continued throughout 1944, when Brian Windross was on leave in Beirut.

[not dated]: I've had another leave! This time Tel Aviv. It's a smashing place to stay, the best seaside place I've struck. Everything is laid on… all the hotels have hot swing bands — they know their Benny Goodman! In retrospect, I think a Beirut and a Tel Aviv leave go a long way to balancing our three and a half months on the beachhead.

Tel Aviv was very much an early twentieth century city, which grew together with Zionism and the idea of a nation state of Israel — not exactly the setting for 'hot swing bands', though Goodman and a great many of the musicians in the American bands were Jewish! Just like the American jazz bands in the '50s in Germany, the bands in Tel Aviv will have been for the GIs and British troops. Brian is not oblivious to the wider problems:

I spent a lot of time with waiters and barmen — they were all refugees, and I collected a lot of gen from them on Central Europe, Poland, the USSR and, of course, Zion. They could tell harrowing tales and most wanted to get the hell out of Palestine. One Czech ex-officer was a personal friend of E.E. Kisch ('Secret China') and could tell some good stories about him.

**

1/8/44: we all read the news avidly and hope for Ted's early downfall — it seems to be on the cards now….

Not the first time he uses 'Ted' to refer to the Germans. Derived from *Tedeschi* the standard Italian for 'Germans', it must have caught on amongst the soldiers fighting in Italy. He has crossed out the CMF ('Central Mediterranean Force') and corrected it to MEF ('Middle East Force') which suggests he has now been posted to Palestine. The letter is dated 1 August and sent as usual to Mrs D. Windross, 2 Montreal Street. It was, however, redirected to *10 Chatsworth Square* (Gran's address) and re-stamped 11 August at Carlisle post-office.

By the end of October, he is definitely with the MEF in Palestine:

29/10/44: A lot is laid on in ME Camps. Generations of soldiers have seen to that. There is the barber and the tailor, the NAAFI which sells beer of varying quality, early morning tea in some places (from a Chai Wallah) and washing either by kids or by an officially appointed Dhobi Wallah.

25/11/44: Are the swaddies in Blighty wearing collars and ties? We have just been issued with them. My God, isn't Hitler persistent. Wish to Hell he would pack in!

30/11/44: I have recently been on a week's 'Pay Duties Course' at Jerusalem and got 'Distinguished' (92%) which quite pleased me. I know a bloody sight more about pay now than when I was in the Pay Corps. It wasn't exactly a holiday. I now know my Jerusalem pretty thoroughly (my 3rd visit) and can give most of the arguments for and against the sites of this or that biblical event. I ran into two of my former compatriots from Edinburgh, Bill and McArthur. I was a bit shaken to realise that if only I had stepped to a certain side of a certain room back in Edinburgh Pay Office (the same side as McArthur!) then now I should be completing my second year in the Holy City.

He goes on to discuss the difficulty he has in settling down to the normal exchange of courtesies, like letters of thanks which he owes to his Mother and to Auntie Mina:

We have many unpleasant memories of the still too near past, our present is a blink, and there is always the possibility of having to return to that past.

On a lighter topic:

[not dated]: The Battalion is trying to resurrect its newspaper. The Padré called me in tonight and said he had been told I was a 'sort-of-communist bloke' and asked me for contributions — I must be getting 'sort-of-notorious' or something. So now I've got to be controversial for the Battalion's sake!

I laid on a Mackenzie scarf for you for Christmas — has it arrived? I did it through a bloke here who knows someone who works in the factory at Elgin. This Bn incidentally has its headquarters at Elgin, its known as 'Morayshire's Own'.

The envelope bears the usual address, 2 Montreal Street, and although the letter itself is not dated, the post-office at Carlisle has redirected it on 16 January 1945, 'c/o Graham' at 73 Currock Road' — the first occurrence of the first address I knew as a child! The next letter is to this Currock Road address; it is not dated but he is still with the MEF, presumably in Palestine:

The weather is surprisingly like blighty. We change back into battledress in the winter… I can imagine the sherry going down the sink [at New Year 1945?] — I don't believe there are any good wines or spirits left in the world — except for those 'Margaret's father' is hoarding.

The latter is in reply to something Doris has written. Margaret (Jim's sister) was Brian's eldest cousin, born in 1908, the daughter of Mina and Tom Hetherington, 'Margaret's father' refers of course to Uncle Tom (see above). At one time, some married couples tended to avoid a direct use of the first name of their spouse in conversation, and I suspect he is taking a disguised pot shot at this habit of speech — probably at Mina's expense!

He goes on:

> Everyone is very excited at the Russian offensive — I would hate to be in E. Germany now.

Prophetic. It must be mid-January 1945. He adds:

> I shall soon have been a year with this battalion, and over two years in the Infantry

which helps a little in forming the chronology of his military service. He had been with the 6th battalion since sailing from England in December 1943, and presumably in infantry training camps and the Pay Corps before that.

In the following letters England is very much in his mind:

> 21/2/45: Have you got any prints of the two snaps we had taken at the Hastings YCL camp? If you have, I wonder if you would send me them sometime.

One of these snapshots (taken at the Young Communist League summer camp) has indeed survived.

> [No place or date: addressed to Currock Road, now stating 6th Batt. BLA 'British Liberation Army'] I was interested to hear about Michael's expedition — I did the same myself, being found in Marks and Spencers (then the Penny Bazaar) reading, I think, 'Beauty and the Beast', but not at such an early age.

If this is a reference to my getting lost in Binns (which I mentioned early on) then I was only just two years old! That cannot be right, for I have a detailed memory of the occasion — it must indeed have been a habit of mine!

> 14/3/45 — BLA... I am now in Belgium — still getting around! I am in private billets at the moment, and very much appreciate it. The Belgian people are very kind, though of course they have not much they can offer us. I do, however, get a coffee and cognac each morning before setting out. Just the job!
>
> Belgium is much as I imagined it — rather like industrial Britain. The houses and people, in contrast to Italy, are very clean. Clogs much in evidence... We get the London papers here, one day late. The news is good isn't it. I'm keeping my fingers crossed!

I seem to remember the English papers were still a day late when I first arrived in Belgium.

> 26/4/45: I can't tell you exactly where we are or what we are doing, so I'll just give you my impressions of Germany. It's a well-kept and pleasant

country, except where the Royal Artillery has been busy. The Bosch looks pretty much like a Bosch, the peasants wear blue smocks and bus-conductor hats on their square heads. The roads are lined with trees and there is a constant stream of Polish, Russian, Belgian and French refugees on every conceivable kind of vehicle. Whole families mit (sic) children perched on top of carts. The Russian and Polish women wear bright scarves on their heads and the French, of course, have a tricolour prominently displayed somewhere... I have spotted Mongolians, Turkestans, etc. amongst the slave workers; one bright family had commandeered a motor-car which was being drawn by oxen. It does one good to see it!

The atrocities reported in the press recently are quite true — the bosch prisoners are all shit-scared of the Russians, as well they might be!

From 'Hofbesitzer Sprätz, Barum (Bez.Hann)':

6/5/45: Guess they've had it — the end has been pretty messy for Mussolini and Co., but 'who sews the wind...'. Since last writing, I've had a few tense moments, including 60 hours without sleep. But thank God it's over and I've reached the other end of the tightrope....

I must brush up my 'social and class consciousness'. I'm cutting out drink when I get home and I also want to be a *good European*. It seems to me that the pre-requisite for this is another language — so I hope it's not too late to finally learn some French... All this based on the assumption that I don't go to Burma! I don't think there is any chance of that — but I will be glad to hear Govt. policy re Far East drafts just the same. I have written to Mother and have posted some parcels — let me know when they arrive. The prospect of a bouncing boy is enchanting. Will write again soon.

Wanting to be a 'good European' was not perhaps the most obvious aim for someone whose war had been fought largely on European soil. Nor was it shared by some of his fellow-countrymen. In the post-war reconstruction of Europe, American investment — the 'Marshall Plan' — played an important role. Marshall himself later observed that Britain was all too ready to benefit from the European Recovery Program - while maintaining that it was not wholly a European country.[43]

He talks of 'having reached the other end of the tightrope', but his time of service was not quite over.

Same address 21/5/45: The paper AND the typewriter was liberated. I expect to leave here on the 28th May. The period of leave has been extended to 11 days in the U.K!

After crossing the Elbe, we moved into the town of Lübeck, which surrendered without a fight. Lübeck is a Gothic town completely surrounded by canals and lakes, I found it extremely beautiful and romantic, though it has been rather badly bashed about by the RAF.

At Hayton, I was always fascinated by a small black and white print of the Hanseatic *Holsten Gate* of Lübeck which hung on the wall. It was difficult to explain my excitement to others when I was confronted by similar tower-gateways in Flanders, at Ghent and Mechelen, when I first arrived there in 1964, since it had to do with a feeling inside me rather than the gateways themselves — almost a déjà-vu. One of the few times that Father talked to me about the military side in the war, it concerned this final push into Northern Germany. While hundreds of thousands of German troops surrendered, there were pockets of fierce resistance (which he experienced) with heavy Allied losses. On 29 April there was a British assault crossing of the Elbe followed by a rapid advance. So rapid in fact that my father's platoon found itself ahead of the front-line! Lübeck was in Allied hands by 2 May.

> I now live in a country mansion in rather pretty surroundings. Have a soft bed and a light bedroom, next door to where I work. It's all very quiet but pleasant — but leave is the only thing I can think about at the moment....

Throughout the correspondence there has been an assumption that they would be living again in London when the War was over:

> [undated] Any ambitions I have also have a pre-requisite that I live in the centre of a metropolis. In short, I long for Bloomsbury, Kensington or Hampstead.

And when Doris writes that she will be looking for somewhere in London for them to live, he asks her to wait until the danger of 'rocket bombs' (V1s and V2s) has passed, and adds:

> The nearer Soho the better, and suburbs proper barred. London's my village!

In mid-June he reminisces about the leave he has spent with Doris and talks about his return journey via London (where he made a pilgrimage to Fleet Street and St Paul's) and Folkestone, where they were put up at a hotel — serving as a transit camp:

> Folkestone, next morning looked so fresh and the air so sweet, that I almost regretted that London is to be my future home.
>
> 14/7/45: I have just returned from five days leave in Brussels — I couldn't resist the enclosed postcard of the Mannikin statue — it's not very high brow, but it makes a change! Brussels isn't a bad place and I enjoyed myself there. Belgium is a hell of a place for the black market, and this has resulted

in prices being very high. The Army did us quite well — we stayed in hotels in the centre of town. I was impressed most of all by the Market Square and Town Hall — there is a photo of it in the German Hanseatic book I brought home on my last leave.

***

When I began reading Father's wartime letters, I hoped they might provide a window to that world just out of sight. As I read on, the more it came into focus, and by now I was no longer looking through a window at all. It was a mirror — and the room behind it was familiar.

The final letter is dated 27/8/45:

… Now you are in London, will you please have a shufti round Charing X Road and try and get … [there follows a whole list of art books] and Verve numbers I to V.

What do you think of 'the smoke' now? Let me know what you are doing.

All my love,

Brian.

P.S. Just been issued with my kilt!

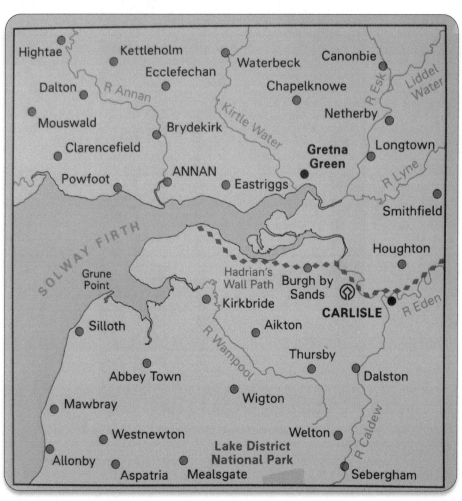

Solway Region. By courtesy of Ordnance Survey

Family memorial at Hoddom 1779

Langholm Parish Register 1772

Ambrotype c.1860

JCL and Barbara Elliot

The Little family c.1890

Group photograph with James Little (left) c.1880

Reverse with studio details

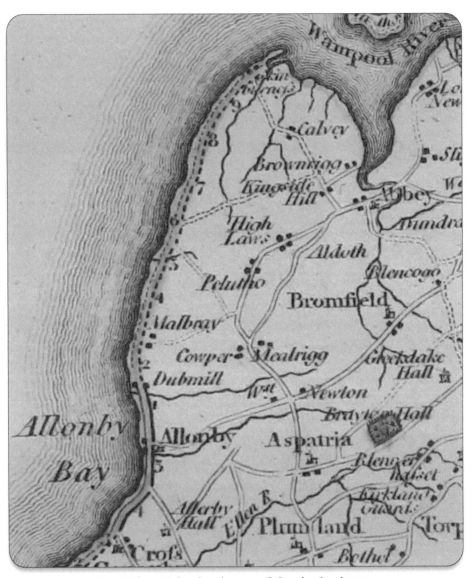

Detail from John Cary's map of Cumberland 1793

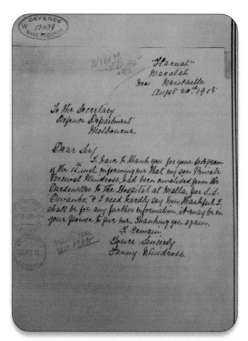

Fanny's letter to the Defence Department Melbourne

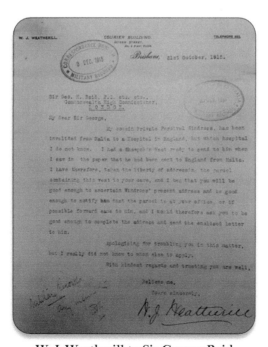

W. J. Weatherill to Sir George Reid

Lieutenant Percival Windross 1916

Captain Windross 1919

Miniature from the Smith family

Reverse

Eve Hamilton

W. E. Norton Piccadilly, 1890

HMS Queen, by permission of the National Maritime Museum

Jack Spong and crew of HMS Coventry c.1941

From Indenture 11 January 1900

OBITUARY.

MR JAMES LITTLE, CARLISLE.

We regret to announce the death, which occurred on Thursday at his residence, 5 Aglionby Street, Carlisle, of Mr James Little, one of the oldest and most respected commercial travellers in the North-West.

Mr Little, who was 82 years old, had been in failing health for several months, but his end came suddenly. He had represented Messrs J. Robertson and Sons, Ltd., preserve manufacturers, in Dumfriesshire, Cumberland and the Furness district for 45 years, and retired about eight years ago. He was a man of very kindly disposition, and took the keenest interest in helping young men who were beginning their careers "on the road."

Having been born at Ecclefechan, he was greatly interested in the works of Thomas Carlyle, and he was also very fond of Burns. His recreation was bowling, and he was one of the oldest members of the Carlisle Subscription Bowling Club He was also an active Churchman, and at one time was a sidesman of Christ Church, Carlisle. His wife predeceased him five years ago. He is survived by four daughters.

The funeral will be at Carlisle Cemetery on Monday afternoon, following a service in Christ Church.

James Little's obituary

Brian and Allen c. 1924

Brian and Gran c. 1929

Brian with James Little c. 1930

Brian still in Carlisle c.1934

Brian reading The Daily Worker 1937

Doris Spong c.1928

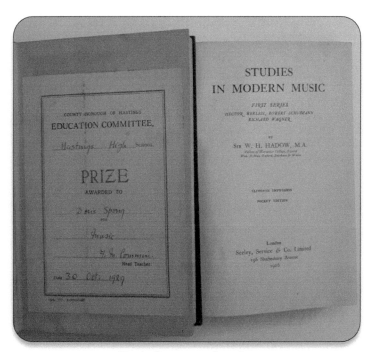

Doris Spong music prize

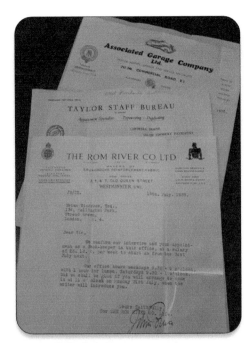

Brian's job correspondence

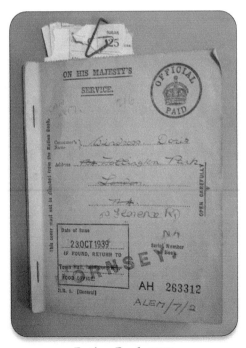

Ration Book 1939

Brian's report from Anzio

Mother and me

You probably think: "Christ, what a tall order!"-
but, provided you have received all the other books
I have sent you (please acknowledge!), these will complete my Art Collection and one of my war aims.   I
will send you the money if you will let me know the
bill (can you borrow from the Bank?)   I suggest
Zwemmers, Foyles, the Phiadon Shop near the British
Museum and Faber & Fabers (Covent Garden). 2nd. hand
(provided they are not too ragged or dirty) will do
for any but the Phiadon books and the Verves - Foyles
Art Department may have some of the others 2nd hand.

We are still in the same wee village, an occasions
mobile cinema and the preparing of a supper in our
bedroom at night are about the only things that break
the monotony.

What do you think of "the smoke" now, let me know
what you are doing?

     All my love,

     Brian.

P.S. Just been issued with my kilt!

Full circle

ENDNOTES

1   NOTES

Part One: Time's Cycle

On 4 February 2005, I bought the *Times* at Brussels South to read on the Eurostar. On the property pages under a heading 'A fortress against marauding Scots' I was surprised to read a full-page article on Edmond Castle, now referred to as 'Hayton Hall'. It was a good article, well researched, and full of admiration for the building — though I felt it was encroaching rather on my territory! Hayton Hall was then on the market for £875,000.

2   Often these tunes are hard to place and 'anonymous' — that is part of their charm — so it detracts a little from one of my favourites now I know it is 'Jumping Bean' by Robert Farnon!

3   As a child, I heard these first-hand, by word of mouth, but they have now been put down in print — see *Solway: Past and Present*, September 2014, and see note 23 below.

4   It is a 9 mm bullet made at Steeton ordnance factory in April 1943, according to the headstamps.

5   More recently, at Antwerp Central, catching the train to Brussels, I had to settle for the *Telegraph*, 27 Feb. 2019. On one of the inside pages, I noticed the following: 'Hadrian's Wall: archaeologists discover rude graffiti — along with a figure of a penis — carved into the face of a long-abandoned quarry in Gelt Woods, from which stone to build part of the Roman Wall was hewed'. My initial surprise gave way to annoyance, no doubt because I felt it was taking the wind out of my sails, but also because it was a misrepresentation. It sounds as though this is all a recent discovery. The press release from the University of Newcastle in fact makes it clear that these are new and interesting discoveries — to be added the ones *already known*.

6   The Society of Women Artists.

7   The tour was at the invitation of the English-Speaking Union, United States, in gratitude for the proposed American Memorial Chapel in the restored east-end of the Cathedral. The background is more fully treated

in Peter Chapman's *A History of St Paul's Cathedral and the American People*, 2009.

8   See James W.P. Campbell, *Building St Paul's*, Thames & Hudson, 2020. Further: *A History of St Paul's Cathedral and the men associated with it*, ed. W.R. Matthews and W.M. Atkins, Phoenix House, London, 1957, in particular chapter vi, 'A brief history of the fabric' by Martin S. Briggs. For a wider view, placing it within the rebuilding of the city after the Fire, see Eric de Maré, *Wren's London*, the Folio Society, London, 1975.

9   G.E. Milton, *Beautiful Britain: St Paul's Cathedral*, Black, Soho Square, 1914 p.6, and Martin Briggs in Matthews and Atkins op. cit. p.352.

10   E.H. Gombrich, *The Story of Art*, Phaidon, 1950, p. 134.

11   I don't know who coined this. I read it (quoted) in Colin Renfrew's book *Before Civilization* (Pelican edition, 1976).

12   See *The Travel Journey of Antonio De Beatis: Germany, Switzerland, The Low Countries, France and Italy, 1517-1518*. Edited by J.R. Hale. The Hakluyt Society, London, 1979. By kind permission of the Hakluyt Society.

13   London was another, where the 'Fleet' was such a sewer. The Dutch *vliet* is pronounced in almost the same way as the English 'Fleet' and in this context they have a shared etymology: a 'stream' or 'creek'.

14   Translated from the Latin by John Stow in *A Survey of London*, (1598). [See www.buildinghistory.org].

15   Charles Green, *Sutton Hoo — the excavation of a Royal Ship*, Merlin Press, London, 1988, pp. 108-113.

16   Antwerp saw a mushrooming of pop groups in the early '70s. We generally played our own material, written by our vocalist/lead guitarist, Frank Storms — I played Hammond organ and a bit of saxophone. Decades after the demise of Prudence, people still tell me how good we were — I wonder *where* they all heard us? The closest we came to the 'bright lights' was when we played at the Arena (Deurne) as supporting act for *Sha Na Na* — of Woodstock fame: 'reflected glory' you might say!

17   It all looks so beautifully set up. Bruney was accepted into the St Lucas guild at Antwerp in 1602. Originally the guild of the painters, it had expanded to include other crafts: engravers, printers, bookbinders, virginal and harpsichord makers. John Norton (1556-1612) was a Shropshire man who started business as a bookseller in Edinburgh in 1586. He moved to London around 1603 when James VI of Scotland came to the throne of

England as James I, and he was appointed King's printer in Latin, Greek, and Hebrew. He built up extensive contacts with the Continental book trade and participated at the Frankfurt book fair from 1600 on. John Bill (1576-1630), also from Shropshire, arrived in London as apprentice to Norton. He also became King's printer, and he had good relations with James I, for whom he collected books on the Continent, and also served as a part-time spy.

What went wrong? 1605 was not the best year to approach the king for someone with Verstegan's Catholic background — moreover, the man in charge of the gunpowder, Guy Fawkes, had acquired his expertise while serving in the Spanish army in the Low Countries. Furthermore, Verstegan himself worked as a papal spy in Antwerp. Was it perhaps a case of spy/counterspy?

18 See my article 'Language, Earth, and Water in Richard Verstegan' in *Dutch Crossing: A Journal of Low Countries Studies*, vol. 24/1 2000.

19 From Philip Lovell, *The Story of England*, Lawson and Dunn, London, 1946. This note to the 'young reader' precedes the paginated text.

20 D.A. Robinson and R.B.G. Williams, 'The Sussex Coast Past and Present' in *Environment, Landscapes, and Society*, Sussex University, 1983.

Part Two: The Family Circle

21 Thomas Williams, *Viking Britain: A History*, William Collins, London, Paperback edition, 2018. By kind permission of the publishers.

22 See the collection of photographs in Raymond Hood, *Old Ecclefechan, Eaglesfield, Kirtlebridge, and Kirkpatrick Fleming*, Stenlake Publishing Ltd., 2017.

23 *Cambridge Guide to English Literature*, Michael Stapleton, London, 1983, p. 144.

24 Christopher Lowe, *Excavations at Hoddom, Dumfriesshire*, 2006. Published by the Society of Antiquaries of Scotland, this book is based on excavations carried out in 1991.

25 Cf. David Grigg, 'Farm size in England and Wales from early Victorian times to the present' in *Agricultural History Review*, 35/2, 1987. Further, Dennis R. Mills, 'Farm statistics from censuses 1851-1881', in *Agricultural History Review*, 47/1, 1999.

26　The pioneering antiquarian William Stukeley notes during a visit to the Esk Valley in 1725, 'I even beheld here and there a castellated house, whither at night the cattle are driven for security from the borderers'.

27　For a detailed discussion see Mike McCarthy, *Carlisle: a frontier town and border city*, Routledge, 2019.

28　For a view of nineteenth-century Silloth in photographs see *Solway Past and Present*, 14 August 2017.

29　Michael French, 'Commercials, careers and culture: travelling salesmen in Britain 1890-1930' in *Economic History Review*, vol. 58, 2005.

30　John Harris, *Moving Rooms: The Trade in Architectural Salvages*, Yale University Press, 2007.

31　There is a sequel to this. Quite by chance, a neighbour of ours in Schoten (Antwerp), Eddy De Wispelaere, hearing that we had had connections with Brighton, informed me that his great-grandfather, P. De Wispelaere, had an atelier in Bruges in the early 1900s specializing in altarpieces in the traditional Flemish manner. The firm was known throughout Europe, and was responsible for the reredos in St Michael and All Angels Church, Brighton. I knew St Michael's, having sung there in the early '60s; it is one of a number of Victorian Gothic revival churches in Brighton and Hove, all on a grand scale and Anglo-Catholic — hence their rich furnishings. It turns out that St Michael's also has a sixteenth-century Flemish altarpiece, at present boxed away awaiting restoration. De Wispelaere also provided the altarpiece at St Aiden's Church, Carlisle (1931). Quite a coincidence.

32　Both here and below, the military (and other) details are based on Peter Hart, *Gallipoli*, Profile Books, London, 2013.

33　See Bryan Jamison, *A great social force making for order and morality*, (pp.274-318). PhD dissertation, University of Queensland (2011). www.researchgate.net Pdf file. Last consulted October 2020.

34　See David Carter, *Carlisle in the Great War*, Pen & Sword Military, Barnsley, 2014, which contains a wealth of information on the period.

35　In *Darwinism tested by Language*, published in 1877, arguing against the theory of evolution, the author, Frederick Bateman M.D. writes: 'The novelty of Mr Darwin's views has had something to do with the ready reception of them by the rising generation, who, in this age of electric telegraphy and *underground railroads*, are always seeking the sensational and marvellous.' — My italics.

36   Fu-Chia Chen, *Cab Cultures in Victorian London: 1830-1914*, PhD, University of York, 2013. In the sixties — so long after Hansom cabs had been replaced by motor taxis — we still 'called a cab' by phone or simply stepped off the pavement to 'hail a cab', which serves to show how deeply engrained the 'cab culture' is in the English psyche!

37   Figures taken from Fu-Chia Chen, op. cit.

38   The only evidence I have found is in the 1939 register for England and Wales, just before the War. In the section for Merton and Morden, Surrey, 57 Arundel Avenue: Spong- John, H. b. 18 July 1888, Club Steward; and Spong — Mona, b. 28 August 1892, Club Stewardess. The right people in the wrong place.

39   I have benefitted greatly from reading Lloyd Clark, *Anzio: The Friction of War*, Headline Review, London, 2006, and my brief commentary is largely drawn from its early chapters.

40   I was struck by a letter to the *Times* on Thursday, 3 January 2013, 'Staying Sane', where the writer talks about her father's war correspondence from North Africa and Italy: 'Unlike many of his colleagues, who requested supplies of socks, my father asked for books... He said that reading was the principal factor towards maintaining his sanity'.

41   The following summary is based largely on Peter Mansfield, *The Arabs*, Penguin Books, 1985, pp. 197-205, 216-218, and James Barr, *A Line in the Sand*, Simon & Schuster, 2011, pp. 201-294.

42   Elie Kedourie, *Nationalism*, Hutchinson University Library, London, 1960, p. 135.

43   See Ian Kershaw, *To Hell and Back: Europe 1914-1949*, Penguin Books, 2016, p. 516.